Object Studies

Cyrus Mulready

Object Studies

Introductions to Material Culture

Cyrus Mulready
Department of English
State University of New York at New Paltz
New Paltz, NY, USA

ISBN 978-3-031-09026-4   ISBN 978-3-031-09027-1 (eBook)
https://doi.org/10.1007/978-3-031-09027-1

© The Editor(s) (if applicable) and The Author(s), under exclusive licence to Springer Nature Switzerland AG 2023
This work is subject to copyright. All rights are solely and exclusively licensed by the Publisher, whether the whole or part of the material is concerned, specifically the rights of translation, reprinting, reuse of illustrations, recitation, broadcasting, reproduction on microfilms or in any other physical way, and transmission or information storage and retrieval, electronic adaptation, computer software, or by similar or dissimilar methodology now known or hereafter developed.
The use of general descriptive names, registered names, trademarks, service marks, etc. in this publication does not imply, even in the absence of a specific statement, that such names are exempt from the relevant protective laws and regulations and therefore free for general use.
The publisher, the authors, and the editors are safe to assume that the advice and information in this book are believed to be true and accurate at the date of publication. Neither the publisher nor the authors or the editors give a warranty, expressed or implied, with respect to the material contained herein or for any errors or omissions that may have been made. The publisher remains neutral with regard to jurisdictional claims in published maps and institutional affiliations.

This Palgrave Macmillan imprint is published by the registered company Springer Nature Switzerland AG.
The registered company address is: Gewerbestrasse 11, 6330 Cham, Switzerland

For my students

Preface

Begin with an object. You may choose anything you'd like, but it is best if it is something important to you: a prized possession, a souvenir from a memorable trip, a family heirloom. Once you have your object, place it in front of you (if it is small) or sit next to it (perhaps it is a piece of furniture). Touch it or hold it in your hand. What are the object's dimensions? How would you describe it to a friend or family member who couldn't see it? Take your time (and jot down some notes, make sketches, or take photographs, if you'd like). After you observe the first features that come to your awareness (color, shape, texture, weight), look to see if there are any details that you have never noticed before—a nick or scratch, a label, an imperfection that remains from when it was made. Do you know the materials that went into its manufacture? Are they natural or synthetic? Do they require their own process of creation in order to be made into an object (like plastics, or fabric, for instance)? Do you know where your object was made? Is there a story behind how it came to be in your possession? You may need to do some quick research to find clues, but that's fine. Talk to a family member who might have some knowledge of it, or search for the maker's name on the internet. This is your object and you may use whatever tools you need to tell its story.

Once you began looking at your object carefully it may have stoked your curiosity. What was that story that you once heard about your great-grandmother? How *are* ballpoint pens made? Why did teacups that were designed and manufactured in China become popular in Europe? If you take some time with this exercise, you might be surprised at how many questions and how much descriptive detail you can generate from the careful observation of even a small object. We process the elements of our environment so quickly that we rarely find opportunity to appreciate the wonders of the material world. Objects usually sit in the background of our awareness as tools that help us carry out essential tasks or decorations within our surroundings. Moreover, objects of the kind that you may have selected (clothing, jewelry, furniture, tchotchkes, photographs) are not typically the things that students, even in college courses, are asked to think much about. The last time you were asked to describe an object may have been in the earliest years of your schooling, if at all. When I began my education in Object Studies I was studying for my Ph.D. and, ironically, my professor would frequently encourage us to "think like a Kindergartner": he wanted us to see objects such as books and paintings with a curiosity and appreciation for subtle details that we had unlearned through many years of higher education.

Those first experiences in bringing attention and a different kind of analytic rigor to the study of material culture were some of the most thrilling of my years as a student. As a literary scholar I learned to see books not merely as vessels of information, but as unique objects with layered histories of creation that involved editors, bookbinders, typesetters, and readers. I began teaching a course at my university inspired by the theories and practices I developed in the years after those early experiences. I wanted to invite my students to the excitement of discovery I have had as a scholar working with material culture. Teaching those courses, I saw both a need and an opportunity for a textbook that could support students and faculty interested in in this mode of inquiry: thus, *Object Studies*.

Once we attune ourselves to details of the kind you observed just now with your own object, new and unexpected avenues of interpretation and understanding often appear. The first purpose of this book therefore is to provide readers with a wide variety of entry points into the study of material culture. My hope is that in these chapters the model essays, exercises, and projects will give readers a first-hand experience with the many possibilities for scholarly and creative work that the study of objects can open. The structure of this book brings these experiential forms of learning to the forefront: the first three chapters are organized to take readers on a progression from the personal and individual experience with objects to local perspectives and then, finally, to the global and wider historical frame. "In the Middle," Chap. 4 of this book, will then introduce readers to key theoretical concepts and offer suggestions for further reading and engagement with the philosophy and conceptual dimensions of Object Studies. This structure is intentional—too often in material cultural studies new learners are asked to begin with difficult theoretical readings before reflecting on how objects are meaningful to us and our histories. *Object Studies* instead prioritizes learning as a material experience by allowing readers to approach important theoretical questions with a sure grasp of methods and examples. The remaining chapters of the book then introduce a variety of applications for Object Studies in diverse fields of study, including psychology, literary studies, philosophy, history, neurology, and museum studies.

From personal narratives to historical research and psychological experiments, material cultural studies offer a rare opportunity for integrated interdisciplinary study. Indeed, it is this kind of intellectual work that I believe to be the future of a thriving academic culture in our universities. In higher education there has been a notable shift over the past generation away from teaching that "delivers" knowledge to students and toward more active and authentic learning opportunities that emerge from the shared experiences of the professor and student. The second purpose of this book therefore is to provide an integrative model for teaching the skills that I (and others) believe should be at the core of modern higher education:

Preface ix

Authentic Research: Students using this book will engage in research that will lead them to new discoveries. Through the application of various skills toward a wide array of object-based projects, they will learn to ask questions that create opportunities for new knowledge about their lives, their community, or even within a broader discipline.

Intensive Writing: The projects in this book will encompass various modes of writing: from personal essays and traditional thesis-driven papers to descriptive writing, journalistic reporting, and critical note taking. There are further suggestions for students and instructors within the book on how to find opportunities for digital publication and other outlets for sharing their writing.

Scholarly Collaboration: Most of the projects in *Object Studies* are designed to be carried out collaboratively, either among students or with the help of librarians and other research professionals. Students will learn from each other by working together on stimulating projects.

Experimental and Experiential Learning: *Object Studies* is designed around a practice-oriented, experiential pedagogy. This approach encourages students to seek out problems and questions rather than simple answers. Objects and the materials of our culture are themselves products of multiple, layered histories and therefore require this mode of critical thinking.

Chapter Organization

Each chapter will follow the same format, designed to offer both practical advice to students and instructors about how to carry out the projects and research described in each unit. These chapters will also provide a discussion of additional materials to include in a course or for supplementary reading and viewing. Here are the headings you can expect to see in each chapter:

Overview: This section sets up the general ideas, key theoretical concepts, and an initial description of the project to be undertaken in the unit. These can be read as a brief introduction to the particular focus each chapter will bring to the practice of Object Studies.

Model Essay: Few textbooks on material culture offer useful examples for students of how this kind of scholarship can be practiced. Therefore, the core of each chapter in this book is an essay (or a series of essays) that demonstrates the work and methodologies described in the overview. These are designed to be read as models for the kinds of writing and scholarly approaches one can take in Object Studies. Students may want to imitate the structure and approaches taken in these model essays, or they may also use them as points of departure for their own innovations.

Procedures and Methods: After the model essays, I offer a discussion of the particular skills and methods modeled across these chapters. These build a kind of Object Studies toolkit that you can use and adapt in various ways over each section of this book. Just by way of overview, here is a list of some of the skills that we will develop through the course of these projects:

Descriptive Writing, Collaboration, Interviewing, Creating Detailed Field Notes, Project Design, Archival Research, Formulating a Question, Curating a Collection

I believe that writing and research (like all forms of learning) develop syncretically—through repetition of skills that reinforce one another by being combined in novel ways over time. The chapters of *Object Studies* are structured accordingly, with projects that build upon work done in previous chapters. Each chapter of this book will also invite the student and instructor to invent new ways of thinking about these projects. For example, there are some projects that I formulate as individual research but that can easily be adapted into collaborations in small groups or even for a full seminar.

Resources and Research: One of the main challenges students face in undertaking a research-heavy course of study is a lack of experience or understanding of how professional research in the humanities or social sciences works. A core objective of this book is to make research more accessible for students by focusing each chapter around clearly defined guidelines for carrying out the projects described in the model essay. This will include advice about source selection, databases to use, note-taking techniques, and even important research resources for the work described in each chapter.

There are also many novels, plays, films, television shows, and internet resources that could be used in conjunction with the projects outlined in this text. Each chapter will include suggestions that can be included on a syllabus or used for additional exploration of the topics covered in the unit.

Ideas for Further Project Applications: Course instructors and students will hopefully find inspiration in these chapters for adapting new projects based on the skills and ideas they read about. Most chapters include related projects that I or others have undertaken, along with assignment prompts and questions that suggest further possibilities and directions for these studies.

New Paltz, NY   Cyrus Mulready

Acknowledgments

The work of Object Studies is fundamentally collaborative; likewise, this textbook would not have been possible without the support, encouragement, and material assistance of many students, colleagues, friends, and collaborators. It is a pleasure to acknowledge them here.

First and foremost, Ben Doyle, then at Palgrave, supported the project from the very start and helped me develop it from a fuzzy sketch to a viable proposal. I am grateful to Lina Aboujieb for picking up where Ben left off, and to Molly Beck for seeing the project through to completion. I am also greatly indebted to Bernadette Deelen-Mans and Samriddhi Pandey for their careful and attentive work on the many details that went into producing this book.

This textbook originated with a series of courses I taught through the New Paltz Honors Program, and I have been incredibly fortunate to work with the director, Pat Sullivan, in developing and teaching "The Materials of History, Art, and Thought." Her unwavering excitement and support for my teaching in the program have been essential. I worked with so many brilliant students in these seminars and thank them all for their generous feedback on what worked (and didn't work) in our courses together. The book is dedicated to them. I am especially grateful to those who agreed to share their work with me for this book: Carina Kohn, Caitlin Cummings, Kimberly Blum, and Elise Bruce.

My colleagues at New Paltz have offered their time and energy in countless ways to support me in writing this book. Nancy Johnson gave me the best advice in simply telling me to write it, and my department chair, Vicki Tromanhauser, and dean, Laura Barrett, helped me secure a sabbatical to do the work. My thanks to our provost, Barbara Lyman, and the institution for granting me this indispensable leave. Andy Evans, Jackie George, Kris Jansma, Jed Mayer, and Tom Olsen all read drafts of various chapters, saving me from errors and helping make the work as good as it can be. I also thank Ann Gaygan and my dean's office for providing financial support that enabled reproduction of some of the images used in the text.

My community of scholars and friends beyond SUNY New Paltz also played a vital role in this book and the course that inspired it. My sincere thanks to the anonymous readers for Palgrave whose thoughtful feedback helped give the book its final shape. David Scott Kastan was a champion from the start and enlivened my thinking about books and pedagogy. Kurt Schreyer and Jared Richman each helpfully read chapters when I needed their insights. Jane Degenhardt read and gave crucial feedback on the entire manuscript. Our many conversations about this project were integral to its substance and scope.

Most of this book was written at home while my family and I were in relative isolation due to COVID-19 restrictions. I couldn't have wished for a more encouraging group of people to support me in its composition. My children, Mo and Des, gave me space or distraction as needed. Colleen Mulready, my wife and partner in all things, was my first reader and ideal audience.

I would be remiss if I didn't finally acknowledge the two mentors whose example inspires me: Margreta de Grazia and Peter Stallybrass. My first lessons in the excitement and pedagogical potential of working with objects came in their seminars. In my classroom, theirs is the model of excellence I always hope to achieve.

Contents

1 Personal Objects 1
2 Objects and Local History 19
3 A History of the World in Coffee Cups 43
4 In the Middle: Subjects, Objects, and Theories of Things 63
5 Collecting Things: The Psychology of Accumulation, from
   Museums to Hoarders 81
6 The Things We Read 103
7 Consuming Objects 123
8 Thinking with Things 141
9 Epilogue: A Department of Object Studies? 159

Index 163

List of Figures

Fig. 1.1	A pair of cufflinks. Photo by the author	3
Fig. 1.2	*RMS Adriatic.* Wikimedia	8
Fig. 1.3	Entry detail from the Irish Deaths Register, 1901. Irish National Archives	11
Fig. 1.4	Entry detail from the Irish Deaths Register, 1896. Irish National Archives	12
Fig. 2.1	Jean Hasbrouck House Cellar Fireplace. Historic American Buildings Survey (Library of Congress)	22
Fig. 2.2	The Jean Hasbrouck House. (Photograph Courtesy of Historic Huguenot Street)	24
Fig. 2.3	Floor Plan of the Jean Hasbrouck House Basement after renovations in 1786. (Courtesy of Historic Huguenot Street)	27
Fig. 2.4	Rotating circular shelves in Jean Hasbrouck House cellar, constructed in 1786. (Photo by the author)	28
Fig. 2.5	Door separating main rooms of Jean Hasbrouck House cellar. Historic American Buildings Survey (Library of Congress)	30
Fig. 3.1	Coffee Cup from the Safavid Empire, Persia, late seventeenth century, The British Museum	46
Fig. 3.2	*The Lady Sultan Taking Coffee from a Black Woman*, 1755, by Charles-André van Loo, *Musée des Arts Décoratifs*, Paris	52
Fig. 3.3	Stewart's Coffee Cup Lid, photo courtesy of Stewart's Shops	57
Fig. 5.1	Thai Lintel from the San Francisco Asian Art Museum. (Image from *United States v. Lintels*)	87
Fig. 5.2	Photograph of Manhattan, 1999. (Photograph by the author)	96
Fig. 6.1	Hampden Family Memorial. (Photograph by Iain McLauchlan)	109
Fig. 7.1	Infographic depicting the material make-up of a Pilot pen. (Illustrations by Kimberly Blum)	137
Fig. 8.1	St. Jerome, Florence, the Church of Ognissanti. Image courtesy of Alamy.com	154

Chapter 1
Personal Objects

In this project, students select and carefully describe an object that is important to their personal history. They conduct research, including interviews with family members, to create an "object story" or personal narrative based on their object.

Overview

One of the reasons we keep objects is for the stories they enable us to tell. Even beyond their real worth, objects can accumulate value through the associations they bring to us or that have been added to them by others. Many such objects have a physical connection to us: jewelry, clothing, tattoos, keychains, and other accessories often serve this story-conveying function—"conversation pieces," we call them, a kind of social lubricant that lets us share something about ourselves with friends and acquaintances.

To begin in Object Studies—to understand the potential this approach has for our scholarship and developing an understanding of the world around us—it makes sense to start with something that has such a personal connection. What are the stories, well-known or hidden, that the things in our lives communicate for us? In pursuing this question we will find one of the fundamental truths about studying objects: our sense of self, the idea of who we are that we may think of as immaterial, actually connects profoundly with the material world. Many of our memories and stories would not exist without objects in which we can encode those ideas. Objects transmit the past into our lives today—this is one of the reasons families and societies collect "heirlooms," objects that help preserve the stories of a family or community. This is perhaps most apparent in the case of books and writing technologies (a topic we will look at various points in this book) but even a wordless object can often "speak," or allow us to speak, in sharing our story.

Object narratives have become a popular subgenre of biographical writing and memoir in recent years for this reason. Edmund de Waal's family memoir, for instance, *The Hare with Amber Eyes: A Hidden Inheritance*, is a must-read for students and lovers of objects. De Waal tells the story of his remarkable ancestors, the Ephrussis, a family of bankers and aesthetes who built one of the world's largest financial empires in the nineteenth and twentieth centuries. As a Jewish family living in central Europe during the twentieth century, their fortunes were mostly lost during the Nazi invasions of Austria and France. What remains for de Waal to tell their story is a collection of Japanese *netsuke*, small carved figurines originally collected by his connoisseur great-great-uncle in Paris in the nineteenth century. Through his immense curiosity and assiduous research, de Waal reconstructs the path that these *netsuke* took from Paris to Vienna to Japan and eventually to his home outside London. It is a remarkable tale of survival that touches on almost all major threads of history from the past 150 years: the rise of Impressionism in France, anti-Semitism in Europe, the Holocaust and Jewish diaspora, American occupation in Japan, and the rise of a global economy. Yet it is also an incredibly intimate story of his family and the hands that passed these small *netsuke* from one point in the story to the next: the avid art collector, the woman who was one of the first female recipients of a Ph.D. from the University of Vienna, the fashion designer who quietly lived in a same-sex relationship in Japan through the end of the twentieth century.

De Waal is an inspiration for this kind of storytelling because his focus always remains on the materials themselves. "I really don't want to get into the sepia saga business, writing up some elegiac Mitteleuropa narrative of loss." Such an approach would create a "thin" and nostalgic narrative—"…I am not interested in *thin*," de Waal writes. "I want to know what the relationship has been between this wooden object that I am rolling between my fingers—hard and tricky and Japanese—and where it has been" (16). What de Waal implicitly encourages us to do with this kind of "object biography," as some have called it, is counterintuitive. We normally start with the person, the story, the lived experience of another human as shared orally or written down. Objects of course can't tell us where they have been in the same way a person can. To tell the story of an object requires a different approach.

Objects are stubborn remnants of the past. We may try to fit them into our grand narratives, but the things themselves remain as silent fact checkers. In Object Studies, we try to question stories about the past, whether personal or cultural, by relying on the hard evidence that things give to us. The stories we tell or that others have told are still important. An essential part of studying an object is gathering as much information as we can about it from those who have owned it. If we are lucky enough to know the people who originally owned the object, then we can interview them: the simple question "Tell me what you know about this thing" can be the start of an instructive conversation. But the object itself should be at the center of the story. I begin mine with a pair of cufflinks (Fig. 1.1).

Fig. 1.1 A pair of cufflinks. Photo by the author

Model Essay

Her Mark: The Objects and Stories of Family Loss

Before I ever saw the cufflinks, I somehow knew their story.

My great-grandmother, Catherine Mulready, coming over on the boat from Ireland, was out for some fresh air. On the deck of the steam liner, she talked her way into a game of shuffleboard with her fellow passengers. The game was a welcome distraction. Having only the money to afford tickets in third class with her children and mother, she was seeking a moment of respite on an anxious voyage. "Ma," as her family called her (an Irish term of endearment for "mother"), apparently was a good hand at the game and by the end of it, she walked away with a hard-won prize: a pair of golden cufflinks depicting, in miniature, the ship where she won them.

The cufflinks are now mine, and as I look at the scuffed metal and majestic ship's prow in the small portrait, I imagine her holding them in her hand, tucking the pair into her pocket with a smile of triumph. Her luck had changed. She was a widow with six children and an elderly mother in tow, but better days were ahead. One of the founding myths of my family is this voyage, and my great-grandmother is the undoubted heroine of the tale. The story of the cufflinks reflects the reverence we hold in my family for Ma. She was determined, crafty, gritty. This is the woman who not only emigrated from Ireland as a widow, but also set up a boarding house in North Dakota to get her family on its feet in America.

I inherited the cufflinks about 20 years ago, and ever since I have wondered about this story and its protagonist. As much as I wanted it to be true, I have also had my doubts. The object and its story don't fit with the other facts I know about the family's crossing. Firstly, the Mulreadys arrived in Canada during the early months of winter. My grandfather badly burned his hands on a stove in the immigration processing building while trying to warm them against the frigid Quebec air, he would later recount. Shuffleboard strikes me as an unlikely pastime on the cold waters of the North Atlantic and cufflinks as unusual winnings for a casual game. There are other possibilities for the object's origin: even if the shuffleboard story is a fabrication, perhaps the cufflinks were simply a memento purchased by my great-grandmother to commemorate her family's migration from Ireland to America. But it seems even more improbable to me that she would purchase such trinkets while her family was in crisis. When I begin thinking, too, about how this object could have arrived in my possession I am even more skeptical of the story. My grandfather had four older brothers. Surely one of them would have been more likely to receive this family keepsake from their mother.

The enigma of my cufflinks fascinates me because they are a rare physical trace of both my grandfather and my great-grandmother. As the youngest grandchild, my connections to the Mulready family consist almost entirely of objects: these cufflinks, a pocket watch, a tie tack, a shaving kit, a few photos. And a name. As inheritances go, it's not much. Most of these items fit in the top drawer of my dresser, hiding behind my socks and a few other cherished possessions. Peter Mulready, my grandfather (and Ma's youngest son) died when I was seven, but I do have a few scattered memories of him that I hold onto along with these objects. For a year or so toward the end of his life we shared a bedroom and he often looked after me while my parents were at work. I remember the leather case he kept his reading glasses in, always in his chest pocket, stories and songs he would share with me, his red leather recliner, his kind voice. He was a teacher (maybe another part of my inheritance): he built and served as the principal of the trade school and industrial arts programs at Father Flanagan's Boys Town in Omaha, Nebraska. The shaving kit I have was made as a retirement gift from the boys in his leatherworking shop.

Over the years, I have dabbled in research into my family tree, trying to find the clues and hints that might unfold something about my personal story. Genealogy is one of the most popular hobbies in the world, and with the internet and new technologies like personal DNA kits, it has never been easier to find out information about our ancestors and trace family lineages. Television shows like Henry Louis Gates, Jr.'s *Finding Our Roots* and "*Who Do you Think You Are?*" speak to a wider popularity in the media, as well, for stories that tell us something about our origins and the people in our ancestry. But my own experiences with this kind of research have been disappointing. While my Ancestry.com app holds a large set of names, birth and death dates, and perhaps an occasional grainy photo or grave site, it seems to me more like a roll call than a family. What does it really tell me about the lives that these people lived: their loves, fears, and frustrations? There is an inherent emptiness that accompanies the fascination with these people I may have never known. They seem spectral, insubstantial.

Objects like my cufflinks are an antidote to this empty genealogical history. In his beautiful memoir *The Hare with Amber Eyes,* Edmund de Waal reflects eloquently on the fullness of narratives that derive from the things that constitute our material history. Writing of his collection of Japanese *netsuke*, de Waal describes how such items pull him into their physical lives: "I want to walk into each room where this object has lived, to feel the volume of the space, to know what pictures were on the walls, how the light fell from the windows. And I want to know whose hands it has been in, and what they felt about it and thought about it—if they thought about it. I want to know what it has witnessed" (15-16). In the act of recovering an object's life we can also come to know the people who owned the things that survive them.

But things can also conceal. These remnants of the past take us to unexpected places and hidden truths. In my case, the sentimental version of family history that had been handed down to me was a fabrication that covered up a profound episode of family trauma. The boat in the miniature portrait on my cufflinks was not what it seemed.

I.

When I hold the cufflinks in my hand, they are lighter than I would expect them to be. Each link has two oblong-shaped discs that are connected by a metal link roughly ½ inch in length. One of the oblong pieces is a smooth piece of rosy gold metal that is also about ½ inch long. The other disk is the decorative part: a miniature portrait of a ship at sea on a smooth enameled surface. The image is small, about the size of the nail on my pinky finger, but I can see that the ship has four masts and a long black hull. It sits in front of a sky that is creamy white with a hint of pink. On the reverse side of the disk are two words that were stamped into the metal when they were manufactured: "QUIKFIXR" and "PATENT".

It is hard to make out these tiny words, but once I do, I find my first real clue to the origin of the cufflinks. With some quick internet searching of these terms, my screen fills with images of a virtual fleet of cufflink ships like mine. I also find the manufacturer and patentee: Henry Owen and Sons of 72 Caroline St., Birmingham (UK). An advertisement for the firm from a 1929 trade show, the "British Industries Fair," describes their business:

> Manufacturers of Links, Collar Studs, Dress Studs in large variety; Gent's Collar Pins, in Rolled Gold, Gold Fronted, Silver Mounted and Mother of Pearl, Patentees of the "Neverseen" Stud, "Quikfixr" Link, etc. Birmingham Jewellers; and Silversmiths Association. (*Catalogue*)

This early twentieth-century commercial language makes me smile; the company makes practical yet decorative fasteners for men's and women's clothing. The "Quikfixr" cufflink is just the thing for the professional man on the go (I can picture the advertisement). According to an online antiques appraiser, "rolled gold" is an alloy invented in England in the nineteenth century that became popular during the 1920s and '30s, "especially in utilitarian objects such as watches and fountain pens" (Segal). So the cufflinks I have before me were made in England in the early twentieth century. They strike me as the kind of souvenir middle-class travelers still pick up today, maybe as a gift for a husband or something to tuck away for Father's Day.

Sometimes we refer to objects and styles as "timeless" but more often the things in our lives are layered with age. That is probably the reason why I have held on to this pair of cufflinks for so long. They are rich with time. I don't wear shirts with French cuffs that require the accessory (and probably never will). These are also not the kind of item that I would put on display, nor can they be reused for another purpose. They have no practical utility in my life. But as witnesses to the world that my grandfather inhabited, they are invaluable to me. Between the image of this old ship and the darkened patina on reverse side of the portrait, the objects in my hand immediately evoke another era. Cufflinks themselves are a holdover from a time before shirts came with buttons sewn into them, and while some people still wear them today for style, they proclaim to me a slightly retro flourish. They are time travelers, but not the kind that step into a machine and pop out immediately in the future. They carry the wear of the decades with them. There's a bit of dexterity involved in flipping the fasteners so they sit properly in the shirt to hold the cuffs together. I imagine my grandfather rubbing his thumb over this surface to ensure a snug fit against his cuff, just so. The clasps now have a dulled shine on their metallic surface from his countless touches. Although we think of objects as being separate from us, most of our things bear such marks, residue of their connection to our lives. To me these cufflinks are more than a reminder of my grandfather, they are part of him.

I am thrilled to put my cufflinks into their historical place and find that they are not some one-off item of curiosity. But the discoveries of my research present even more problems for my family's shuffleboard story. Henry Owen and Sons became incorporated in 1900, and while I cannot find the exact date for the Quikfixr Patent, the manufacture of these cufflinks almost certainly came sometime after 1901. I own a copy of the ship manifest for my Mulready family's transatlantic voyage, so I know the trip took place in November of 1901 on board a ship called the *Corinthian*. And it is when I find a photograph of that ship that I put an end to the speculation about the family story: even with the tiny dimensions of the portrait on my cufflinks I can tell immediately that the ship is not the *Corinthian*. It only had two masts, and in the photo is less imposing than the ship on the cufflinks. The hard evidence of this object has made the conclusion clear, and it is with some sadness that I accept my cufflinks were almost certainly not won or purchased on that trip.

As I researched the *Corinthian*, I came across a record from a 1913 Parliamentary discussion of regulations involving emigrant ships. It seems that there were complaints about conditions on-board the ship, particularly for its 200 third-class passengers, "who complain of overcrowding, poor bedding, and of having no place to sit down on except their bunks during rough weather." The complaint received a typical bureaucratic response:

> I am informed on inquiry that she [the ship] fully complied with the requirements of the Merchant Shipping Acts. Nine hundred and seventy-nine steerage passengers (equivalent to 828 adults) were embarked at London and Plymouth, and the clear space allotted to emigrants was much more than sufficient for the number carried, according to the scale laid down in the statutory rules. Besides the usual dining rooms, additional rooms were provided for recreation. (*Steamship "Corinthian."*)

This exchange and discussion of regulations brings me closer to what my family may have experienced—"additional rooms for recreation" sounds like a far cry from a shuffleboard court. I wonder whether the Mulreadys even ventured outdoors during their trip.

While I have found this family legend to be false, these objects are still a puzzle to me: why do I have them, how did my grandfather get them, what is the ship pictured on them (if not the *Corinthian*) and why would he hold onto them well past the time he retired from professional life? Maybe they were a gift from someone else? Did he find them in a secondhand store or charity shop? Was it then that he slyly spun the tale? I am especially intrigued by the English provenance of the cufflinks. My grandfather never left the United States after he emigrated, so far as I know, and while purchasing British-made items in the middle of America is not unheard of, my research showed me that these cufflinks were originally purchased, in all likelihood, on board a transatlantic carrier. They were likely originally a part of a set that included a tie clip; I found just such a set on eBay depicting a different ship. Owen and Sons, I can speculate, had an agreement with these carriers to produce souvenir cufflinks and tie-clips depicting voyaging vessels. It was a good way for the young company to place its products. This must have been how my cufflinks were originally purchased, the tie clip now lost to time.

Searching a UK database that documents passengers on transatlantic voyages, I come across an unexpected breakthrough. My unusual last name is a gift for this research, and when I search the name "Mulready" I find "Catherine Mulready," my great-grandmother's name, on a passenger list for another voyage, this one back across the Atlantic. In 1926 the database records her as a passenger on a ship that passed through Southampton, the RMS *Adriatic* (*Passenger List*). I learn from my mother (who probably heard the story many times around family gatherings in North Dakota) that Ma took this trip back to Ireland so she could see what was left of her family and old homestead. She also wanted a handful of dirt from County Mayo to be buried with her, perhaps revealing her own longing for a material connection to her past.

When I find an image of *The Adriatic* online, it is indeed a near perfect match for the portrait on my cufflinks (Fig. 1.2).

The ship in the picture was a starkly different vessel than the *Corinthian* that carried my great-grandmother with her family 25 years prior, as described in an advertisement for the *Adriatic* from 1907:

> The seating accommodation is of the most comfortable type, and for ladies there are work tables, while cozy corners have been arranged for conversation, tea, or cards. The lounge is as delightful a place as is the reading and writing room, or the smoke room, to enjoy a book from the well-selected library. ("White Star Liner")

The *Adriatic* was part of the White Star and Dominion Line, the same company that produced the *Titanic*. In fact, the *Adriatic* was dispatched in 1912 from New York to help with the rescue and recovery of passengers following that historic disaster. It had luxury accommodations, including an indoor pool and Turkish bath (the first cruise ship to offer these amenities). The features of these baths sound

Fig. 1.2 *RMS Adriatic*. Wikimedia

sumptuous even by twenty-first century standards: "They consist of the usual hot, temperate and cooling-rooms, with shampooing rooms, a plunge bath, and massage couches. It is likewise worthy of remark that three electric baths have been provided" ("White Star Liner"). By 1926 the RMS *Adriatic* was one of the older ships in the White Star fleet and probably not as posh as other transatlantic steam liners, but it still must have seemed like stepping into another world for my great-grandmother from rural North Dakota.

And so, a new story emerges for these cufflinks, but this one is about a successful immigrant who is now an American citizen, travelling back to Ireland to visit family, friends, and the graves of her husband and two children that she had to leave behind. My great-grandmother has been in North Dakota for almost a generation. For over 20 years her family has thrived running a boarding house in Jamestown, a town bustling with workers for the railroad needing a place to stay for a few weeks or months. This was an all-hands-on-deck operation: anyone in the family old enough to hold a broom or fry an egg would have been put to work. But by 1926, her sons and daughter are all college graduates or successful in a trade: her oldest, Jack, has become a lawyer and would eventually work in the office of US District Attorney for the State of North Dakota. My grandfather, Peter, is a relatively recent college graduate himself, beginning his career as a teacher of mathematics and industrial arts. Ma, approaching sixty, is probably not taking in boarders any longer. Some days she helps out with running a business owned by the family, a machine shop that performs contract work for the railroad and other local businesses. Her daughter, Nellie, is a bookkeeper there, and another of her sons, Mike, runs the shop.

Looking at the photographs of the *Adriatic* and reading the descriptions of its accommodations, I know immediately that this is the place where my cufflinks originated, the room where they first lived. There is an image online of a biscuit tin printed with pictures of the *Adriatic* (with those famed Turkish baths) that could be purchased on-board the ship. She must have picked out the cufflinks in a gift shop on that journey as a souvenir gift for my grandfather. Perhaps she bought matching sets for all her sons. Maybe she saved the biscuits for herself. I am struck for the first time that these cufflinks are mementos not of a migrant's voyage, but of a tourist traveling overseas. They speak to me of the pride she must have had in her sons for their aspirations and successes. I still can't know for certain if they were won in that apocryphal game of shuffleboard. It is possible she played the game on that trip and came up with the story.

As I follow this voyage to its end, I also find the re-entry record at Ellis Island for my great-grandmother. That place looms so large in the imaginations of descendants of American immigrants, but when the first Mulready passed through there it was not as a foreign national. Her papers show her home address, 921 2nd St., Jamestown, N. Dakota, and that she became a naturalized citizen 10 years earlier in 1916 (*Passenger Record*). This was not the traumatic journey that had brought her to America a quarter century before. In fact, it may have been a voyage of healing, a way to sort out the personal losses that had sent her to American in the first place. I didn't realize the scope of that loss until I started looking for the story of these cufflinks. And that takes me to another set of objects, and another story.

II.

Over 100 years ago my family were victims of another global pandemic. I learned this, unexpectedly, while I was conducting research about my cufflinks. Objects preserve stories, but in this case, they also hide things: the cufflinks proved one of my family's prevailing stories to be false, even a purposeful fabrication. Documents I found in my research revealed the more stunning truth about the circumstances under which my family left Ireland. As objects they were boring and bureaucratic: a series of entries in a registrar's account book. At the time this discovery was a cause of some curiosity but didn't seem related to my research, so I filed the documents away. But in 2020, living during a more recent medical crisis, my family's experience with a nineteenth-century outbreak gained new relevance.

From 1896-1901, my great-grandfather, his sister, and two of his (and Ma's) daughters all died in Ireland of tuberculosis. How could this tragedy have been hidden from me for so long? My beloved grandfather was at least partly to blame. When Peter Mulready emigrated with his mother, siblings, and grandmother from County Mayo to North Dakota he was just a toddler, not yet two. What I know of this trip and the circumstances that led to the Mulready family leaving Ireland comes from an oral history my grandfather recorded on a cassette tape shortly after I was born. That recording is one of my most prized possessions. I have listened to it countless times over the years, to the extent that I have probably internalized much of what I know (or think I know) about my grandfather and my Irish immigrant family from these stories.

The tales he tells are riveting; with remarkable detail, my grandfather recounts his family's journey from Ireland to North Dakota, their hardships and successes, and his own life as an educator and director of the trade school at Father Flanagan's Boys Town in Omaha. This story begins with the narrative of the Mulreadys' life in Ireland and their final years there before they emigrated. They lived in a stone house on eight acres, where they had been for 400 years, according to my grandfather. The one-room house had an earthen floor and a loft they reached by ladder, where they slept on mattresses made from hay-stuffed sacks.

One detail that I have always remembered from this oral history is the story of my great-grandfather, Pat Mulready, sitting in the loft of his cottage at home reading the newspaper to his family and neighbors:

> Another thing about my father he was one of the only, the few men who could read in the village. Every night he'd come back he'd bring the Londonderry newspaper back with him. All the neighbors would gather in the house and he would sit on the ladder going up to the loft and read the news. (Mulready)

The image of my great-grandfather reading aloud in the loft, like the story of the cufflinks, has been with me from an early age. I can picture Pat Mulready in his home sharing the day's news, gossiping, singing, reaching out to a neighbor in need. We latch onto such stories because they forge intergenerational affirmations of our identity. Am I a reader and educator because of my great-grandfather? Stories like this help us make sense of our present by looking to the past.

My great-grandfather worked for the railroad in Ireland, where he earned a good salary, which is probably the reason the family was able to stay in the country even decades after famine had driven away so many others. But tragedy struck when he suffered an accident while at work: "…his job consisted of throwing out [railway] supplies at the different stations, and unfortunately they were throwing out a tie from a car and it hit him in the side. He came home and he was laid up for six weeks or so. In fact, he never did go back to work again. He died at the age of 33" (Mulready).

I love my grandfather's own political spin on the story of his father's death: "Now, in Ireland at the time he died, approximately 1903, there was no Social Security, no Aid to Dependent Children, nobody carried any life insurance, there wasn't such a thing." This is my grandfather using the story of his family's past to cast his own identity, now as a proud American. A New Deal Democrat who worked as a part of the WPA in North Dakota during the Depression, my grandfather believed innately in the importance of government support for the poor and elderly. I hear the strength of conviction in his voice as he speaks: this would never have happened in his adopted country. He goes on to say that as poor as the poorest American was during the Depression, it was nothing compared to the poverty his family left behind in Ireland.

It only occurred to me in recent years, when I shared this recording with my own children, that my grandfather did not experience first-hand much of what he reports in these stories. As the youngest in his family of six children he could not, for instance, have remembered the transit from Ireland, the reasons why his mother (my

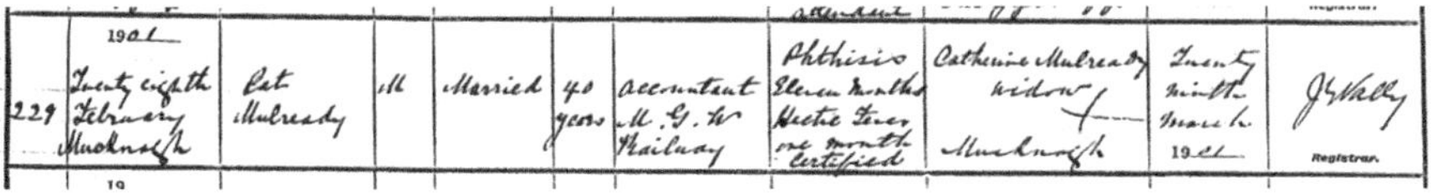

Fig. 1.3 Entry detail from the Irish Deaths Register, 1901. Irish National Archives

great-grandmother) chose to leave, or even many of the colorful tales he shares about his brothers. These are all part of an oral tradition that circulated within his family, shared many times over tea (or something stronger) with his brothers and sister. He tells them well, and with a remarkable level of detail ("the Londonderry newspaper," Colonel Blake, the name of their landlord, the stops the ship took on its way to America). In the end they are stories—quite good stories—but largely unsubstantiated.

What do objects add to our stories? How can materials like jewelry, books, documents, furniture, clothing, and other keepsakes help us better understand the past? These objects of history elucidate, enhance, but sometimes reveal inconsistencies in stories such as my grandfather's. The first document I found that upended his narrative was an entry in an Irish death registry. Here is the record from March 1901 recording my great-grandfather's death (Fig. 1.3).

Two key pieces of information directly contradict the oral account handed down through my family and change the way I now understand my own story. First, my great-grandfather was not a laborer working on the rail lines, a "supply man" as my grandfather calls him in his story, but an accountant for the Midland Great Western Railway Company. I had always thought that I was descended from poor Irish farmers, not a member of the professional class. This detail, though, fits with the story of his reading in the loft and earning a living wage. Second, and even more jarring to my view of this man and his family, he died not from a work-related injury but from "phthisis," the lung disease caused by tuberculosis. I also found entries for his two daughters, Anna Marie (13) and an infant Delia, indicating that they had suffered the same painful death before him, as had his sister, Eliza Mulready. According to the death records, Catherine, my great-grandmother, attended to all four of them in their final months and days.

These documents tell a new story of their own: of a compassionate sister-in-law who takes in and tends to a fatally ill family member even though she herself had just given birth. Of a mother who had to watch that infant suffer from "convulsions" that led to her death in just a few days. Of a mother and father who, with increasing panic, watch their 10-year-old in anguish with a debilitating lung disease over the course of three years. Of a wife who sees her husband of 20 years succumb to the same fate over the course of a miserable year. In the end he suffers through a month of wildly spiking temperatures, "Hectic Fever," as it is described in the register.

None of this was part of my grandfather's story. Before seeing these documents, I had never heard or seen the name "Eliza Mulready," most likely patient zero in my family's four-year struggle with tuberculosis. She is listed as a "Servant" in the Registrar's account book, and I wonder if she contracted the disease working in

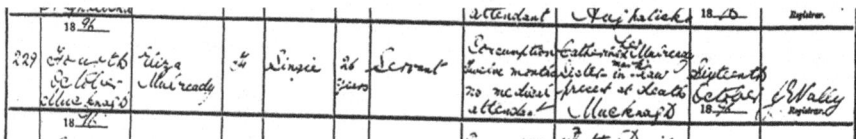

Fig. 1.4 Entry detail from the Irish Deaths Register, 1896. Irish National Archives

another household, finding herself vulnerable as many service workers have in the COVID-19 pandemic. My great-grandmother nursed her in her final days, as indicated by the X in the account book: "her mark," the Registrar recorded on the document (Fig. 1.4).

Like migrants caught in the tides of war, disease, and environmental catastrophe today, the Mulreadys left Ireland in hopes of finding safety, better employment and economic opportunities abroad. Ireland in the early twentieth century was in the grips of a widespread tuberculosis pandemic; the bacterial infection killed at least 13,000 people there at its peak in 1904, accounting for 16% of all deaths that year. Even in the age of COVID, TB remains the deadliest infectious disease in the world. I feel both empathy and pride for my great-grandmother as I look at these documents. According to my grandfather, their landlord, a kindly man named Colonel Blake, advised her to take her five boys and young daughter and move to America. They left Ireland on October 31, 1901, a little more than six months after Pat Mulready's death.

III.

Our stories can be things, too. They begin as thought and breath, material of infinitesimal weight. But as we record and retell them, they gain a power disproportionate to their physical size. The fiction my grandfather passed on of his father's workplace injury and death was a kind of talisman that I imagine my great-grandmother crafted to ward off fear and stigma. It was a protective covering that could see her frail family through their journey. Diseases like TB and COVID-19 continue to mark their victims and their families with shame and fear. Maybe Ma sat her oldest boys down and told them sternly that *this* would be the story they would tell to Colonel Blake, to the medical staff that would screen them on-board the steamship *Corinthian,* and to the American immigration officials on the Canadian border when they arrived (the same border that was shut down in an effort to stop the spread of the coronavirus).

I speculated before that my cufflinks, with their portrait of the luxury ship *Adriatic*, were originally something of a metaphor for the Mulreadys' life in America; they manifested the achievements of an immigrant family. With the knowledge of my great-grandmother's grief and loss, I understand them differently. I wonder if these gifts, like the trip back home itself, were a small way that Ma could reclaim something in her past. Maybe my great-grandfather wore cufflinks when he went to work as a part of his accountant's professional uniform. Perhaps she saw her son carrying on the same legacy and wanted a material connection, something to link past and present.

For Peter Mulready these objects meant something different. He wasn't burdened by the unshakable memories of family death as his mother was. And as I imagine my grandfather wearing the cufflinks, I glimpse, I think, the origin of the story that came with them. "These? Oh, my mother was a shark of a shuffleboard player," I hear my grandfather say, "she won them on the boat from Ireland." My grandfather, the storyteller, would have turned this one out with aplomb, raising his wrists and showing off the cufflinks while spinning the tale, maybe with a wink and a sparkle in his eye. At some point he passed the story along to my mother and her siblings, its transmission assured by the objects that give it substance. When it comes time for me to pass along the cufflinks, I might recount that story, but I think I'll say more about what is really remarkable about these items: that they were loving gifts purchased by a woman whose strength preserved her family.

My research started with a novelty, an object with a curious story from my family's lore. What it led me to instead was more complicated and more valuable: the four Xs, the "marks" that my great-grandmother recorded for her signature as she reported a series of deaths in her family. I see the bold determination that carried her through that crisis in the large, final mark that she placed under "widow" for her husband. In these documents, Ma's resiliency through that pandemic arrives to me as if in a time capsule, intact and palpable. Her story is an unanticipated inheritance that, as I share it during the pandemic today, helps again to sustain the hope of our family.

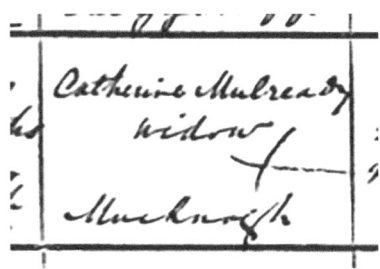

Procedures and Methods

In the forms of storytelling that are most familiar to us—novels, films, television series, comic books—people and human narratives are the focus. We are accustomed to protagonists, antagonists, heroes, biographical plot structures, and other human or subject-oriented methods that serve as the building blocks of the fictional and non-fictional worlds we create and consume. To tell a story from the point of view of an object is therefore a radical act in reimagining narrative. What happens when we put a thing, rather than a person, at the center of our story? How to craft an "Object Story" is also one of the key skills of this book, one that will serve as some part of the procedure in all the work that we undertake.

An object story begins with shifting your point of view, of bringing something that stands in the background to the forefront. This type of storytelling, however, also requires the incorporation of other skills: it is important to develop a series of close observations and descriptions so that you can offer your readers an immersive experience of the tactile and visual features of your object. Edmund de Waal, whose *Hare with Amber Eyes* is one inspiration for telling object stories, warns that when we ignore the details of objects in our history the result is a "thin" or "nostalgic" narrative. He calls his *netsuke* carvings "a small, tough explosion of exactitude" that require a similar "exactitude" in the way he tells their story (16). From a narrative perspective, such description is important because objects typically can't be given dialogue or tell of an experience. Their way of recording history is more indirect and emerges only when we can observe all the physical traits they present to us. Patient descriptions will also help you in your research to understand when and where the object comes from, how it was made, and how its original owners might have used it.

Two researchers in design theory, Jacob Buur and Preben Friis, have developed a method for telling object stories that aids designers in understanding how people, objects, and environment interact in the formation of experience: "object theatre." Buur and Friis recommend creating a puppet show (even a makeshift one will do) to help you perceive the dramatic interactions between "object-characters" and human characters. Can you imaginatively inhabit your object(s) as a character in a story, seeing and feeling how they would perceive the people around you? When you switch back to the perspective of a human actor, how has your perception of the object changed? What do you understand better about the story you are telling having taken on these multiple viewpoints? While their "object theatres" are intended to help product designers empathize with users, such an approach may also be helpful to you as a writer imagining your object's use and history.

In this chapter, I use one of the objects I inherited from my grandfather to delve into the history of my family's emigration from Ireland to the United States. While this work is meant to be a model for your personal object memoir, it is truly only one of many approaches one could take to such a project. You should select an object that has some kind of personal meaning to you or your family. This could be anything from a quilt to a book, a small piece of jewelry or a building. Even a set of documents like letters or papers from an archive (like the kind I turn to at the end of my story) can work as a starting point. But try to choose an object that you are genuinely curious about, or that has some kind of exciting or strange story attached to it—these tend to be the best objects for the project. If the object is too large or precious to get a hold of, or if it is in the possession of a family member who lives far away, photographs or copies are fine. Just be sure you get detailed images of the object from multiple angles so that you can see the various details that will help you in your research (especially maker's marks, dates, patent numbers, or other identifying information). If nothing comes to mind immediately for you, begin asking other family members about heirlooms, sentimental objects, or other items that might illuminate your personal story.

My students have uncovered remarkable stories by engaging in this process of personal object study. Here are a few examples—

- *A Ticket from a Spanish Bullfight* sold in 1931 connected my student to her great-grandfather's teenage years as a diplomat's son in Europe.
- *A Cache of Letters* sent from Nuremberg documented life in occupied postwar Germany from the point of view of an American Army Colonel's wife.
- *A Humble Belt* was the inspiration for a memoir that tells the story of a family's harrowing escape from Soviet-occupied Ukraine.

From there it is essential to interview relatives, friends, experts, and anyone else who can help you find the story of your object. If you have never recorded a grandparent's or great-grandparent's oral history, this is a perfect time to do so. If it's possible you should have your object with you for these interviews (or photographs of it) so that your subject can feel and examine it. You might be surprised at what comes out of such conversations, as objects are often keys to memories that have been locked away. Remember, though, that stories may be a good source of information, but your research might reveal a more complicated history behind your object. Unlike stories, objects bear material traces that are more resistant to change. They witness and verify the past in was that our imperfect oral traditions cannot. As such, to tell an object story is to experiment with new forms of narrative and to see opportunities that may depart from the human-oriented stories that we know.

In my courses, students often write their object stories over several weeks through a shared course blog. This allows us to break down the components of the story into more manageable pieces: descriptions of the object, accounts of the object's history in the family, research into the manufacture and creation of the object, stories of the object's significance today. These "short assignments," as the writer Anne Lamott calls them, are also good exercises to help students develop the new ways of seeing and writing encouraged by Object Studies (16-20).

Resources and Research

Genealogy is a hugely popular hobby, and so there are many resources available to find dates, facts, photographs, and other valuable information about your family. You may be fortunate to know someone in your family who has already carried out this work—if possible, be sure to look at primary documents they may have that can tell your family's story. If you are starting from scratch, companies like MyHeritage or Ancestry.com offer an easy way to set up a family tree and gather information quickly about your family. These sites are often pay-based but offer free trial periods that may be long enough for you to make good headway in your research for this project. Many of the resources that Ancestry (or others) charge you for are, in fact, freely available on the internet if you know where to look. In writing this chapter's model essay I found ship manifests, country entry and departure records, and other key documents to my research by searching through freely available databases hosted by British, Canadian, and American government sites (these are listed in the bibliography). Another important resource for genealogical research is the local library. Particularly if you are researching someone who lives or lived near to where you are working you may be able to find extensive information about them in your local public library. Many larger libraries have dedicated staff for their genealogical collections, so you can try contacting them by phone or email for additional assistance. I received helpful advice from a volunteer librarian in Ireland in the course of my research for this essay.

There are special challenges in conducting research on your family if you have African or South Asian heritage, or if you are the member of a first peoples or indigenous group. Some of the internet resources mentioned above may or may not contain information about these groups, especially if your ancestors were enslaved or didn't travel to your country through a government entry point. In researching my family in Ireland, I found that while the British colonial government kept some records of deaths and births in the nineteenth century, other documents from that period were hard to come by. I had to rely on my grandfather's claim that Mulreadys had been living where they were for "hundreds of years." I will cover more about conducting research where few records exist in the next chapter, but here it is worth mentioning that general historical narratives (such as those I consulted about tuberculosis in Ireland) can help give shape and content to the stories you are looking into, even if you can't find specific information about your family members. Historical newspapers can also be helpful in documenting births, deaths, marriages, and special events, even if you have found little else in government databases. Once again, if you are able to locate a specific place where an ancestor of yours lived, contacting a local historical society or librarian may be the best course of action for developing your research portfolio.

Further Applications

Object Memoirs

Object biographies and memoirs have become an increasingly popular genre and there are several wonderful examples that would work well as companion texts for a unit on personal writings and objects. Here are just a few:

Mudlarking: Lost and Found on the River Thames, by Lara Maiklem. Maiklem writes in lyrical beauty about her experiences with "mudlarkers," a community of treasure hunters and scavengers who have scoured the banks of the River Thames for generations in search of treasures. Her book is partly a memoir and partly an idiosyncratic history of London told through these objects.

All That She Carried: The Journey of Ashley's Sack, a Black Family Keepsake, by Tiya Miles. An inspiring narrative about the history of slavery and freedom told through an embroidered bag and the chain of ownership that connected three generations of African-American women in the South.

Crying in H-Mart, A Memoir, by Michelle Zauner. Zauner's memoir of grief and loss is also a remarkable story about food, cooking, and the ways in which we make (and are made) by the things we eat. Zauner, a Korean American, finds an intimate connection to her deceased mother by learning to cook the foods from her culture.

Braiding Sweetgrass: Indigenous Wisdom, Scientific Knowledge and the Teachings of Plants, by Robin Wall Kimmerer. The author, a botanist and member of the Citizen Potawatomi Nation, demonstrates how the knowledge of plants and the ecological world transmutes the boundaries of scientific and indigenous knowledge. Kimmerer's narrative expresses that the human transformation of the natural world is, for her, a process of being in tune with the material properties that surround us.

The Object Lives of Others

Many families do not pass down objects of sentimental or real value, or you may find it hard to gain access to your family's material history. Adoption, migration, fire, flood, or other natural disasters can also erase material family histories. In my experience, many students find personal object stories difficult to uncover for other reasons, as well: divorce, rifts within families, a reluctance in grandparents or other members of their kin to reveal painful memories.

There are nonetheless ways of telling personal object stories outside of your family history that may be of interest to you. In an essay published in *The New Yorker*, Kathryn Schulz writes eloquently of how the encounter with other people's things in thrift shops, antique stores, or jumble sales can connect us with a sense of the past: "The beauty of a true junk shop is that it is a kind of island in the stream of time. Things wash up there and are granted temporary clemency from the all-devouring future; people stop by and mingle, like time travellers at a rest stop, with fragments of the past" (31). You may want to discover what has "washed up" in the "stream of time" through your own "junk shop" project—for Schultz it was the discovery of a book by Langston Hughes that she found, miraculously, inscribed by the author himself to a now obscure twentieth-century African American writer. Wander around an antique store, jumble sale, flea market, or yard sale (it's remarkable how many names and venues we have for this type of object bazaar). Much of what you find may be anonymous, or bear few markers of its past. But you may be surprised by what you can find out about the original owner of an object from a signature or other mark of ownership, or even from the shop owner who may have known the person who donated the object. I recently purchased an old Canon camera from eBay and in communication with the seller found out that its original owner, her deceased partner, was a member of the Iowa State Music Hall of Fame; she graciously shared articles, photographs, and some of his artwork with me. Even if your object story is unable to connect directly to personal ownership, you might find it interesting and valuable to explore the past of an unusual object (there is a reason we call such things "curiosities").

"Significant Objects" (significantobjects.com) is another project that embraces "object stories," but with a monetary twist. The creators of "Significant Objects" describe it as a "literary and anthropological experiment" whereby authors take an item of little value, craft a story about it, and then sell it on eBay with their description (with the proceeds being donated to charity). Their website and subsequent book record 200 of these stories: a chocolate tin with a picture of Elvis, a Fred Flintstone Pez dispenser, or an old stapler all become more precious with the added value of a story attached to it. A former student of mine has replicated this project on a smaller scale in her creative writing classroom, asking students to "sell" their objects to each other in a mock silent auction. However you approach it, this exercise highlights in real terms the value that objects accrue when they have stories connected to them.

Works Cited

Buur, Jacob, and Preben Friis. "Object Theatre in Design Education." *Nordes,* vol. 1, no. 6, May 2015. archive.nordes.org, https://archive.nordes.org/index.php/n13/article/view/379.
Catalogue. *Board of Trade British Industries Fair Catalogue.* 1929, p. 130. *Grace's Guide to British Industrial History.* www.gracesguide.co.uk/1929_British_Industries_Fair.
de Waal, Edmund. *The Hare with Amber Eyes: A Hidden Inheritance.* Picador, 2010.
Ireland Deaths Registry. https://civilrecords.irishgenealogy.ie. *Irish Genealogy.*
Lamott, Anne. *Bird by Bird: Some Instructions on Writing and Life.* Random House, 1994.
Mulready, Peter. Interview. 1976.
Passenger List. Passenger Lists Leaving the UK, 1890-1960. Findmypast.co.uk.
Passenger Record. Ellis Island Passenger Entries. Libertyellisfoundation.org.
Segal, Troy. "What Is Rolled Gold?" *The Spruce Crafts.* https://www.thesprucecrafts.com/rolled-gold-jewelry-149521.
Schulz, Kathryn. "The Lost Giant of American Literature." *The New Yorker,* Jan. 22, 2018, pp. 26-31.
Steamship "Corinthian." Hansard Online, vol. 55, 21 July 1913, Column 1719, https://hansard.parliament.uk.
"White Star Liner *Adriatic.*" *The Marine Review*, vol. 35, no. 20, May 1907, pp. 17–19. *Gjenvick-Gjønvik Archives.*

Chapter 2
Objects and Local History

Working collaboratively with a museum, archive, or historical site, students perform research on an object that illuminates one or more narratives of their local culture or history. This community-based project connects students with librarians, historians, and other professionals to carry out work utilizing archival research.

Overview

In the first chapter of this book, I began with a curious object that served as a starting point for a research project into my family history. You may have found a similar object once owned by a relative, or perhaps you worked with an object from a more recent chapter of your past. The goal of that exercise was, in part, to give those who are new to Object Studies a personal experience with this kind of research. That chapter also oriented you to the importance of honoring the specificity of the thing itself. We saw how objects sometimes contradict or complicate the personal stories that we have inherited from our families. This "material first" approach is the foundational methodology of Object Studies. As I discussed in the introduction, starting with an object and the material world is a practical application of theoretical arguments that tell us to prioritize the physical presence of things to shift our critical eye.

But what if we have a compelling research question that doesn't yet have an object in its focus? These are the circumstances that usually arise in my collaborative teaching with a local historical site and museum. In New Paltz we are fortunate to have a well-established institution that maintains several stone houses built by the town's original European settlers and their descendants—a group of Protestant emigrees who first came to this area in the late seventeenth century. In addition to maintaining the homes and providing guided tours of the structures (most of which are now interpreted as museum spaces), Historic Huguenot Street (HHS) also keeps a library, archive, and collection of material objects related to these families and their centuries-long history in the region.

My students and I have worked closely with the expert staff at HHS, as well as with a colleague in our college's Archaeology department, to explore the history of our community through the objects found at this site. This includes things left behind by the indigenous people of our area, the Munsee, whose objects form the oldest material record at the site. Sometimes the projects my students undertake start with an odd or beautiful object: a chiseled stone knife, a button, a waffle iron, a chess set. Just as often, though, my students want to know something about the lives of the people who lived here: what was a woman's experience like in one of these stone houses in the eighteenth century? How did the Munsee live? What was their diet and how did they prepare food? How did the people who lived on Huguenot Street experience various events in American history?

The questions that you generate in your chosen project will be unique to your interests and specific to the place you live. In recent years, the questions that my class and I have been asking persistently (and that I explore in more depth in the model essay of this chapter) are about the history of slavery in our community. My students are usually surprised to learn that many of the Huguenots, and all of those who built the houses that remain a part of the historic site, were enslavers. When we tour the homes on Huguenot Street, we are walking into spaces that were built with enslaved labor and that housed many enslaved people over generations. In America, many still do not think of Northern states (like New York) as part of the history of slavery. The American Civil War (1861–1865), as the narrative is broadly and simplistically told, pitted Southern "slave states" against the "free states" of the North. That geographical alignment of enslavement remains deeply ingrained in the popular imagination—even Lin Manuel Miranda's Alexander Hamilton perpetuates the idea that Northerners didn't have slaves. In *Hamilton*, he taunts Thomas Jefferson: "your debts are paid 'cause you don't pay for labor." But in the late eighteenth century, the moment when the real Hamilton and Jefferson lived, enslaved labor fueled both the Northern and Southern economies. In 1790, the first federal census recorded 40,000 enslaved people in Northern states, 80% of whom were in New York and New Jersey. By 1799, New York had the largest population of unfree people in the North. The earliest Huguenot settlers here generated their income and wealth from growing and trading wheat, a lucrative agricultural business that benefitted from slavery. Almost from their first arrival in New York, these settlers enslaved people of African descent—in 1674 a member of the DuBois family made possibly the first purchase at a Kingston (NY) slave market. In 1790 the enslaved population of Ulster and neighboring Dutchess Counties climbed to nearly 3000, or about 15% of the area's population (Heidgerd 20–1). In New Paltz alone there were 300 enslaved people in the community's 344 households (Diversity and Inclusion 9). This is an uncomfortable legacy, but fortunately one that HHS has made a part of its educational mission to preserve and share.

The project in this chapter involves a collaborative process that will connect you with people in your campus, school, or community. Local museums, historical sites, and other regional archives are marvelously untapped resources for Object Studies that are available to many if not most colleges and schools. The process of generating your research question and identifying the object of your study will probably begin differently in each case. As an example, I will outline a project and research that focuses on a house (a cellar, in fact) and that began with a conversation with my knowledgeable colleagues at Historic Huguenot Street.

Model Essay

"Watch your head, Cyrus," Ashley says to me as we turn toward a narrow staircase. As I crouch, I have the feeling, as I often do in historical homes, that the space was not made for my six-foot frame. I am in the "Jean Hasbrouck House," New Paltz's oldest structure, making my way down to the stone building's cellar with Ashley Campone, Historic Huguenot Street's Collections Manager, and Carrie Almendinger, the Archivist and Librarian. Large beams of wood cross the ceiling, enormous hewn logs that are over 300 years old. The space is dusty and divided into two rooms. Each has a fireplace and, in the center of one of the rooms sits a large, unusual circular shelving unit that is built into the floor and ceiling. I feel the bubbling thrill of discovery, as I am getting to enter a part of the house that few visitors ever see, but my physical discomfort in the low-hung space also matches a mental unease: I know that this is the place where dozens of enslaved people owned by the Hasbrouck family spent most of their hours during a period that spanned more than 100 years. The only sign that this space once served that function is the fireplace that stands in a southwestern corner of the building's basement. Built sometime around 1786 during a renovation, it was used to keep the space warm enough for dwelling, heating water, or even cooking. Prior to that time, it was possibly the main cooking area in the house, as well, but when the structure was expanded in a 1786 renovation all cooking for the household moved upstairs. The buttress that reinforces the floor for the weight of the large upstairs fireplace can be seen in the photo. This small fireplace in the basement would have been strictly for the enslaved members of the household (Fig. 2.1).

Unfortunately, there remains only a scant material record of slavery in this region. The enslaved individuals on Huguenot Street lived in close proximity to the families they served. Unlike in the South, where separate slave dwellings were more common, New York quarters were typically in the enslavers home. To be enslaved, to be property, meant that you had no legal right to ownership of any object. Whatever few things the unfree may have kept in their possession, therefore, were legally a part of the enslaving family's possessions and therefore almost impossible to identify as belonging to the enslaved. The activities carried out by these enslaved people, too, were the sort of day-to-day labors that may not leave a significant identifiable material trace: cooking, sewing, cleaning, and farming. While these occupations have objects associated with them, these are the kinds of things that usually are not saved or handed down. Or they may be items like clothing, which in a pre-industrial world would have been used and re-used into oblivion. This is yet another way in which African Americans, Afro-British, and all members of the African diasporic community have been and continue to be dispossessed: their material culture has been largely erased.

Fig. 2.1 Jean Hasbrouck House Cellar Fireplace. Historic American Buildings Survey (Library of Congress)

Reclaiming this history, as literary scholar Saidiya Hartman incisively puts it, "requires excavations at the margins of monumental history in order that the ruins of the dismembered past be retrieved, turning to forms of knowledge and practice not generally considered legitimate objects of social inquiry or appropriate or adequate sources for history making …" (11). Although Hartman's language here is partly metaphorical ("margins of monumental history"), she is also calling on scholars to use physical records and archives as a way to view the struggles of enslaved peoples with the "politics of domination" that controlled their lives (11). Similarly, Martha Katz-Hyman, an expert in historical preservation and a leading scholar of the material culture of slavery, encourages research that takes a broad viewpoint when considering what constitutes the objects of that history:

> … everything used by the enslaved, whether these were goods found in their own slave quarter houses, or their work tools, or the ceramics, furniture, textiles, and other goods used by them in the course of their work, *or the houses they lived and worked in as well as the landscapes in which they were situated*, the clothing they wore and how they wore it, their food and how they prepared it, even their hairstyles and oral traditions, was a part of their culture. (109, emphasis added)

Object study of this kind is valuable because it can help to shift the prevailing, sometimes toxic narratives of history from people and politics (Europeans vs. Africans, white vs. black) to the physical and economic realities that all people inhabit. One historian of slavery in the New Netherlands (today's New York) describes such scholarship as an act of "discursive restitution," a way of using research to correct for past narratives (Goodfriend 238). When (and if) we tell the story of enslavement in the New Paltz community, we begin with the European settlers who purchased the land that would become New Paltz from Munsee Indians in 1683. The names of these families can be found everywhere in this area of the Hudson River Valley: Hasbrouck, Deyo, Freer, DuBois, LeFevre, Bevier.

I wanted, therefore, to begin this project as locally as possible to understand the material conditions of slavery in this place. What remains, and what can it tell us about the institutions of enslavement, the history of the period, and, most importantly, the lives of the people whose presence here was the product of violence and systemized oppression? These are perhaps the most important historical questions we can ask today, particularly during a time when around the world we continue to struggle with the intolerable consequences of slavery. Object Studies might provide us with a way to recover this history in a way that can help us gauge its real material aftermath. How can we truly understand the lasting impact of this institution without knowledge of its material consequences in our world, even today? As Hartman and Katz-Hyman show us, however, we need to look to the margins—places like basement or attic slave quarters—to find the people, stories, and struggles that have been lost.

It is difficult for me to imagine this dark basement as permanent living quarters. The contrast between the comfortable, even stately rooms on the first floor of the house, where the family lived, and this dusty dark area is profound (Fig. 2.2). Sojourner Truth, a woman born into enslavement in a nearby community (just a few miles from where I write this), described the experience of living in such a space in vivid detail; the conditions constituted some of her first memories (the voice is in the third person as she reported to the editor who compiled her *Narrative*):

> A cellar, under this hotel, was assigned to his slaves, as their sleeping apartment,–all the slaves he possessed, of both sexes, sleeping (as is quite common in a state of slavery) in the same room. She [Truth] carries in her mind, to this day, a vivid picture of this dismal chamber; its only lights consisting of a few panes of glass, through which she thinks the sun never shone, but with thrice reflected rays; and the space between the loose boards of the floor, and the uneven earth below, was often filled with mud and water, the uncomfortable splashings of which were as annoying as its noxious vapors must have been chilling and fatal to health. She shudders, even now, as she goes back in memory, and revisits this cellar, and sees its inmates, of both sexes and all ages, sleeping on those damp boards, like the horse, with a little straw and a blanket; and she wonders not at the rheumatisms, and fever-sores, and palsies, that distorted the limbs and racked the bodies of those fellow-slaves in after-life. (14–15)

There are no boards in the current cellar at the Jean Hasbrouck house. Large flagstones cover the ground. In an earlier period, when it was a dwelling space, there were likely wood planks in place to cover the floor and keep sleeping bodies away from the dampness. But maybe not. It was not uncommon for straw bedding, as Sojourner Truth attests, to be the main covering for the floor.

Fig. 2.2 The Jean Hasbrouck House. (Photograph Courtesy of Historic Huguenot Street)

Slave quarters, as one scholar notes, "… materially represent the dynamic negotiation between slaves and masters as to the location and design of shelter, living and working conditions, household composition, and social life" (Katz-Hyman and Rice 448). Looked at from this point of view, the Hasbrouck house in the 1790s created the physical conditions that set and reinforced a literal hierarchy (much as British manor houses did in the same period). You feel this in the space itself: although the ceiling is high enough to allow one to walk upright through the cellar, even a person of average height needs to duck slightly to avoid the heavy wood beams overhead. It is as though the basement was intended to make its inhabitants bow in perpetual subservience. Sojourner Truth's description captures the physical impacts of living in this environment; the cellar "… distorted the limbs and racked the bodies" of those who lived there with her.

In the case of the Hasbrouck home cellar, there are further layers of "material representation" to consider. Since the late eighteenth century, the basement has comprised two rooms, separated by a stone wall. The West Basement is the section that housed the enslaved people described above. It is here that the small "English type" fireplace was constructed, probably in 1786, during a major renovation of the house as Josiah Hasbrouck took over primary residency there. As a detailed architectural report carried out in 2002 indicates, this fireplace was used for heat rather than cooking and indicates the use of the space for dwelling. The room has a small window and a door that leads outside—a separate entrance and exit that would have allowed the people who lived in the basement to enter without using the main floor of the house. I wonder what the door indicates about the social relationships in the house; was there a level of trust between the Hasbroucks and the people they enslaved that allowed for a separate access? Or was it so important to the enslavers that their slaves not use the main floor entrances that they were willing to take the risk of an escape? We have documents that show Hasbrouck was a part of a "bounty society," a group of local men who pledged to pay one another for the return of a fugitive slave. Perhaps "Colonel" Josiah Hasbrouck was confident enough in his ability to track a runaway that he didn't worry about the access they had to the world outside that door. It is hard to know for certain, but these possibilities suggest how a seemingly simple material artifact like a door creates interpretive possibilities for exploring complex social dynamics.

The home that Josiah inhabited with the people he enslaved in 1800 had been in his family for four generations: in 1721 his grandfather, Jacob, built the large stone house on the site where his father, Jean, first established the homestead in the seventeenth century. Although it would be difficult to perceive this from the perspective of the meager lodgings in the basement, this house is one of the most significant examples of early Dutch-American architecture today. To modern eyes the exterior of the stone house may seem quaint, even simple—the homestead of a successful yet modest farmer. But it was a marvel of early eighteenth-century colonial material culture. At that time stone conveyed wealth within this community, and the Jean Hasbrouck home (even today) stands out as a large and ostentatious expression of that material. Jacob Hasbrouck, who built the house in 1721, was making a bold statement to his neighbors and the broader community about the status of his family. Unlike other neighboring houses, which were smaller, two-bedroom homes built in stages over years or decades, the Hasbrouck house was constructed all at once as a four-bedroom structure. Furthermore, no other home or structure on Huguenot Street used as much stone in its construction. Stone was an expensive material for building: labor intensive to gather and transport, it also required the hiring of skilled craftsmen who could cut the stone to size, arrange it properly to bear the load of the house, and stack and mortar it into place. The names of the stonemasons who carried out this work are almost entirely lost to history, as are the identities of the carpenters who framed the windows, the glaziers who made the windowpanes, the bricklayers who built the steep chimneys, and the various other skilled and unskilled laborers who had a hand in constructing the house. Two of those men, though, were likely enslaved by Jacob Hasbrouck in 1721: Garret and James. Built during the winter months after their work on the harvest was complete, the home would be theirs, too, if not in title then in habitation.

By 1798, the Hasbrouck family owned and enslaved at least thirteen people. Eight of them, three men and five women, lived in its basement dwelling space. A woman identified only as "my Winch [wench] Kingo," gave birth to a girl named

Dian in the house, maybe in the same cellar space where I stood. We know this because in 1800 her owner, Josiah Hasbrouck, recorded the birth as the first Town Clerk of New Paltz (he created the position, in fact). As such, he was required to register the names and birthdates of all children born to enslaved people after 1799. New York State introduced a policy of gradual manumission in 1799, whereby anyone born in that year or after would be technically free but beholden to an apprenticeship with their master until their twenties. We thus find in the record the odd rhetorical position of the slave-owning Clerk referring to himself in the third person:

> One Thousand Eight Hundred & one October the Twenty Secon [sic] Coll [Colonel] Jos. Hasbrouck Farmer of the Town of New paltz Did Deliver to me a note in Writing the purport of it was that he had on the Ninth Day of last July a black female Child born of my Winch Kingo and named (Dian) Recorded by Me. (Josiah Hasbrouck, Town Cl.) (*New Paltz Register of Slaves*)

The name in the registry, "Kingo," is all the evidence we have of this woman's existence. Perhaps her name was an alteration of "Kongo," the embattled African nation that was the origin point for many of the enslaved people of the Atlantic world—a reminder of her foreignness to this environment. Penned in the book, the name survives as a reminder of New Paltz's larger place in the global mercantile economy. New York, and before it, New Amsterdam, was part of the broader Atlantic slave-trading world: by the 1660s, enslavers constituted one in eight citizens of New Netherland; persons of African descent made up a quarter of the colony's population. When the English took over control of the colony in 1664, their regulations broadened the economic incentives for using enslaved labor by limiting the number of white Europeans who could be brought to the colony for labor (Wright 104).

The "Register of Slaves," as it is called on the cover of the manuscript book that still survives in New Paltz Town Records, also documents the institutionalization of slavery in the community. It highlights the Hasbrouck family's central role in that institution, especially Josiah, who by 1799 was one of the wealthiest members of the New Paltz community. The value of his estate was estimated at over $10,000, making him the second richest man in town. The people he enslaved comprised an essential part of that value, not only because they themselves could be sold or traded, but because their labor generated sources of valuable income for the family. If Josiah Hasbrouck made money as a "farmer" as it indicates in the slave ledger, then it was in large part because Kingo and the other enslaved members of his household kept his labor costs low.

Looking in the basement of the house leads us to another important source of income for the Hasbrouck family. The other half of this level, the East Basement, is an open room with four shelves in it: three rectangular units that hang from ceiling, and a custom-made spinning shelf in the middle of the room (Fig. 2.3). These shelves were constructed at the same time as the other renovations took place in the cellar (1786) and were likely put there to house merchandise for a general store that operated from the main floor of the home. One of the shelves in the basement is especially striking: a large, tiered circular unit that spins on a central axis extending from floor to ceiling (Fig. 2.4).

Model Essay

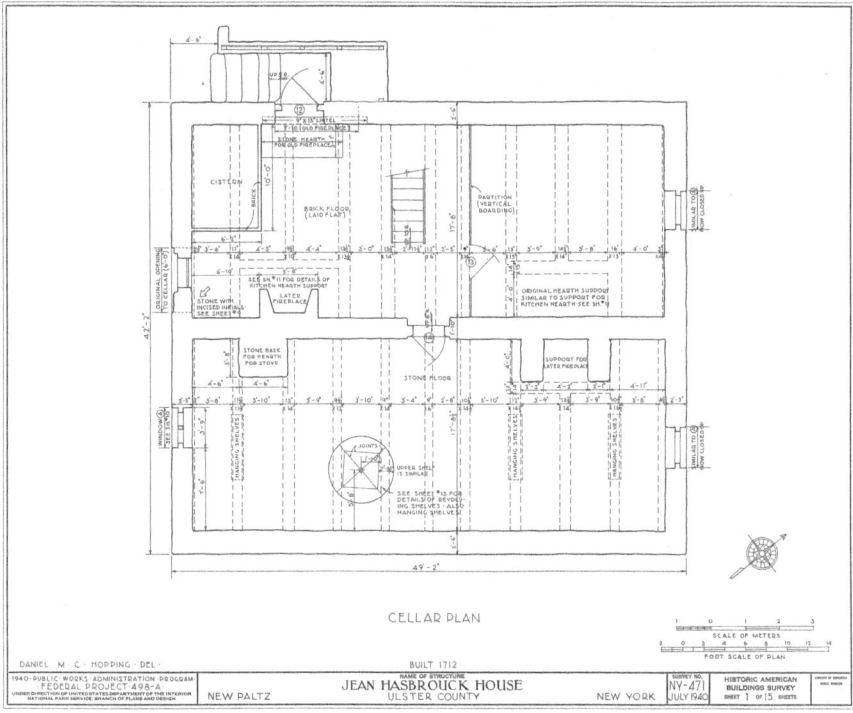

Fig. 2.3 Floor Plan of the Jean Hasbrouck House Basement after renovations in 1786. (Courtesy of Historic Huguenot Street)

The shelves were crafted by hand and remain a fine example of woodworking technique. Each tier or plate is comprised of planed boards that fit together like a large jigsaw puzzle to form perfectly circular shelves. Even after nearly 250 years, the shelves are un-warped, undamaged, and could clearly hold a significant weight. Most remarkably the shelves still spin smoothly and easily around their central axis, with no creaking or seizing. Even though the shelving unit was built for purely utilitarian purposes, the family clearly invested some money in having this unique shelf made. As "bespoke" work (the term craftspeople use for one-off specialty orders) it would have been more labor-intensive and therefore more costly than basic shelves (such as the other three in the same room).

The architectural report from 2002 dated the circular shelf to the 1786 renovation and speculated that these storage additions were for preserves and other food storage for the household. But canning and food preservation relied on techniques and technologies that wouldn't become widespread until later in the nineteenth and twentieth centuries. Food storage in the eighteenth century was more likely to take place in barns, outhouses, and external larders and root cellars that, in New England, were built into the ground. Cellars were actually too warm for this purpose, especially this one with its fireplace and source of heat. It may be that the shelves were

Fig. 2.4 Rotating circular shelves in Jean Hasbrouck House cellar, constructed in 1786. (Photo by the author)

used for food storage later on, but given the time they were built it makes more sense that they would have been additions designed for the family's new business venture: a general store that operated on the first floor of the house. As the population around New Paltz grew, the Hasbroucks understood a business opportunity when they saw it; Josiah established a general store in New Paltz sometime before 1790 to service its growing population. The new store probably started operating around the time of the household renovations and stayed open through 1811. Surviving ledgers show that the store traded in various foodstuffs, as well as "liquors, textiles, household supplies, farm tools and supplies, and construction materials in exchange for marketable agricultural products, such as wheat, flax and flaxseed, butter, ashes, nuts, and beeswax" (Crawford & Sterns 1.26). It also operated as the local tavern. The venture would grow into Hasbrouck and Company, a business that was one of the first mercantile operations in the area.

The expansion and renovation of the cellar in the 1780s, including new shelving, seems that it was associated with the opening of this business. The circular shelf would have been well-suited for the purpose of storing items for the shop. Like smaller circular shelves used in kitchen cabinetry today, the design allows for more objects to be stored in a smaller space. It also enables easier view and quick access to the various objects on the unit. The heavy construction of this particular shelf indicates that it was designed to hold a large amount of merchandise. As you enter this room of the cellar the turning shelves are directly in front of you; I can see a clerk or assistant speedily coming in to grab needed items for restocking.

Thinking back to one of the framing questions of this chapter, how do slave quarters "materially represent the dynamic negotiation between slaves and masters as to the location and design of shelter, living and working conditions, household composition, and social life," I am struck by the way this split basement space—part slave quarters, part storeroom—brought together the pieces of the Hasbrouck family's "property." It is an unsettling observation: on one side of the cellar the family held commodities and merchandise that would be sold in its thriving shop. On the other the Hasbroucks held what they viewed as the human property of the household, its labor supply. The space represented but also created a material equivalency between these two categories of "objects"—and as repugnant as that idea is to us today, that is what enslaved human beings were in the eighteenth century. Just as the Hasbrouck family's wills itemized homes, furniture, and kitchen implements, they also included the names of their "negro slaves," along with their monetary value; the cellar of this home is a material manifestation of that brutal economy.

One of the first histories of the Huguenots was written in the early twentieth century by Ralph LeFevre, a descendant of "the Duzine," the families that colonized New Paltz. His history therefore reveals the biases one might expect from a person with close connections to the community. Here is his first-hand description of the basement of the Jean Hasbrouck house, written more than 100 years before my visit there:

> Descending to the cellar we find a higher ceiling than in the other old houses. There is one dark room, without a window, in the cellar, but we do not find the sub-cellar which two or three of the other stone houses in the village had and which we are informed was to store liquor in or to put things in for safe keeping, to have them out of the way of the slaves. Doubtless this dark room and the sub-cellar in other old buildings were for the same purpose. Part of the cellar is paved with stone, part of it with brick, an evidence of comfort we have not seen in other old houses. (LeFevre 399)

By LeFevre's account, the basement sounds like a cozy den, a characterization drawn in striking contrast to Sojourner Truth's despairing depiction of living in such quarters. What arrests me about LeFevre's story, though, is how he brings up the presence of unfree people in the home. It is not that the stone and brick floor was where they slept, that goes unmentioned, but that the cellar lacks a special storage space for liquor or "things ... for safe keeping." Other homes, he suggests, have these to be "out of the way of the slaves," but no such secure space is here. It may be that LeFevre thought the Hasbrouck's enslaved people slept in the attic, "out of the way." In fact, the organization of the cellar space in the Hasbrouck house I offer here presents a direct challenge to LeFevre's racist supposition that enslaved people would steal liquor or needed to be separated from valuable goods. The East

Fig. 2.5 Door separating main rooms of Jean Hasbrouck House cellar. Historic American Buildings Survey (Library of Congress)

Basement, with its storeroom of goods, was not kept under lock and key. The passage between the spaces is an open archway today, but as recently as 1933 the original door and its hardware were still there, and it shows no evidence of a lock or bar (Fig. 2.5).

Josiah Hasbrouck seems to have trusted the people he enslaved with a cellar full of valuable merchandise—perhaps (contrary to LeFevre's suggestion) including liquor for the tavern upstairs.

I wonder if that confidence was extended to those he enslaved because some of them were already involved in operating the shop and, therefore, had to be trusted daily with its merchandise and operations. Was there a role for slave labor in the family store? Although enslaved Africans and their descendants in the area largely carried out agricultural and domestic roles, it was not uncommon in colonial America to find enslaved labor used for other jobs, including more skilled professions like shopkeeping. In a recent examination of the broad economic impact of slave labor, historian Joe William Trotter summarizes: "Working as general laborers, domestic servants, building and construction laborers, deckhands, sailors, ship pilots, artisans, and factory workers, African people were indispensable to the growth and development of the new nation" (3). City newspapers in New York and around the country regularly advertised the need for enslaved workers with particular trade skills, Trotter notes. It was not uncommon, according to Juliet Walker, to find enslaved people operating as what she calls "intrapreneurs," individuals with "decision-making authority in managing their owners' business enterprises" (69). Such arrangements were a part of slave society throughout the colonial period. It isn't hard to imagine the Hasbroucks employed enslaved labor on the "back end" of the operation, as it is called in retail today: maintaining the storeroom, taking and unloading deliveries, fetching and restocking merchandise, and keeping inventories. As the labor historians Ira Berlin and Philip Morgan observe, "Exactly how slaves worked for their owners depended most vitally upon the requirements of particular crops and crafts, which shaped the nature of the work force, the organization of production, and the division of labor" (3). A successful business like the Hasbrouck shop demanded (and benefitted from) the free labor that the family's enslaved could provide. It is at least conceivable that in this household part of the division of that slave labor involved work in the store.

Although I couldn't find records that directly show the use of enslaved labor in the shop, there is a suggestive piece of local evidence that illustrates African American involvement in mercantile business during this time, and that fills out the portrait of Josiah Hasbrouck. It comes again from Ralph LeFevre, who in his history recounts a story that had been handed down to him through the community's oral tradition. He heads the story with the title "The Springtown Merchant of 1800"; it refers directly to the Hasbrouck store, as well as a second store that had opened on Huguenot Street by 1800:

> The following story dates back to about 1800, when Col. Josiah Hasbrouck kept a store in what is now the Memorial House and Ezekiel Elting and his brother-in-law Philip Elting kept a store in the stone house with a brick front ... A negro living at Springtown [a nearby road], had a little store, his goods being kept altogether in a large chest. He sold molasses by the pint and whatever other articles he had for sale in like proportion. In those days flax seed was one of the principal articles sold by farmers, and purchased by the village merchants. One day our Springtown merchant came to the village and having quite a high idea of his importance as a business man dropped in at Col. Hasbrouck's store, saying that as spring was approaching he thought he would come to New Paltz so that he and Col. Hasbrouck and the proprietors of the Elting store might "put their heads together" and dictate what price they would pay the farmers for their flax seed that spring. But Col. Hasbrouck did not take kindly to the idea of putting their heads together in this matter and the Springtown merchant left his store in a hurry. This story shows that although the slaves were not set free until long afterwards, a negro kept a store at Springtown, even if it was a small one; it shows, moreover, that the organization of a trust in those old days was attended with difficulties. (LeFevre 129–30)

This is a remarkable story on many levels. Firstly, as LeFevre rightly comments, it demonstrates that even at a relatively early date (1800—decades before general manumission in New York) there was a business operated by a free black man in New Paltz. At the time, there were a handful of enslavers granting manumission—the Ulster County Land Records include an entry stating that one John York of Kingston "set my negro man Charles on his liberty" in September of 1803 (*New York Land Records*). The "Springtown Merchant" must have been among those who found freedom at this early time. His prospects for operating a mercantile business that would compete with the Hasbroucks and Eltings, however, were limited at best. Perhaps the white shop owners were artificially setting the price of flax low to pinch the black man's profits. Or maybe he simply wanted to have say in setting a fair price for this important commodity. We can't know more than LeFevre tells us, but his description only thinly covers the violence (or threat of it) that took place: "Hasbrouck did not take kindly to the idea of putting their heads together in this matter and the Springtown merchant left his store in a hurry." The Hasbroucks and Eltings in this time were not freeing slaves—quite the contrary: the records of the period show that they continued to trade, inherit, and even hunt down runaway slaves throughout the early decades of the nineteenth century. Their names each appear on agreements among various enslavers in 1810 and 1811 to "Sell and Dispose of the Said negroes and retain the one moiety thereof for their troubles & Expences" anytime someone escaped (*Bounty Hunters Agreement*). This was a hostile environment for such an entrepreneur to operate.

Between 1784 and 1821, when he died, Josiah Hasbrouck would serve two terms in the US Congress, was the founding Town Clerk for the Village of New Paltz, and also served in the New York State Assembly (among other roles in local and state government). He is the kind of person that the metaphor "pillar of the community" was invented to describe. This may be the reason that the unnamed "Springtown Merchant" came to discuss business with him. Thinking about the possibility that Hasbrouck used his enslaved people in his store, I also wonder if this small-scale merchant felt more comfortable going to the shop to meet with the owner and "put their heads together." Had he spoken with one of the black workers there first before approaching Hasbrouck? It seems that he operated in good faith that a fellow shop owner would be willing to make a basic agreement with him—the kind that happens all the time in a market economy. I take offense at LeFevre's suggestion that the Springtown Merchant had "quite a high idea of his importance as a business man." But perhaps Josiah Hasbrouck and Ezekiel Elting were not only trying to force out the competition—and that is the gist of LeFevre's story—but also trying to show the people they enslaved, possibly some who were working in the shop, their place. The threat that the Springtown Merchant presented was not to their business, exactly, but to their worldview. If a black man could own his own business, what kind of hope might that offer to Kingo, the enslaved woman who gave birth in the same year of this alleged incident? Just as the Hasbroucks physically kept their enslaved laborers in the cellar, they enforced a mental diminution on them as well.

In conducting the research for this chapter, I have found the basement to be an operative historical metaphor. These stories remain hidden away, difficult to find in the darkness of the past. It seemed at times that there was, even, a willful eradication of slavery's legacy here. That erasure runs deep in New York's history and mythology. One founding document of that tradition is Washington Irving's 1809 *Knickerbocker's History of New York*, a pseudo-historical satire that retells the colonial struggles between English and Dutch settlers during the formation of the state. It is a complicated, multi-layered narrative, but one of the guiding ideas of the story is that the simple, sometimes oafish Dutch settlers (of whom the Huguenots would have been included) were usurped by a more canny, conniving group of English or "Yankee" colonists. The Dutch, for Irving, are known for their pipe-smoking and convivial drinking, as well as a general silliness. His catalogue of Dutch families is typical of these traits:

> First of all came the Van Brummels, who inhabit the pleasant borders of the Bronx: these were short fat men, wearing exceeding large trunk-breeches, and were renowned for feats of the trencher [eating]; they were the first inventors of suppawn, or mush and milk. Close in their rear marched the Van Vlotens, or Kaats-kill, horrible quavers [drinkers] of new cider, and arrant braggarts in their liquor. After them came the Van Pelts of Groodt Esopus, dexterous horsemen, mounted upon goodly switch-tailed steeds of the Esopus breed; these were mighty hunters of minks and musk-rats .... Then the Van Nests of Kinderhoeck, valiant robbers of birds' nests, as their name denotes; to these, if report may be believed, are we indebted for the invention of slap-jacks, or buckwheat cakes ... Then the Van Grolls, of Antony's Nose, who carried their liquor in fair round little pottles, by reason they could not bouse [drink] it out of their canteens, having such rare long noses. Then the Gardeniers, of Hudson and thereabouts, distinguished by many triumphant feats: such as robbing watermelon patches, smoking rabbits out of their holes, and the like, and by being great lovers of roasted pigs' tails ... (*Knickerbocker's History* Ch. V)

The family names Irving gives here are real, as are the geographic locations, many of which are neighboring communities to New Paltz in the Hudson Valley (Esopus, Anthony's Nose, Kinderhook, Catskill). Irving's Dutch are an unthreatening people: benign and humble, they are more interested in eating than a slave economy. He later shows them fearfully fleeing the English, who took over New Amsterdam and renamed it New York in 1664: "Every member waddled home as fast as his short legs could carry him, wheezing as he went with corpulency and terror. Arrived at his castle, he [the typical Dutchman] barricaded the street-door, and buried himself in the cider-cellar, without venturing to peep out, lest he should have his head carried off by a cannon ball" (*Knickerbocker's History* Ch. IX). These portraits of a meek and congenial people do not fit with the more common contemporary image of the violent enslaver, nor do they suggest a people capable of the shrewd economic calculations of slavery I saw in the Hasbrouck family.

Irving's account fits neatly with the version of the Huguenots LeFevre painted in his 1903 portrait of the Hasbrouck house and its symbolism, as he saw it:

> From cellar to garret the house is full of quaint reminders of the olden time—over two centuries ago, when the country around was a wilderness and New Paltz a little hamlet in its midst, where a handful of French Huguenots, fleeing from persecution, had found a home and a refuge, where they might worship God in peace and rear their families in comfort. (299–300)

With these stories in the background of the region's history, it is no wonder that 200 years later the early colonial history of New Paltz is still difficult to understand. As a team of architectural historians who compiled a report on the Jean Hasbrouck house wrote in 2002, "It seems that the satirical image created by Washington Irving of plump Dutch Boers, prospering from the natural bounty of the Hudson Valley Eden despite their sloth, still characterizes the interpretation of the region's past and its material culture" (Crawford 1.9–1.10). There is an accretion of false historical knowledge that makes it difficult to see this dimension of the community's history. While the lives of these former enslavers have been given a rich historical accounting, those of the enslaved who served them remain obscure.

But this past came to the foreground on my campus in 2017–2019, when, as part of a larger societal reckoning about the cultural remnants of slavery in America, we grappled with renaming buildings on campus that bore Huguenot family surnames. At SUNY New Paltz, Hasbrouck Hall was home to the largest dining center, a building that nearly every student living on campus would pass through daily. LeFevre Hall was a dormitory next door. The historical connections between the college and these families are deeper than names, though: the first version of the institution was established as the New Paltz Latin and Greek Academy by descendants of the Huguenots in the early nineteenth century. The New Paltz Normal School, the direct predecessor of the current college, was established in the 1880s on orchard lands that were once owned by the Hasbrouck family; Ralph LeFevre, who wrote the history quoted in this chapter, was a key advocate and actor in the creation of the school. Huguenot descendants served as members of the college's board of trustees from this time and throughout the twentieth century.

The process for changing the names of these campus buildings went on for two years, and involved collaboration between faculty, students, campus administration, and various members of the family organizations that continue to support Historic Huguenot Street and preserve its history. Student government, faculty government, and college president Donald Christian all supported the call for changing the building names. By a slim 4–3 majority, the College Council approved a resolution to remove Huguenot names from campus buildings. Starting in the fall semester of 2019, Hasbrouck Hall became Peregrine Hall, and five other buildings exchanged their Huguenot names for titles associated with local geography, ecology, or Native American traditions. As a member of the faculty, I supported these changes because I saw them as serving our educational mission. Our campus chief diversity officer, Tahena Pacheco Dunn said in a public statement: "We have re-imagined a SUNY New Paltz that not only accounts for its complex history but also invites the next generation of students to add to the story" (Hasbrouck Renaming).

Object Studies helps us to better understand debates like these over taking down monuments from the past that commemorate racist ancestors: Confederate Army statues and memorials, statues commemorating those who built and promoted the Atlantic Slave Trade and British Colonialism, the names on buildings, awards, museums, and other cultural institutions. The importance of these material practices is not merely symbolic, as it is sometimes argued. As objects that take up the spaces we inhabit and share, they are real places and discourses that make an imprint on the environment. If you are a descendent of someone who lived a life in enslavement, there is a physical significance to you if the place where you sleep is named after a slaver. But in removing the names, the campus also leaves open a gap in our history. If students were unfamiliar with the legacy of New Paltz slavery when we had buildings on campus named after slave owners, how will residents come to know about this regrettable legacy after years have passed and these names fade into memory? Even if the name "Hasbrouck Hall" no longer exists, I would want future students on my campus to understand the history of the place and who lived in the community.

The lessons of material cultural study show us that objects and places offer opportunities within our communities to use things to create new memorials and archives. I can imagine a project on my campus, for instance, of the kind the historian James Grossman describes:

> [Students] could work with design and architecture students to create historical markers—maybe even small monuments—that reside alongside and speak to a named campus building or statue, both historically and aesthetically. The students would be required to do the necessary research, write text, collaborate with colleagues in appropriate disciplines to prepare and submit proposals for construction, and perhaps use digital media to disseminate their work beyond the campus. ("Whose Memory?")

The stories and objects I have explored in this chapter lay bare the oppressive power dynamics and struggles for freedom that constituted the experience of those who lived in slavery in our village. These materials could, however, be an important part of community reconciliation with that past. I can imagine a plaque near the former Hasbrouck Hall dining and rooming complex that explained what sleeping conditions were like for these enslaved people, including images and the account of Sojourner Truth (after whom our campus library is named). Perhaps the story of slave labor could be told in a display with maps that show the fields where they worked that extend around New Paltz. Further research could tell us more about LeFevre's "Springtown Merchant" and the history of black entrepreneurship in the community, a monument to which could be part of a display in today's bustling business district. If the physical record of slavery in the community has been hidden away, then these measures could, even in a small way, bring those stories into the light.

Procedures and Methods

This chapter details how you can use the study of objects as a gateway to research on issues that are relevant to the history of your community—your college or university, the town or city in which you live, or even the broader region (as you or others define it) that is your home. The two central components and methodologies to this research are (1) working with those who have expertise in the "community" you have defined: librarians, archivists, historians, archeologists, or even eyewitnesses to important historical events, and (2) utilizing archives and other primary source material that you have access to in your community to develop your research.

Collaborations with Professionals

Each semester that I teach my courses in material history, I plan several weeks of the semester for this project. This includes a visit to Historic Huguenot Street, where my students and I tour the houses and talk to my colleagues there. We learn about the history of the people there through these homes and by hearing the stories that the tour guides use to interpret these houses. I have worked with the Collections Manager Ashley Carbone and Archivist and Librarian Carrie Allmendinger for several years, and their knowledge and insights about the history of "the street" as they call it is incredibly varied and rich. My students usually come away from our visit with a number of questions about the visit and ideas for projects—an initial step in the process is for them to email me about these possibilities.

We also have a class meeting where I invite a colleague from our Archaeology and Anthropology department, Prof. Joseph Diamond, to come and share his knowledge, as well as items he has collected from the many digs he and his students have carried out at the site over the years. This is one of my favorite days of the semester, as tiny bags of treasures circulate around the table: seventeenth-century clay pipe bowls, old coins, arrow heads and stone knives, buttons of various materials and patterns, as well as examples of pottery shards and pieces of stoneware from across the centuries. If the visit to the houses on Huguenot Street shows us how we interpret and imagine the lives of these people in the past through coherent interior spaces, the archeological record gives us a more dispersed but equally fascinating picture of the past.

Since I am neither a historian of early America nor an archeologist, I share with my students curiosity and wonder about our local community, but not expertise. I enjoy the challenge of learning along with them, in an authentic way, the subject matter that constitutes this unit of our course. This puts a special emphasis on having my students develop contacts and relationships with these experts; they are essential to the work of carrying out our projects together.

If you are in a course on material culture, your professor may have already established such professional contacts for you. Perhaps you visited (or will visit) a historical site as a class, be given a list of objects to choose from that you will work with, or be assigned to work with a pre-selected set of items from an archive. At some point, though, you will need to engage in personal communication with one or more experts who have knowledge about your project or who oversee an archive that is important to your work. Here are some examples of how you might reach out to such professionals:

Exploratory Email—Preliminary Research

Dear Dr./Ms./Mr. Librarian/Scholar/Expert,

My name is Cyrus Mulready, and this semester I am working with Prof. X on a research project related to slavery in early Huguenot society. Prof. X recommended that I contact you for your expertise on Huguenot cooking practices and how those enslaved in the household were involved in carrying out this work. She also suggested that you might be aware of some cookbooks or other archival materials that are a part of the holdings at Historic Huguenot Street.

I would be grateful for any resources you could refer me to, or, if you have time, to meet in person and discuss possible research opportunities in this area.

Many thanks in advance for your time,

Cyrus

[If you aren't sure if you are reaching the right person, don't be afraid to include that in your introduction: "I'm not sure if you are the person to contact with my inquiry, so thank you in advance if you can direct my question to the right place." If you can, try to ask a specific question or give a specific idea about your area of research.]

Archive Appointment

Dear Dr./Ms./Mr. Librarian/Scholar/Expert,

My name is Cyrus Mulready, and this semester I am working with Prof. X on a research project related to slavery in early Huguenot society. I see from your website that your institution has archival holdings related to Jacob Hasbrouck, Jr., and his son Josiah. I would like to set up an appointment to meet with you and look at these materials. The website indicates that you are open on Wednesday and Thursday afternoons from 12–4. I am available during those times, so please let me know if there is a time we can meet to discuss.

Thank you for your time,

Cyrus

Archival Research

An archive, broadly defined, is a collection of primary source materials relating to a particular person, place, institution, or topic. These often include objects such as diaries, letters, newspapers, and photographs, but archives can also hold rare books, government documents, business records, or other unique items that register details about people and places. Archives are important because they are *primary materials*, they come from and there for link us directly to the person or time that we are studying. In many cases they have not been interpreted or even found by previous researchers, and so can provide new or unexpected insights about the topics and objects you are studying.

Working within archives is also challenging because they are not usually as neatly organized as, say, a book with an index; you also cannot typically search archives in the way you can using a digital resource or search engine. Many librarians have created "finding aids" for items in an archive, and occasionally you will find that items from an archive have been digitized and therefore are available online or have search functionality built into them. But you might also find that you need to comb through pages of old documents, leaf through disorganized sheaves of letters, or carefully look through an old book in order to find what you are looking for. Oftentimes the best first step to working in an archive is a conversation with a librarian or scholar who is knowledgeable about its contents. They can save you time by pointing you in the right direction.

Archival research therefore offers a different kind of experience than you might be accustomed to as a student, but it also opens more possibilities for exploring questions that interest you. Often your professors might ask you to research a question that has a large body of literature associated with it. You may be able to find extensive digital resources on a topic like "Slavery in the Northern United States," for instance, by working with the online resources available through your library. But what if the topic is a local figure, like Josiah Hasbrouck, a key player in the model essay in this chapter? Research on people like him is limited in the scholarly literature, even though he was a major figure in the local economy here. The best place (perhaps only place) to find records on Hasbrouck is HHS as well as other local archives (see more below on Resources and Research).

But the resources that you find may not directly answer the question you have. Unlike a history book, where you find historical documents that have been interpreted by another scholar, archival materials can be more indirect. They can also be more surprising. In carrying out my research on Josiah Hasbrouck, to return to that example, I was amazed and troubled to find his name on a document signed by a group of New Paltz enslavers who were agreeing on a kind of contract whereby they would capture and return any escaped slaves owned by the others. This "bounty" document, as it is called in the archive, gave me an unexpected look at how slavery functioned in this society and the brutal behavior carried out by its practitioners. Such research will inevitably send you in new and unexpected directions in your research.

When you are using an archive, be sure that you research ahead of time the policies of the institution. Do they require you to make an appointment and do they have a time limit for research trips? Do they allow photography? Can you bring in a laptop? What are their policies on publishing the materials you are working with from the archive? Most institutions will give detailed directions on how they want you to work with their rare and valuable materials, so be sure to pay attention and follow their guidelines to the letter. If you are unsure or can't find such policies, contact the librarian or archivist you are working with or ask your professor.

Resources and Research

This chapter was spurred by the question: what material remains did the legacy of African slavery leave in this community? What can we see and touch that connects our present to that past? When working with local or regional history one of the research challenges can be a lack of widely published resources on your topic. Unless you are fortunate to live in a major city or a locality with an extensive record of historical research attached to it, you may find that even your college's research library does not have specific information about your topic. Internet resources such as Google Books, HathiTrust, and the Internet Archive can help fill in the gaps, but oftentimes your best research support will come from local librarians or archives. For this chapter I made extensive use of a deeply researched architectural report prepared specifically for the historical organization I was working with—such items can only be found with the help of local historians and archivists.

There are three main categories of research that you will want to gather to do the work outlined in this chapter: (1) general local histories and surveys (2) material cultural research related to your chosen object and (3) archival materials to elucidate specific biographical, cultural, or historical background.

General Histories and Surveys

You may or may not know much about your local history, so it is good to find a general source that is easy to read and gives a broad overview of the events that have shaped your area. Historical societies will often publish pamphlets or booklets for visitors that cover these broad details and are a great place to start. Such organizations sometimes have produced videos or will have other multimedia materials available online for you to review. The goal of this level of research is to educate yourself broadly about the place you are studying, but also to begin identifying important themes, events, people, and other possible topics that you might use to develop your research question. These local histories can perform another function—it became important to me in the model essay in this chapter to look at the interpretations of earlier historians and identify where blind spots or biases had developed. In comparing historical accounts written at different times in your community you may be able to get a sense of how historical interpretation has changed over time. When it comes to working with objects, such insights can help you understand the layers of historical narrative associated with the items of material history that are before you.

Material Cultural Research Related to your Object(s)

Students sometimes get frustrated in their research on local historical objects because they can't immediately find any specific scholarship on their object. The problem is usually that they are thinking too narrowly about their topic. In this chapter, for instance, I would have had a hard time finding research on cellars in Hudson Valley Dutch Architecture, or even slave labor in Ulster County. There are only a few resources that are so precise in their scope. But looking for scholarship on the material culture of slavery, labor histories, Dutch American architecture more broadly, and even on the history of cellars was much more fruitful. This is also an area where the advice of an expert can help. I have had students, for instance, who became interested in a particular item of furniture and who reached out to woodworkers or appraisers who deal in these items. Such individuals can be an invaluable resource in exploring niche topics in material culture.

Scholarly resources can be important models for you as you are starting your scholarly work in Object Studies. Reading in the scholarly area you are working can show you the kinds of methods used in that field, the way in which you might approach evidence, and even how you can formulate a better question about your object. This can be especially important as you work to make some careful logical connections when working with an object that doesn't have a robust history attached to it. In this chapter, for instance, I had to make some suppositions about the implications of my research on slave labor in the local economy by looking at broader histories of black labor in Early America. I also found great inspiration from scholars of material history such as Martha Katz-Hyman and the contributors to her *World of a Slave* volumes in developing these connections.

You may already have identified sources like these through your course readings, but if not check in with your professor or other experts for guidance in finding these key studies. If you are doing independent research, you might find it helpful to read review essays by scholars who survey large volumes of literature on a given topic. In this chapter I found such a piece in Theodore Landsmark's essay "Comments on African American Contributions to American Material Life." As is often the case in research, we follow the guideposts of scholars who worked before us to orient ourselves to new discoveries.

Archival Materials

One of the key skills outlined in this chapter is archival research, in part because your information on your object and topic in this project may only be accessible through such unpublished materials. This is especially true if you are lucky enough to be working with an object that has a well-documented provenance (ownership history) associated with it. Knowing the name of that owner will give you a starting place for searching in an archive, even one as simple as a local newspaper collection (an incredibly rich resource in many cases). Working in archives is itself a lot like working with objects—they require patience and an open mind. You might find that your ideas about an object are radically changed by what you find, or that you switch directions in your interpretations as a new set of documents comes into view. Such was the case for me in working on this chapter when I first encountered an archival image of a simple cellar door (Fig. 2.5). Preserved through a digital archive at the Library of Congress, this photo documents an object that is no longer a part of the basement space I was exploring. It helped me better understand the uses of the two rooms in the cellar and even potentially how the Hasbrouck family related to those it enslaved. Although it is more labor intensive than a Google search, archival work is also more rewarding as it helps produce knowledge about a topic that has not been widely circulated.

Further Applications

The project modeled here works with materials from centuries ago, but students with an interest in a community's recent material history can use the same methodologies to explore more contemporary objects. A student in my course wrote about an artifact from 1960s New Paltz culture, a pin advertising a local bar that implored "Make Orgies, Not War." She carried out research by interviewing the bar's ownership (it remains a local institution), delving into newspaper stories about campus war protests, and interviewing alumni who remember a time when the bar would make hand deliveries of beer to the campus quad. The same methodologies and principles of the chapter (consulting with experts, working with archives, developing a connection between the object and local history) were all applied equally well through this and other similar projects.

The work described in this chapter, when done at the scale of a class-size, can be developed into a special exhibition on local objects. This is a great opportunity to collaborate further with your local institutions, many of which have exhibit space available that they rotate regularly. Such an exhibition can be thematic (kitchen objects), period-based, or even broad in scope. You can also take such a project online through virtual exhibition software like Omeka. With the work produced by students in my class, and in collaboration with a local library council, I created *Storied Objects,* a freely available online resource on objects related to New Paltz history.

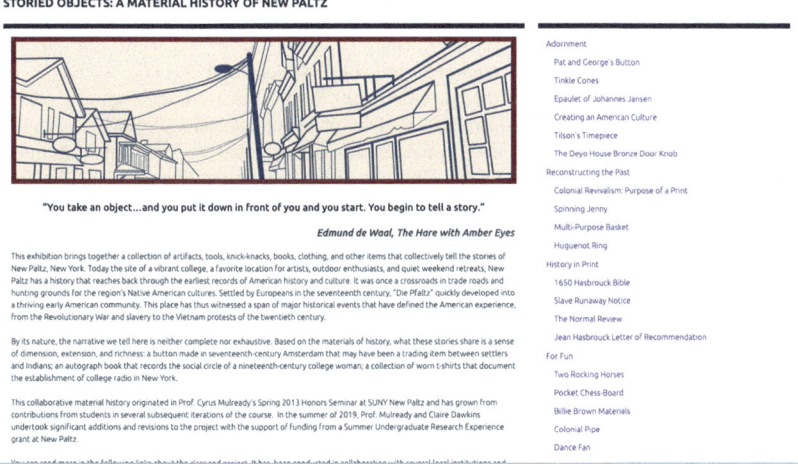

Acknowledgments This chapter would not have been possible without the contributions of the phenomenal staff at Historic Huguenot Street: Josephine Bloodgood, Ashley Campone, and Carrie Allmendinger. My immense thanks to them for providing me with ideas, research, and access to the Jean Hasbrouck house.

Works Cited

Berlin, Ira, and Philip D. Morgan. *Cultivation and Culture: Labor and the Shaping of Slave Life in the Americas*. U of Virginia P, 1993.
Bounty Hunters Agreement. 6 June 1811, Historic Huguenot Street Archives, https://cdm16694.contentdm.oclc.org/digital/collection/hhs/id/578/rec/102. Manuscript.
Crawford & Sterns Architects and Preservation Planners, and Neil Larson & Associates. *Historic Structure Report: The Jean Hasbrouck House*. 2002.
Diversity and Inclusion Council. *Hasbrouck Building Complex Renaming Dialogue Report and Recommendation*. SUNY New Paltz, 1 May 2018, p. 160, https://www.newpaltz.edu/media/diversity/Hasbrouck%20Renaming%20Report-Web.pdf.
Goodfriend, Joyce. "Merging the Two Streams of Migration to New Netherland." *The Worlds of the Seventeenth-Century Hudson Valley*, edited by Jaap Jacobs and L. H. Roper, SUNY Press, 2014, pp. 237–52.
Grossman, James. "Whose Memory? Whose Monuments? History, Commemoration, and the Struggle for an Ethical Past." *Historians.org*, 1 Feb. 2016, https://www.historians.org/publications-and-directories/perspectives-on-history/february-2016/whose-memory-whose-monuments-history-commemoration-and-the-struggle-for-an-ethical-past.
Hasbrouck Renaming. SUNY New Paltz. https://www.newpaltz.edu/hasbrouck-renaming/.
Hartman, Saidiya, *Scenes of Subjection: Terror, Slavery, and Self-Making in Nineteenth-Century America*. Oxford UP, 1997.
Heidgerd, William. *Black History of New Paltz*. Haviland-Heidgerd Historical Collection, Elting Memorial Library, 1986.
Irving, Washington. *Knickerbocker's History Of New York*. W. B. Cockney, 1848. *Project Gutenberg*, https://www.gutenberg.org/files/13042/13042-h/13042-h.htm.
Katz-Hyman, Martha. "Furnishing Slave Quarters and Free Black Homes: Adding a Powerful Tool to Interpreting African American Life." *Interpreting African American History and Culture at Museums and Historic Sites*, edited by Max A. van Balgooy, Rowman & Littlefield, 2014, pp. 105–14.
Katz-Hyman, Martha, and Kym Rice, editors. "Slave Housing." *World of a Slave: Encyclopedia of the Material Life of Slaves in the United States*, vol. 2, Greenwood, 2011.
New Paltz Register of Slaves (1799–1825). 1825 1799, New York Heritage Digital Collections, https://nyheritage.org/collections/african-american-presence-hudson-valley. Manuscript.
Landsmark, Theodore. "Comments on African American Contributions to American Material Life." *Winterthur Portfolio*, vol. 33, no. 4, Dec. 1998, pp. 261–82. doi:https://doi.org/10.1086/496755.
Le Fevre, Ralph. *History of New Paltz, New York and Its Old Families (from 1678 to 1820): Including the Huguenot Pioneers and Others Who Settled in New Paltz Previous to the Revolution*. Fort Orange Press, 1903.
New York Land Records, 1630–1975. 15 Sept. 1803, Ulster County Archives, https://familysearch.org/ark:/61903/3:1:3QS7-L9WR-NHCQ?cc=2078654&wc=M7CX-XTL%3A359005801%2C360664401. Manuscript.
Trotter, Joe William. *Workers on Arrival: Black Labor in the Making of America*. U of California P, 2019.
Truth, Sojourner. *Narrative of Sojourner Truth: A Northern Slave, Emancipated from Bodily Servitude by the State of New York, in 1828*. Edited by Olive Gilbert, Boston, 1850.
Walker, Juliet E. K. *The History of Black Business in America: Capitalism, Race, Entrepreneurship*. U of North Carolina P, 2009.
Wright, Donald R. *African Americans in the Colonial Era: From African Origins through the American Revolution*. John Wiley and Sons, 2017.

Chapter 3
A History of the World in Coffee Cups

Students select an item from a museum or from everyday life and trace its development through world history. This allows them to find and explain connections between cultures through objects and generate new questions based on the evidence they find in their research.

Overview

If you were to write a history of coffee, where would you begin? In the hills of South America? Perhaps in a coffeehouse in Vienna, London, or Istanbul? What about with a heavenly visitation from an angel? Or on a merchant ship sailing to Europe from India? What about with a simple coffee cup? Can a small item contain such a vast subject?

In my research, I am particularly interested in the representations of non-Western cultures within English history (my own area of expertise is sixteenth- and seventeenth-century British culture). In my day-to-day life, like millions of others around the world, I'm also a coffee drinker, and one who (I'll sheepishly admit) takes his morning brew pretty seriously. I would estimate that between our supplies at home and regular trips to coffee shops, my wife and I spend upwards of $80 per month on our coffee habit. We are not alone: In the United States we spend, collectively, $40 billion per year on coffee, and the average American consumes more than three 8-ounce cups of coffee per day (Harvard University). But coffee is one of those ever-present *things*, like many others, whose history and materiality are remarkably blurry to us in the modern world. Where does coffee come from today? Where was it grown originally? How did the rituals of coffee making and consumption come to be such normal parts of our lives? What does this mild stimulant and the objects we use to prepare and consume it tell us about our culture and history?

I came to these questions only after I happened upon something I didn't expect to find while browsing the British Museum's digital collection: a 300-year-old coffee cup from Persia (modern-day Iran). Perhaps it is because of both my personal and our societal obsession with coffee that I was quickly drawn in by the many examples of coffee cups held in the museum's collection. Over 300 results come up for a simple search of "coffee cup," artifacts ranging from pottery shards created in the Ottoman Empire to intricate pieces of porcelain manufactured in China for wealthy British buyers. The museum's search engine conveniently lets you organize results by date, so I was able to home in quickly on the many coffee cups held in the collections that date to the seventeenth and eighteenth centuries. I do not immediately associate the history of coffee with Iran, yet as I quickly found it was at the center of the region where the drink was first consumed. This discovery led me to an unexpected story of how and where coffee became an indispensable commodity of the modern world.

My ignorance of this history no doubt stems from the images and language that coffee companies now use to sell their goods. Walk into a Starbucks, Lavazza, or other local coffee shop, and you will see an impressive range of geographic and cultural signs: the names of the drinks speak to the European cultural heritage of today's market. Espresso, cappuccino, Americano, and barista are all words that originate with the Italian coffee bars that were the direct ancestors of Starbucks. Coffee from a "French Press," or prepared in a "French Roast," as well as Café au Lait (literally coffee with milk) reveal the Parisian influences on our café culture (a word that is itself, of course, French). Coffee retailers also tap into the exotic geographic origins of their beans to market them (Colombia, Sumatra, Kona, Java) and often use images of remote, mountainous regions in their packaging (primarily in South America or the South Pacific).

There is only scant evidence in today's local or mass-market cafés, however, of where coffee first originated. Hidden in the name of a sweet, chocolatey espresso drink (served with whipped cream, please) is an important clue: the Café Mocha. Mokha, an ancient port city on the coast of the Red Sea in Yemen, was the center of the coffee trade for centuries and a key link between the British Museum's Iranian cups and today's coffee drinkers. The central location of cities like Mokha on and around the Arabian Peninsula made these places important way stations for merchants sailing to and from Europe in the sixteenth and seventeenth centuries. Trading firms, primarily the English and Dutch "East India Companies," began moving products such as silk and spices from the "Spice Islands" and the "East Indies" (India, Sri Lanka, Indonesia, Malaysia, in today's geographic language) to Europe through these ports. Most of us know about this history of European trade and expansion, but we might be surprised to find out that coffee developed as a world commodity from the Middle East rather than the Indies. As one historian points out, it is the only "psychotropic substance" (tobacco, chocolate, tea) that did not originate in either the Western Hemisphere or East Asia; by the 1680s, coffee became the most significant commodity traded in the Arabian region (Barendse 221).

Coffee, like other examples of our material culture, shows us the ways in which humans transform the natural world to create new foods, building materials, and other products. As with many of the commodities in our global consumer society, however, we can forget their origins in the natural world: that the silicon and lithium that serve as the media for our microprocessors and batteries are mined from the earth (as we will see in Chap. 7), or that the pages of our books are refined plant fibers (the word "book" is itself etymologically related to "bark"). Foods and drinks like coffee, too, can be easily removed from their origins and the human labor necessary to bring me my morning cup: harvesting, roasting, grinding, brewing. Even as some of these steps can be carried out in our homes, I would guess that most of us don't know where our coffee beans came from (beyond the supermarket). Even if we have a vague sense that these plants are foreign to Europe and America, there is nothing about my store-bought coffee (beyond a potentially misleading label) that gives me a clue to its origins. One pile of ground coffee looks much like the next.

The same is not true of coffee cups, those items of material culture that I have found to be essential to the story of coffee itself. Decorated mugs, espresso cups, vacuum insulated tumblers, Styrofoam containers, the iconic blue Chinese coffee takeaway cup, and of course those ubiquitous disposable paper cups with cardboard sleeves and plastic lids; the containers we drink from today speak to the popularity and varied circumstances in which coffee is now consumed. In my case, I have no fewer than 15 coffee mugs stored in my kitchen at any given time. In my limited cupboard space, I am willing to dedicate nearly two shelves to these items. My coffee maker and storage containers for beans and grounds, likewise, occupy precious counter space in my small kitchen; we even keep a backup French press maker in case the power goes out. Yet when and if we think about coffee, we don't normally reflect on the objects we use to transport the drink in our hands. What, if anything, can these seemingly insignificant things reveal to us about the way we live now or how others have lived in the past? In the course of this chapter, I will look at three different objects: a cup made in seventeenth-century Persia, one depicted in an eighteenth-century French painting, and a more familiar cup from our world today. Each of these offers an insight to the connections between coffee production, consumption, and larger narratives of global history.

Model Essay

Introduction

"All of Europe is in the Orient. Everything is cosmopolitan, interdependent."
—*Compass*, Matthias Énard

The cups held by the British Museum are elegant but humble objects: they are small in comparison to our modern coffee mugs and do not have handles. Their dimensions vary a little, but most are only 4–6 cm in height (around 2 inches) and about 7 cm in diameter—roughly the size of smallish tea cup. Since I don't have the object in front of me I grab a ruler, and as I'm imagining the dimensions of these cups, I lay the tool across my hand and realize these cups are perfectly palm sized. The images and reported measurements show me that they taper from a wider brim to a

Fig. 3.1 Coffee Cup from the Safavid Empire, Persia, late seventeenth century, The British Museum

narrower base, allowing the holder's smaller ring or pinky finger at the bottom of the hand to form around the cup's lower rim. Contemporary designers call features like these "affordances," the ways in which objects quietly enable us to use them (Norman). I imagine the warmth of the filled cups sitting gently in the hands of their original owners, the smooth glaze of their exteriors pleasant to the touch. These are objects that ask to be held, cradled, spun softly around in the hand to distribute their heat. The cups and their contents fuel conversation. I see circles of coffee drinkers on a cool evening in Isfahan, once the Persian capital, sipping and gossiping, reciting the Persian poetry of Hafez, discussing the news of the day (Fig. 3.1).

A central idea of Object Studies is that the things in our world are containers of hidden meaning. Because they do not "speak" (in the way that the language of a Shakespearean sonnet does, for instance) objects are slow to reveal themselves to us. A coffee cup, something we may see and use daily, does not immediately present as anything beyond what it does: it holds a beverage, in this case, or perhaps it decorates a shelf or a room with its beautiful color and pleasing shape. To complicate matters, objects can have different purposes in different times and places. An old collegiate coffee mug I picked up at a flea market is now a pencil holder on my desk; it may later serve as a planter, or a scoop for bird feed. The challenge as a reader of objects is therefore one of patience; we must take care, firstly, to observe everything we can about the object. Even a simple coffee cup is, in its way, a rich source of data (giving us much more, in fact, than the aforementioned poem). As much as possible, we should try to observe without judgment or, even, without interpretation. The first questions we should always ask are concrete and connected to our immediate experience with the object: "What is this in front of me? What are its dimensions, colors? How does its surface reflect the light? What is it made of? What marks are there that provide evidence of how and where it was made?"

In the case of this cup, for instance, a marvelous detail reveals itself that can be found in the British Museum's catalog description: there are three "spur marks" at the bottom of each cup. I learn from my research that potters (even today) use small conical objects called "spurs" in the process of glazing their ceramics. These props elevate the object up off the kiln surface so that the bottom of the pot can also dry. The most skilled potters leave only faintly visible spur marks, but these indentations are almost always present, a fingerprint-like remnant of the object's original creation. It is details like these that connect the coffee cup to the anonymous craftsman whose work we see before us, allowing the object to serve as a point of human connection through history. The image of the cup also reveals a pattern of scratches on the interior, marks that I interpret as accumulated scrapes from spoons used to stir the cup's contents (perhaps a drinker who liked sugar in her coffee), or evidence of how the cups were stored by being nestled inside one another. These remnants of past use bring a ghostly presence to the object.

Coffeehouses and Early Coffee Culture

Once we have taken in the full range of information provided by the object, we can move onto larger scale questions about its history and begin to view it as an artifact of a distant culture. Where was the cup used? How and where did people drink coffee when it was made? Patience continues to be a key critical tool: we need to look at what the objects are presenting to us, rather than just rely on whatever understanding we might have of the past. For instance, the coffeehouse, a place that has been a part of European culture since the seventeenth century, had a parallel existence in Turkey, Persia, and elsewhere in the Middle East. Just as coffeehouses were taking off in European urban centers (London, Amsterdam, Vienna), they were also becoming important public spaces at the time in Persia. John Fryer, an English traveler in seventeenth-century Iran, describes the scene in the coffeehouse this way: "hither repair all those that are covetous of news as well as Barterers of Goods, where not only Fame and common Rumor is promulgated, but Poetry too, for that some of that Tribe are always present to rehearse their poems" (Matthee 24). Fryer's description sets a scene of talk, news gathering, bustling activity, even commercial exchange. As social and commercial outlets, coffeehouses in Persia were an important part of the fabric of daily life for many, especially in urban areas. Another English traveler to the region, Thomas Herbert, was more interested in the drink itself than the social scene of the coffeehouse. He offered this description in 1618:

> Here be coffee-houses, which also are much resorted to, especially in the evening. The coffee, or *coho*, is a black drink, or rather broth, seeing they sip it as hot as their mouth can well suffer out small China cups; 'tis made of the flower of bunny or choava [java?]-berry, steeped and well-boiled in water; much drunk, though it please neither the eye nor the taste, being black and somewhat bitter. (45)

Coffee was clearly not to the taste of Herbert, who compared its delicacy to that of "burnt crusts" of bread. But he also acknowledged that those who drank it were attracted to its reputed health benefits more than its taste: "yet (if it be true as they say) [coffee] comforts raw stomachs, helps digestion, expels wind, and dispels drowsiness" (45). Throughout its early dissemination through the Middle East and Europe, coffee is often noted as an elixir of sorts with the ability to heal various ailments and curb sleep. Keeping us awake, of course, remains one of the main reasons we seek out the drink today and it is fascinating to find that its earliest consumers were also looking for an extra boost of energy. In fact, it may have been its qualities as a stimulant that helped the drink grow in popularity.

Early coffee drinkers were not, however, fueling all-nighters or trying to get through a workday. Rather, coffee's connection to Sufism, a mystical sect of Islam, was likely a key factor in its spread around the Muslim world. Sufis used the drink as part of their devotional practices, long late-night prayer services that were aided by the caffeinated beverage. These men were often workers, shop-owners, and merchants as well as mystics, and therefore spread their prayer habits with them in their travels. This is the theory of Ralph Hattox, a historian of the origins of coffee culture, who notes that "Members of the Sufi orders were not as a rule reclusive, hermitic holy men. They went to their shops or workplaces, bargained in the markets, went to the baths...This involvement of the members of the orders in everyday affairs of the world was, in all likelihood, one of the most important factors in the spread of coffee" (26). The importance of this religious connection was also observed by Herbert, the early English traveler, who repeats an often-told story about coffee being, literally, handed down from heaven by the angel Gabriel: "[coffee] won but of the greater repute from a tradition they have it was prepared by Gabriel as a cordial for Mussulmans [Muslims]" (45). And there, perhaps, is the story of the first coffee break: the angel Gabriel plucks the beans from a plant and prepares them in a drink specially made for believers (or, in some versions of the story, the Old Testament patriarch Solomon).

Thinking of this story and learning of the first coffee drinkers, I am aware (and amazed) at how closely coffee is tied to its origins of place and culture: a plant grown in the mountains of Ethiopia and Yemen develops into a popular drink among local inhabitants, even becoming a central part of their religious culture and spiritual narratives. The word itself is most likely derived from an Arabic word for wine, perhaps related to the fact that coffee became a suitable substitute for a recreational beverage in a culture that prohibited alcohol consumption. The word may also be related to the region of *Kaffa*, Ethiopia, where the plant probably originated. From its very name to the soil in which it was planted, from the religious ceremonies in which it was featured to the networks of markets through which it was first distributed, the drink has a strikingly specific origin story.

Islamic and Iranian Pottery in the Seventeenth Century

What about the cups? Do these have a similar material connection to these cultural and geographic origins? Unless you are a potter, you likely don't think of cups as coming from earth, but they are products, like the plant matter in coffee, whose raw materials are beneath our feet. Thomas Herbert says that in Iran they "eat in porcelain or earth," a curious phrase that reminds us of this close connection: such pottery can also be called "earthenware." Through the eyes and description of Herbert we do, in fact, catch sight of coffee being drunk from one of our "small China cups" mentioned in his previous description of coffeehouses. At first glance this geographically oriented description seems to point away from Yemen, Ethiopia, Bashra, and Persia to more remote China. Like everything else in this story, and like any story with the global reach of coffee, Herbert's "China cups" are not, perhaps, what they first seem. Chinese porcelain and celadon were a significant influence on the ceramicists of Iran (and those in the Islamic World more broadly) (Golembek et al. 123–24). We know that the Dutch, especially, did a brisk business in selling coffee cups, most likely from China, to the Iranians in the seventeenth century. Items of Safavid pottery, in fact, often have counterfeit Chinese marks on their bases as a means of imitation (Lane 74). An eighteenth-century observer noted that Persian pottery was so similar to Chinese porcelain that "the Dutch and English, who bring a great quantity of it to Europe, always sell it under the name of Chinese" with no buyer the wiser (Lane 76). "From about 1603 the Dutch had built up an immense trade carrying porcelain and other Chinese goods to markets not only in Europe, but also in Japan, the Pacific, India, and the Near East." (Lane 75). In 1652, because of problems with the production of porcelain following the fall of the Ming dynasty in China (1644), the Dutch began seeking sources elsewhere: Japan, but also Persia, where craftsmen had been successfully producing Chinese knock-offs for decades. These objects made their way to Europe, as well, as we find evidence in British East India records requesting "Earthenware of Carmania (Kirman) and Mushatt (Meshed) [both in Iran] made in imitation of China ware of all sorts the finest" (Lane 75–6).

What we are looking at with our British Museum coffee cups, in other words, is the careful work of imitation undertaken by potters from these areas. "Porcelain" is a word we often use generically today, like "Kleenex" or "Scotch tape," but strictly speaking only pottery made of particular kinds of clay and fired at high temperatures can be called porcelain. Since these techniques originated in China, "porcelain," "china," and "chinaware" are often used interchangeably and generically to describe this type of ceramic. Potters in Iran adapted to the materials they had available to them in order to develop their own versions of "china."

The details of this translation can be glimpsed in this British Museum description of our cup:

> Stonepaste fabric, white slip, transparent colourless glaze on interior, transparent cobalt glaze on exterior, lustre overglaze. Unglazed base. Interior entirely painted in lustre. Exterior decorated with crudely drawn branching vine? springing from one point near foot.

Stone-paste or "fritware" was a composition technique used by Islamic potters to imitate imported Chinese porcelain. Improvising upon the structure and designs of vessels they saw coming from China, potters in the Middle East used a combination of local clay and quartz or glass to perfect a version of local pottery that was almost as durable as the Chinese examples (Golombek et al. 2; 124). The cups are decorated using various designs or "motifs," mostly floral and leaf patterns. They are coated in layers of different glazes that give them a shiny appearance (and also makes them impermeable to the liquids they carry). They were constructed using a technique that was common to the region, whereby a potter creates a paste from a water and stone mixture that is then pressed into a mold and fired (albeit at a lower temperature than Chinese porcelain). I will delve into the question of how these items found their way to London, but in initially observing their qualities they appear to have originated as everyday objects that you might expect to find in a seventeenth-century Persian household. Indeed, it may have been the case that potters in this period were using earthenware as a way of imitating the metalwork (mainly gold and silver) that were found in court. They show an attempt by middle-class buyers to imitate the behavior and objects of the elite.

The British Museum's description notes a "crudely drawn branching vine?" with a question mark indicating the cataloguers best guess at the design. Since I am accustomed to mass-produced copies of elaborate Chinese porcelain designs, I have to agree with the value judgment of the cup's design as "crudely drawn." I wonder, too, how that description might reveal something about the attitude of the anonymous cataloguer. Is the decoration "crude" from an aesthetic point of view? Or are there hidden cultural biases at play here? Objects, it turns out, sometimes reveal as much about the person who describe them as they do about the things themselves. Whatever the artistic value of these objects to a contemporary observer, they held undeniable commercial value in the seventeenth century. Even as the Dutch found it difficult to supply merchants in Iran with coffee routinely, they continued a robust trade in coffee cups. As the historian Rudi Matthee reports, "Coffee cups, an ancillary commodity the VOC [Dutch East India Company] had begun to import, continued to be in great demand and commanded good prices" (10). In 1644–45, the Dutch imported a staggering 268,998 cups to Iran, and would continue, on average, to bring in 50,000 cups per year to the port at Bandar Abbas. As stated earlier, objects like these Persian coffee cups can work to challenge some of the common narratives of history, in this case the idea that Europeans used Chinese porcelain ("China") exclusively in their coffeehouses and homes. These pieces reveal a more complicated history of trade and European engagement in the East. The pottery that represented China to Europeans was really just that—a representation, an idea of another place. Persian pottery was therefore an essential, if little known, part of the early trade from the East in the seventeenth century.

We know less about the pottery of Iran today because those objects were either used so heavily they were broken (the same fate of many a mass-produced coffee cup in my cabinet) or because the materials used by Persian potters took the wear from hot beverages less well than Chinese porcelain. They were also supplanted in the seventeenth and eighteenth centuries by British, Dutch, and German imitations of Chinese porcelain, pottery with "blue and white" patterns manufactured in Delft (Netherlands), Bristol (Great Britain), Meissen (Germany) and elsewhere that also imitated China (or Persian imitations). And, in a remarkable circular chain of imitation, European "delftware," as it became known, was eventually copied by Chinese manufacturers to be sold back to Europe.

The cups that are now in the holdings of the British Museum were not handed down from earlier homes and shops in London. Rather, they were the spoils of object hunters of the nineteenth century: "Orientalists," as they have been called, collectors, scholars, and raconteurs of cultures like the Safavid Persians. The museum's catalogue gives information on "provenance," a history of object ownership that offers important details of this story. This Persian cup was once part of a much larger collection owned by Frederick Du Cane Godman, a former trustee of the British Museum. Although an avid traveler and collector himself, Godman in fact acquired many of these objects in the nineteenth century from an eccentric French scholar, diplomat, and archaeologist named Jules Richard. Richard, or Mirza Riza as he was called after he converted to Islam, was a notable collector who used his access to the court of the Shah of Iran to serve as an intermediary between European collectors and museums, dealers, or archaeologists in Iran ("Julius Richard").

This period of collection marked the second phase of object transfer between East and West some 200 years after the coffee trade first brought goods from the East. Unlike in that earlier time, when the English, Dutch, Portuguese, and other European traders sought predominantly economic contact with the region, these coffee cups emerge from a time of empire. The British and French, especially, sought political and territorial power in the region; such power could be expressed in politics or warfare, of course, but it could also be expressed culturally. In an influential study of the relationship between the West and the East in this period, Edward Said argued that the British and French used their "orientalist" knowledge of Persia, Egypt, and elsewhere to assert power over these territories and their people (*Orientalism* 32). Richard/Riza employed his knowledge of European and Eastern languages for diplomacy (he worked as a translator for the Persian court). He also used his knowledge to gain access to archaeological treasures for military and political leaders in Europe who saw "Oriental" objects as a way of demonstrating aesthetic taste. These small material possessions, following Said's analysis, were part of a larger story of European collectors holding and controlling tangible pieces of the East.

There was a more complicated relationship between France, England, and Persia, too, as the life of Riza shows. In addition to his vast collections of Persian artifacts, Riza was rumored to have taken two new wives each year while he lived in Tehran (behavior that caused a scandal in French diplomatic circles). The provenance of these cups thus adds a new and important layer to our analysis as it also opens further questions. When I look again at the Persian cups, I must now think of the man who sold them to a collector in London. How did they come into Riza's possession? Were they a gift from one of these wives? Did he purchase (or steal?) them from a household that his diplomatic position gave him access to? Did he know their history, or were they merely a business opportunity? What did they mean to him? Does that change what they now mean to us?

Colonial Coffee

As the story of Mirza Riza shows, Europeans through the nineteenth century remained aware of coffee's Near East origins. In France, even as "coffee" was slowly becoming "café," a definitively French beverage, Parisians themselves thought of the drink as Turkish. But with the spread of trade into new colonial territories, the cultural connections with the drink were beginning to change. The painting depicted in Fig. 3.2, *Une sultane prenant café...* works as a near perfect connecting point for the history of coffee as it originated in the Muslim cultures of Turkey, East Africa, and the Arabian Peninsula, and its expansion as a commodity into the East and West Indies. In it, Madame de Pompadour, a French aristocrat, demonstrates her power and importance to the French court by taking on the role of a Turkish sultan (Goodman 16). Paintings like van Loo's are a marvelous opportunity for object study as they give us a figurative window into the past. Paintings are, importantly, a mode of *representation*—they do not present us with reality in the way that a physical object can. Yet because they are able to document and preserve

Fig. 3.2 *The Lady Sultan Taking Coffee from a Black Woman*, 1755, by Charles-André van Loo, *Musée des Arts Décoratifs*, Paris

elements of material culture for us (clothing, food, furniture, architecture), examples from the visual arts are an invaluable resource. When we look at a painting or photograph of people (subjects) today, we look to see in their faces personality, emotion, even a soul. For a painter like van Loo, working in the eighteenth century, it was just as important (if not more) to "compose" his subjects in reference to other elements in the painting. This observation is informed by the insightful work of Ann Rosalind Jones and Peter Stallybrass:

> Portrait painters *composed identities for their sitters* not only by concentrating on the nuances of faces but also by combining an international range of substances for artwork, material objects, and garments to represent those sitters' positions in a world of complex economic…circulation. Aristocratic sitters appear to have played an active role in employing painters to represent them in such positions, to compose an identity for them out of the objects that signaled their participation in different cultures… (49, my emphasis)

Jones and Stallybrass remind us of the multi-layered meaning of "composition" with this analysis: a painting is made by acts of "placing together" images of people and objects that create the identity we perceive. We see precisely this effect in the Sultaness painting, where the objects van Loo chooses to include are as important as his subjects—the characters represented can be more richly understood by observing an interplay between clothing, decoration, and, most important for our purposes, a coffee cup that sits almost at the center of the painting. Van Loo's depiction of the Frenchwoman's "participation in different cultures," dressed in the clothing of a Turkish sultan, consuming the products of colonial power, and served by an African slave, stages for us a complex story of how coffee developed into a colonial commodity.

A woman sits low on the floor, a cushion, or perhaps a divan, holding her weight. She is flooded in layers of lustrous fabric that evoke the silks and expensive materials associated at the time with Turkey and the East. Her legs and arms are spread wide in a masculine pose, amplified, too, by the tobacco pipe in her left hand and the coffee cup and saucer in her right. Although clearly marked as a European setting (the leaded glass and paneled wood interior gives this away) the white Frenchwoman is depicted in a complicated act of cultural and gendered cross-dressing. Her tobacco pipe rests on a table with arabesque designs, an aesthetic that is also seen in floor tiles that peek out in the foreground of the painting. She wears pantaloons and slippers that even today strike the viewer as Middle Eastern, as does the belt and embroidered shirt she wears with it. These signs of masculinity (tobacco, dress, posture) are also counterbalanced by details of femininity. Her hair is long, festooned with pearls, and a decorative flower pins her headdress. The title of the painting points to this double cultural and gendered identity: she is, according the title, a "*sultane*," made-up French for a "female Sultan"; in Turkey, where the word "Sultan" originated, the word and position of power it names are strictly masculine. The sitter is thus a woman inhabiting a masculine identity, as well as a European playing at being an Ottoman Turk.

Perhaps the most striking element of the painting for a modern viewer is the dark-skinned woman, presumably an African slave, shown serving the *sultane* her coffee. While the *sultane's* posture indicates, at once, leisure and dominance, the African woman is depicted in an act of labor. She stoops on one knee, pulling back the heavy metal coffee pot she has just poured from. While her clothing is by no means poor, it lacks the luster of the *sultane's*. The blue and white striped tunic she wears looks like cotton gaberdine, a fabric often worn by and therefore associated with servants and slaves. Her mouth partially opened, perhaps in the midst of speech, asking the *sultane* if she would like anything more, perhaps sugar, perhaps more tobacco for her pipe. Draped over her serving arm is, improbably, more fabric. Is she showing the *sultane* a sample for a dress she's making? Taking something from her that needs to be mended? Carrying an elaborate serving cloth? We don't know, but the visual effect is to show an added burden carried by the enslaved woman. The title of the painting is misleading: the *sultane* is not taking coffee so much as it is being served to her. All of the action, all of the *work*, is performed by this unnamed, subservient presence. Described only as a *"negresse"* in the painting's title, she marks for us the entry of slavery into the story of coffee production.

From Mokha to Jakarta and Beyond

When it began, the trade in coffee remained for a time a relatively local affair, even in the earliest days of European involvement in the venture: a Dutch merchant picks up a cargo of coffee beans in Mokha and ships them around the Arabian Peninsula to the Persian Gulf port of Bandar Abbas. There, he sells the beans (at a profit) or trades them for silks (the more valuable commodities) that have come into port from overland trade routes into Persia. The Dutch merchant then transports the bolts of silk and other merchandise back to Amsterdam, or perhaps makes another stop to trade and collect other valuable merchandise along the way. If we imagine that these early traders were only concerned with delivering expensive luxury goods to European markets, we don't have a full understanding of how they made their money. The history of coffee shows us, in fact, that early traders were more interested in using the commodity to barter for other materials in the Middle East, India, and the East Indies that they thought were more valuable. Not until later did coffee become a product that would sell in Northern Europe.

Dutch merchants successfully marketed coffee to Iranian ports starting in the 1630s, earning profits of as much as 150%. In all likelihood, the Iranian market was so successful that it kept the Dutch (and other companies) from bringing coffee back for sale in Europe. Merchants, after all, are businessmen, and who would risk transporting thousands of pounds of beans to Europe when eager buyers were so readily available nearby? It wasn't until 1661 that the first shipment of coffee arrived in Amsterdam (the 1650s in England). But as the decades of the seventeenth century wore on, the market for coffee in the Middle East became more volatile. Important ports such as Bashra, Masqat, Mokha, Kong, and Bandar Abbas were plagued by pirates and wars broke out between empires. The Safavids in Iran clashed with the Ottoman Empire in Bashra, an important source of coffee for English traders that was effectively shut down by these hostilities. By the turn of the eighteenth century, the Dutch began seeking other areas for coffee cultivation: Java (Indonesia), especially, and Ceylon (Sri Lanka), which would eventually come under English control. This move was the start of coffee as a truly globalized commodity: to escape the vagaries of Arabian and Persian traders, the Dutch, Portuguese, and English set up plantations in other favorable locations to feed the growing demands of Europeans addicted to coffee. It is in that moment, with frustrated Dutch, Spanish, and Portuguese merchants, that the history of coffee begins to break off from the Middle East and develop elsewhere.

Once merchants had seen the commercial possibilities for the coffee trade they were keen to find territory wherever they might to spread the crop. Newly conquered lands like French Martinique and St. Domingue (Haiti), Dutch Cayenne and Suriname, became the first lands in the Western Hemisphere to be cultivated for the crop: Parisian Cafés and Amsterdam coffeehouses were fueled by these early colonial endeavors. The first specimens of *coffee arabica*—the plant's scientific name tells of its origins—had to be carefully transported overseas from Europe, where merchants and early scientists had planted specimens in greenhouses and botanical gardens for preservation. A blight that devastated coffee plants in British-held Ceylon upended production there in the eighteenth century (and may be the event that led to tea becoming the more popular drink in London). When it arrived in the Caribbean, coffee quickly developed into a lucrative cash crop with the help of enslaved labor imported from Africa. Coffee remains a highly labor-intensive plant to cultivate and harvest: it thrives in higher altitudes and the enslaved were required to clear jungle and forest to make room for the plant. Picking the "cherries" or ripe fruit of the coffee tree is likewise arduous, typically carried out in the heat of the day, and requires pickers to carry heavy filled baskets. Like other luxury crops mentioned in this chapter (cacao, tea, tobacco) coffee was a commodity whose very existence depended on a massive force of enslaved labor. Even today, workers around the world who harvest beans live on wages that are barely subsistence-level. The original cup of coffee may have been poured by an angel, but the commodified version we drink today has traveled far from that story.

One legend from this period that I find fascinating because it captures the essence of coffee-as-object, is an apocryphal tale of how Brazil, today the largest producer of coffee in the world, first acquired the plant. A lieutenant colonel representing the Portuguese crown, one Francisco de Mello Palheta, was called on to negotiate a territorial dispute between the French and Dutch in the Guianas on the north coast of South America. During the negotiations, the wife of the French governor fell in love with the Portuguese lieutenant colonel; the two had an affair and when it came time for Palheta to leave after the negotiations, the Frenchwoman gave him a parting gift: a bouquet of tropical flowers. Stashed in the stems of flowers, the story holds, was a valuable prize for her lover: cuttings from the colony's coffee plants. Palheta transported the slips to Brazil, a Portuguese colony, where he used them to begin what remains today a lucrative industry. As a story, true or not, this has a lot going for it—sex, industrial espionage, and a healthy bit of nationalist chauvinism (the Portuguese dupes the French governor for both love and money).

The story also may give us some insight, as origin stories often do, into cultural perceptions of the society that told it. Given the brutal realities of coffee production in Brazil and elsewhere in the eighteenth and nineteenth centuries, I can't help but think that the story allows the teller to give a sentimental sheen to an otherwise ugly history. The institution of slavery persisted in Brazil until 1888, decades after it was made illegal in Great Britain and the United States. As many historians have observed and documented, coffee production in South America throughout the nineteenth and twentieth centuries went hand-in-hand with corrupt government, the exploitation of human and animal labor, deforestation, and a host of other social ills. Colombia followed Brazil into the coffee trade in the nineteenth century, and today the Colombia Coffee Federation (or *Federacion Nacional de Cafeteros*, FNC) operates with a power comparable to the Colombian government. "…at times the FNC has operated as though it were an independent coffee government—establishing export, marketing and structural policies that, while beneficial for its members, were at odds with the goals of the rest of the nation" (Dicum and Luttinger 78). Whether we are looking at the Persian Safavid court, colonial Dutch and Portuguese imperialism, or contemporary Latin American governments, it seems that coffee and politics are always intertwined.

It was a revolt by enslaved workers, in the end, that rearranged the chess board of European power in the Caribbean and helped create the conditions of modern coffee production. French St. Domingue, today's Haiti, was once the largest producer of coffee in the Western Hemisphere, the source of half the world's supply by the 1790s. That was until the island was witness to one of the largest rebellions in colonial history. Realizing the French colonialists derived their power from land and the capital it could produce, the enslaved people of St. Domingue destroyed plantations, burned crops, and effectively ended the French influence in the coffee trade. Returning for a moment to the van Loo painting of the *sultane* and her African servant, we see how profoundly these revolts overturned the fantasy of the French. It is as though the enslaved woman in the portrait, rather than serving the mistress, had dumped out the coffee on the *sultane's* white satin dress.

Coffee for the Masses

Even as I recognize, hazily, the outline of the story of coffee and its connection to global capitalism, I still wonder how the Middle East has been blurred from current knowledge of the beverage's history. How is it that coffee is now so closely associated with the Western Hemisphere, especially Central and South America? Pondering this, an image comes to my mind of a man in a hat standing before a mountain. Is he with a horse? A donkey? My earliest memories of coffee advertising are of a popular television campaign that featured "Juan Valdez," a fictional Colombian coffee grower always depicted with his signature hat and trusty mule (named "Conchita," in fact). "100% Colombian Coffee," the ads announced, "the richest coffee in the world." Since 1958, when a New York-based advertising firm created the character to market Colombian-grown coffee, Juan Valdez has become an international symbol for the coffee trade—literally a "trademark," another important conceptual connection between capitalism and material culture. Today, the Juan Valdez brand has been expanded into a chain of coffee shops in 22 countries. In the twenty-first century, brand names, store chains, and corporate symbols like "Juan

Valdez" make up the dominant visual language of coffee. The disposable cup, adaptable to a range of branded designs and corporate customization, is now the object of choice for drinkers around the world. Unlike small porcelain china cups—like those from Persia or the one in the van Loo painting—the disposable cup can handle the mass consumption of coffee on a global scale.

The National Museum of American History in Washington, DC has a collection of coffee-related objects quite unlike the Safavid examples held in the British Museum. In 2012, architects Louise Harpman and Scott Specht donated 56 items from their much larger collection of plastic "drink through" cup lids to the museum. One of these (Fig. 3.3), the "Stewart's Peel and Lock Lid," comes from a chain of convenient stores in the area where I live. At first glance, the lid looks extraordinarily common, an example of the type of object we use, ignore, and put in the trash bin daily. Yet on closer inspection it really is a marvel of design and manufacture. Around the perimeter are a series of semi-rectangular indentations. I imagine these allow for small spills to collect in the lid (and not dribble onto my shirt as I drink). The rectangles also add rigidity to the lid and help it provide structure to the cup so that when I pick it up by the top (which I do often, especially in my car) the lid won't bend and pop off. The lid also has description words on it: "Black," "Cream,"

Fig. 3.3 Stewart's Coffee Cup Lid, photo courtesy of Stewart's Shops

"Decaf," etc., that can be marked to differentiate my cup from my wife's or a friend's when we order together. But the real innovation in the lid is the "tear back" spout, which can be peeled and fastened into place while I drink from it. This is another excellent example of an object "affordance" (described further in the next chapter), a design choice that allows us to intuit its use. I don't remember ever reading the lid or noting the arrows that show where the tab fastens. The tab that sticks out from the cup shows me exactly where to grab and peel; the feel of the fastener suggests to my fingers how it should be snapped into place. This entire material transaction between person and object happens with barely a thought.

Although they seem an indispensable part of our modern culture, disposable coffee cups are a fairly recent invention. When we look back at the origins of coffee drinking as a leisure-time activity (which it remains in some parts of the world) we can see how the material shift in cups corresponds to the meaning of the drink itself. As Harpman and Specht observe about their collection: "…the true efflorescence in drink-through lid design and production can be traced to the 1980s, when we, as a culture, decided that it was important, even necessary, to be able to walk, or drive, or commute while drinking hot liquids." There are now dozens of patents for these humble objects (my Stewart's cup is marked "U.S. Pat. LIC AH11) with each designed as an attempt to optimize functional concerns such as "heat retention," "mouth comfort," "splash reduction," "friction fit," and "one-handed activation" (Harpman and Specht). The products of designers, government patents, and materials engineers, coffee cups are now firmly a part of the industrialized world.

These objects reveal how the cultural meanings of coffee have changed over the past 300 years. At the core of this is the cultural "decision," as Harpman and Specht call it, that coffee was a drink to be consumed on the go. Anyone who has driven an automobile manufactured before 1995 or so has seen further evidence of this cultural shift: earlier cars do not include cup holders to accommodate all of those disposable coffee cups and travel mugs. I agree with Harpman and Specht that there are broader cultural shifts that have prompted the way we drink coffee (commuting patterns, the increase in two-income households, a work-before-leisure ethos). Just as the saucer made it easier for a servant to deliver coffee by catching spills, the disposable cup fills our need for drinking on the go and in a variety of settings (on the train, in the classroom, at a conference table). But I also think we must consider how these cup technologies, once they became widely available, have themselves enabled the ways in which we consume coffee, tea, and other hot beverages today.

This argument goes beyond our discussion of coffee and speaks to a broader point about Object Studies: once we turn our attention to the things in our world, we have to consider how they actually influence and alter our behavior. We like to believe that we decide how and when we do something as simple as drink a cup of coffee, but what if that decision is already made for us? Or what if, at the least, the material world puts significant conditions on that decision and how or why we make it? The covered drink cup, for example, hides the contents of our coffee cups from us. We may think less about what is inside the cup. We actually taste the coffee less—most of what we experience as taste is, in fact, smell, and our plastic lids block the aromas of the coffee from our noses. The coffee stays hotter longer in a covered cup, but we probably enjoy it less. This is merely speculation, but part of the reason we may be less familiar with where our coffee comes from is that we mainly drink it blindly, perhaps seeking only that hit of caffeine to jumpstart our day or get us through the afternoon. What the modern disposable cup enhances, instead, is the visibility of the coffeehouse logo. Coffee has always been a commodity, but our cups tell us that we identify more now with where we buy it than what is actually in the cup. And that thought lasts only until we throw away it away.

There are discussions in which people consider coffee cups as objects more regularly: concerns about environmental impact have given rise to serious thinking about the materiality of these cups. Starbucks alone uses over 4 billion disposable cups each year. Although the company has attempted to decrease these numbers (offering incentives for those who bring in their own cups into their stores, as well as selling cheap reusable cups) by their own estimates only 1% of Starbucks customers take advantage of these alternatives. Thinking about the sustainability of our coffee habit (a worthy question, to be sure) is yet another way in which the coffee cup today offers a window into our cultural concerns and the historical impact of our things. Looking to the future, it may be that the next coffee cup in this story will be one that is fully biodegradable (like those that are already offered in more progressive shops). Municipalities may choose to ban cups, as they have plastic grocery bags. Or, it may be that we return to the origins of the coffee cup described here and choose reusable ceramic options more regularly, a practice that remains current in some places. As Harpman and Specht report, in their collecting of plastic lids they had a difficult time getting a hold of an example from Paris. When one of their students requested coffee to go, "*à enporter*," the waitress gave her a porcelain mug, asking her only to "bring back the cup."

Procedures and Methods

Objects can make us rethink certain narratives about the past and our present. When we look at an object carefully and study its story in depth, we must deal with the truth of its material presence. As we have already seen, this entails careful description (What is the size, shape, texture, color of this object?); an accounting of its path to our ownership (Where did it come from? How did it get here?); and an understanding of its creation (Who was responsible for bringing it into the world? Who, over time, has taken the care to preserve it?). These are concrete questions that invite precision rather than fuzzy interpretation. Like the famous "five W's" (who, what, when, where, how) of journalistic reporting, these questions force us to get specific, to find hard facts that lead us, even, to truths about our world (and hopefully not the truths we expected we would find).

The premise of this chapter is genuine: before finding the Persian coffee cups on the British Museum's webpage, I had little knowledge of the history of coffee or coffee cups. The inspiration for this essay was a project begun at the British Museum,

The History of the World in 100 Objects, a book (and podcast, television show, and exhibition) that featured the most striking and illustrative objects from their collection. Such research can be undertaken fairly easily with the kinds of reliable resources available to anyone with access to the internet and a basic university library. From there, as I have tried to demonstrate in this model essay, there is a great deal of research material to be found by considering the chains of material and historical connections that exist to other objects. It is worth the time to brainstorm these, or to keep a list of possible further research topics that emerge once you identify your object. Be creative and curious in how you view your objects within this wider network of material connections. You might begin by making a list of raw materials in your object and tracing where they come from today compared to where they came from historically.

Resources and Research

The British Museum in London is a treasure trove for object hunters. Walking through its hallways, you encounter artifacts both humble and grand from every nook and cranny of the globe: the famed Rosetta Stone, which allowed archaeologists to reconstruct the language of Egyptian hieroglyphs, instruments used by the sixteenth-century English occultist John Dee to summon angels, ancient weapons of the Anglo-Saxons, Sumatran calendars…the list goes on. The items that furnish the museum bear witness to the reach and aims of omnivorous British collectors who lived under an empire that spanned the globe. For every object on display, there are hundreds more tucked safely away in storage. As much as I would like to hop on a plane to London and spend some time in the museum itself, the online archive has some decided advantages over its bricks and mortar facility. I work with many cataloguing and searching interfaces, and the one offered by the British Museum is uniquely powerful and user friendly. It allows you to search for objects by not only date ranges but also by object type (weapon, ceramics, documents), geographic location, cultural heritage (Ottoman, Mesoamerican, Dravidian), and so on. This is the kind of research one can get lost in for hours, but even within a few minutes of my work I came up with a set of objects that immediately piqued my interest.

When working with objects from the realm of the visual arts, museum catalogues are also a marvelous resource, and I was fortunate to find a few key exhibition books of Persian Art that shed light on the story of these cups. I found a few key historical sources on the history of coffee with simple searches in Google Scholar and my library catalogue, the most useful of which was Ralph Hattox's *Coffee and Coffeehouses, The Origins of a Social Beverage in Medieval Near East*. Although Hattox mainly writes about the Ottoman Empire, his work has been cited by many later scholars who have developed his story in other parts of the world. I found one of these especially helpful, Rudy Matthee's "Coffee in Safavid Iran: Commerce and Consumption." This essay shows how even one key secondary source can provide a wealth of detail in giving background on a topic. Google Books and Google Scholar are marvelous tools for a researcher working today, but the shelves of a university library, and the assistance of a research librarian, are still the best resources. I found Gregory Dicum and Nina Luttinger's *Coffee Book: Anatomy of an Industry*, one of the indispensable sources for my research, simply by scanning the shelf of books near another source I was tracking down.

As demonstrated in this chapter, when dealing with historical objects it can be illuminating to view paintings or photographs from the period you are looking into so that you can see how the things you have chosen were used or represented. Some historical studies may include such paintings, but you can also browse through catalogues or museum websites that include period paintings or other visual representations of the object(s) you are working with.

Further Applications

Wikipedia, the open-access encyclopedia, remains an under-utilized pedagogical resource—not as a source, but as a platform for publishing student work. The historical objects that students research for this chapter could provide the basis for students to update or create articles based on their findings. This can be done either after students have completed their research or as a way of structuring a unit around historical objects.

I have developed this model for *Wikipedia* editing projects as group exercises:

1. The first thing you should decide, as a group, is what article you plan on editing. If you find that your object or topic has been heavily covered on *Wikipedia*, I suggest that you consider a related topic that was only a brief entry. Generally, I suggest that you stay away from topics that are fully developed and active articles and look instead for articles that have been neglected by the *Wikipedia* community or are in need of serious work. You should let me know by **DATE**, which entry you have chosen (please e-mail me and include a link to the *Wikipedia* page).
2. As a group, evaluate the state of the *Wikipedia* page you have selected. What needs fixing? Is it just more research that is needed, or are there other problems that need to be addressed? You should also create a bibliography of at least **four** sources that you plan to use in your research. By **DATE,** please submit a 300-word evaluation of your page, along with your working bibliography.
3. Your group should then read the resources you have found and make decisions about what should be included in the final entry. What is the most important and interesting information you have discovered? As a group, you will need to make decisions about how to add to the entry, and what you want the final product to look like.
4. On **DATE** your final project is due. You will give a brief presentation to the class that day (no longer than 10 minutes) describing your topic, the major findings of your research, and the work you accomplished on your Wikipedia page. You will turn in to me a final portfolio for the project that should include:

- A printout of the *Wikipedia* entry before you edited it.
- A copy of your 300-word evaluation and proposal (with bibliography)
- A printout of the *Wikipedia* article with your changes to it.
- A concluding reflections statement of 200–300 words that explains the choices you made in your entry, and suggests what further changes you think would help the entry. You should also reflect on the process as a whole: What do you now think about *Wikipedia* as a resource after this assignment? How confident do you feel using it? Did you have interactions with other *Wikipedia* editors? How productive were they? Tell me what you think are some good ways and some bad ways of using *Wikipedia*, and how you think you will use *Wikipedia* in the future.

Work Cited

Barendse, R. J. "Trade and State in the Arabian Seas: A Survey from the Fifteenth to the Eighteenth Century." *Journal of World History*, vol. 11, no. 2, 2000, pp. 173–225.

"Cup and Materials." *Starbucks Coffee Company*, https://www.starbucks.com/responsibility/environment/cups-and-materials.

Dicum, Gregory, and Nina Luttinger. *The Coffee Book: Anatomy of an Industry from Crop to the Last Drop*. New Press, 1999.

Golombek, Lisa, et al. *Persian Pottery in the First Global Age: The Sixteenth and Seventeenth Centuries*. Brill, 2013.

Goodman, Elise. *The Portraits of Madame de Pompadour: Celebrating the Femme Savante*. U of California P, 2000.

Harpman, Louise, and Scott Specht. "Peel, Pucker, Pinch, Puncture." *Cabinet*, Fall, 2005, n.p. http://cabinetmagazine.org/issues/19/harpman.php.

Harvard University School of Public Health. "Coffee by the Numbers." *News*, 4 Oct. 2010, https://www.hsph.harvard.edu/news/multimedia-article/facts/.

Hattox, Ralph S. *Coffee and Coffeehouses: The Origins of a Social Beverage in the Medieval Near East*. U of Washington P, 1985.

Herbert, Thomas. *Travels in Persia: 1627–1629*. Edited by William Foster, Routledge, 2005.

Jones, Ann Rosalind, and Peter Stallybrass. *Renaissance Clothing and the Materials of Memory*. Cambridge UP, 2000.

"Julius Richard Biography." *British Museum*, http://www.britishmuseum.org/research/search_the_collection_database/term_details.aspx?bioId=137664.

Lane, Arthur. *Later Islamic Pottery: Persia, Syria, Egypt, Turkey*. Pitman, 1957.

Matthee, Rudi. "Coffee in Safavid Iran: Commerce and Consumption." *Journal of the Economic and Social History of the Orient*, vol. 37, no. 1, 1994, pp. 1-32. https://doi.org/10.2307/3632568.

Norman, D. A. "Affordances and Design." *jnd.org*, https://www.jnd.org/dn.mss/affordances_and.html.

Chapter 4
In the Middle: Subjects, Objects, and Theories of Things

The relationship between subjects and objects is one of the central areas of inquiry within philosophy, psychology, and even recent studies in biology and neuroscience. This chapter surveys the ideas of several key thinkers within these traditions—including Rene Descartes, G. W. F. Hegel, Karl Marx, Sigmund Freud, and Timothy Morton—and introduces a methodology for tracing keywords that can serve as entry points into these important theoretical discussions.

Our languages are filled with words that reveal a complex history of subject-object relationships. Early on in a semester teaching Object Studies, I give my students a list of vocabulary that has theoretical or historical significance for our work. With a little sleuthing on the *Oxford English Dictionary* online, they can construct a working history of how words like "fetish," "monument," or "talisman" reveal the ways our language encodes these meanings. The shifting definition of "relic," for instance, demonstrates the many layers of meanings this object-oriented word has accrued over time. Today when we call something or someone a "relic," we are most likely employing definition 4.c. from the *OED*: a person or thing that has survived from a time in the distant past. Usually constructed with "of," as in "a relic of a former age," the word has a taste of something archaic in itself. We use it as a way to emphasize the antiquity of the object we are talking about. Perhaps because it sounds a little old fashioned to use the word relic, it is also a term that can be used for sarcastic or humorous effect (Def. 4.d.) so as to skewer people and institutions seen to be out of step with the times. Aging politicians (or even professors) might be called "relics" in this vein of usage.

That current meaning of the word suggests some bias against the old and outdated. But relics were originally of great religious significance as objects that derived their power from a specific material connection to the past. The word came into the English language through French around the time of the Norman invasion in 1066. Derived from Latin, *relique* referred to the "physical remains of, or articles associated with, a saint, martyr, etc." (Def. 1. a.). Within Christian traditions these objects were thought to have the power to heal, confer blessings or good luck, and were therefore treated with reverence. Many churches, shrines, and pilgrimage sites around Europe were created or adapted to house the remains of a saint: Canterbury Cathedral, the seat of the Church of England, enshrines the remains of Saint Thomas Becket—Chaucer's pilgrims in the *Canterbury Tales* are on a journey from London to the cathedral for a touch of grace from those relics.

According to the *OED*, the meaning of the word shifted around the beginning of the seventeenth century. In English, "relic" came to mean *any* object "kept as a remembrance, souvenir, or memorial; a historical object relating to a particular person, place, or thing; a memento" (Def. 1.d.). Around the same time the word acquired an even more basic material meaning (now obsolete) of food scraps or meal remnants. The sacred (spiritual, eternal) had become mundane (from the Latin *mundus* meaning "world," i.e. earthly rather than heavenly). This shift in the register of meaning for relic was the effect of the assault on these objects during the Protestant Reformation in England through the sixteenth century. Reformers saw relic veneration as a form of idolatry and undertook the systematic seizure and destruction of many of the places people would visit to see them. In 1538, Becket's remains at Canterbury were removed and the reliquaries that held them confiscated; what happened to his bones remains a mystery. Like the demystified shrines and their contents, "relic" became another term for any old thing: an antique, heirloom, or curio.

This brief journey into English etymology illustrates that the way we think about things changes over time: there are a host of anthropological, historical, religious, economic, and cultural conditions that shape how we use and perceive our objects. Because of this, the study of objects has been greatly influenced by a range of theoretical teachings and writings. Theory might be defined as the practice of thinking about thinking: it is a form of scholarship that deals in abstract ideas with the hopes of clarifying methods, forming principles, and even critiquing the underlying beliefs that animate our work. In the relatively recent history of material cultural studies, there have been a number of influential theoretical studies that argue for the significance of objects in our world. The relationship between subject and object is such an important topic in the history of ideas that these theoretical readings could form a course unto themselves: Plato and Aristotle (in the Western tradition) each had a great deal to say about the nature of the material world, and the status of objects also figures prominently in many indigenous and non-European belief systems.

This chapter traces one influential trajectory of thought from the seventeenth to the twenty-first century: the relationship between "subjects," humans, and "objects," the materials and things that make up the rest of the world. Are humans really that different from matter? The Bible, Shakespeare, and contemporary science alike acknowledge the materiality of human beings, "this quintessence of dust," as Hamlet calls us. Yet strong religious and spiritual beliefs remain that insist on the exceptionality of the human subject, especially in relation to the mind and/or spirit. I will touch upon several writers and thinkers who have been especially influential, as well as define keywords and concepts that show us the importance of the debate. When we pay attention to the shifts in meaning over time for subjects and objects, we can witness the changing record of how and why objects have value. Moreover, the ways in which philosophers have understood subjects and objects connects with some of the most important world historical events: the Reformation, the history of racism and transatlantic slavery, global imperialism, capitalism, the Scientific Revolution. By anchoring in key parts of this centuries-long discussion I hope to expand our understanding of these theoretical concepts and shed light on the broader consequences of how we think about objects.

Cartesian Dualism

In commonsense thinking we hold onto the idea that humans and objects are fundamentally separate categories from one another. Or, more accurately, that there is something special about human existence that separates us from the material world. We may accept that the body is made up of material components (hair, bone, tissue) that are similar to other objects in the world, but the nature of the mind or soul (some may prefer that word) is categorically different. The material world—including the human body—has substance that can be measured, weighed, and physically described, while there is something special, even *immaterial* about human thought and emotion. "We are such stuff as dreams are made on," Prospero famously says in Shakespeare's *The Tempest*, suggesting that our human "stuff" is effervescent, transcendent. It is more like the alternate reality of a dream than the mere everyday existence implied by "stuff."

Such a view was popular around the time that Shakespeare wrote his plays and remains with us in some part today. Four hundred years ago, the French philosopher and essayist Rene Descartes formulated the now iconic statement of what it means to be human: "I think, therefore I am." That is actually a pithy English translation of Descartes's original Latin: *Cogito ergo sum*, which is more like "I am now thinking and therefore I am in existence" (try putting that on a t-shirt). What Descartes was getting at, and as he expanded at large in his *Meditations on First Philosophy*, was that the only fundamental knowledge we can have (his "first philosophy") is of our own independent thinking state. That's it. All things: the world around us, our homes, our tools, our belongings, our friends, our pets, are external to us and therefore constitute a different, indeed lesser kind of knowledge. Descartes even explores the idea that we (our minds) are being continually tricked by some kind of malevolent spirit or demon to believe that the sensuous world exists (including material culture), when in fact it is all really a great illusion. We should distrust our senses and what they tell us about the physical world, Descartes concludes, and should hold a healthy skepticism about what we think we know from the objects that envelop our consciousness.

Philosophers now call this belief of Descartes "substance dualism," or even Cartesian dualism after the author. Substance dualists hold that the world can be separated into two classes of being (thus the "dual" in dualist). For Descartes these were matter and mind, and as the still-current expression holds, "mind over matter." Important for this discussion of Object Studies vocabulary, Descartes viewed matter as purely mechanistic—it followed its own rules that were determined by nature (or God, for Descartes). The human mind could affect the material world, it could guide or alter the determined path of, say, an arrow being shot through the air. But the mind cannot alter the fundamental design that matter held. This meant for him (and for many of the dualist philosophers who followed in this tradition) that the material world was importantly independent of the mind. Such a belief raised a famous problem for Descartes—how could he account for the interactions that clearly take place between my mind and my body? How can I shoot the arrow, lift my arm, or type these words, if my mind exists as a separate entity from the material world? His answer was that the mind can, in fact, serve as a kind of puppet master for the material body, and its "levers" are in the brain. Descartes was a scientist as well as a philosopher and he had observed a part of the brain, the pineal gland, that he thought was something like the joystick with which the mind operates the body (my image of this is Remy the rat in *Ratatouille* operating his human host Linguini by grabbing handfuls of his hair).

The Cartesian view of the way the world is made up (philosophers call it "metaphysics") has been influential in the Western tradition. Descartes's belief in the power of human thinking (and we should remember he was part of a broader "humanist" movement) helps explain why we still have such difficulty recognizing and interpreting the material world. Whether we realize it or not, most of us remain committed Cartesians; we want to believe there is something special or separate about the mind. For Descartes this belief was rooted in his Christianity. He ultimately challenged his own skepticism about the material world (and the possibility of that evil demon manipulating his thoughts) with his belief that a beneficent God would never allow such demonic forces to deceive him so profoundly. A belief in the afterlife (Christian or otherwise) continues to motivate widespread belief in dualism. Recent work by psychologists has called this "common sense" or "intuitive dualism," "everyday beliefs that the mind can survive death" (Riekki, et al.). 73.3% of Americans and 43.2% of Europeans believe in some kind of afterlife, and several studies carried out on college campuses among undergraduate students from various backgrounds have shown significant belief in the separation of mind and body. Indeed, a number of scholars have argued that dualist beliefs are a kind of default mode in the human brain. The child psychologist Paul Bloom argues this in his aptly named book, *Descartes' Baby*: "…belief in the afterlife is a natural consequence of our intuitive Cartesian perspective" (207). Looked at from the point of view of material cultural studies, this conclusion shows that we must work against some of our ingrained dualist beliefs in order to see the world differently. If we are "intuitive Cartesians," as Bloom suggests, then it also follows that the work of Object Studies may be naturally counterintuitive.

Karl Marx and the Rise of Historical Materialism

Descartes's writings set the agenda for generations of philosophers, who continued to ruminate on the relationship between matter and mind, the material and immaterial. Some, following the influence of the English philosopher John Locke, rejected the Cartesian theory of mind and insisted that all that exists (including the mind) is, at the most fundamental level, material. Such a view of materialism (as it came to be known) would also be informed further by the Scientific Revolution and a growing emphasis on building knowledge from experimentation and observation of the physical world. On the other philosophical extreme, "idealists" argued for a world where the human mind defined all being. There may be an external world, idealists such as Bishop George Berkeley argued, but it only has shape and form when the human mind categorizes and conceptualizes it. The German philosopher Georg Wilhelm Friedrich Hegel, in his still influential *Phenomenology of Spirit*, argued that human consciousness defines and redefines itself through interactions with that which is outside of it. The human consciousness is an ever-seeking and changing being—a subject—that defines itself through encounters with "objects" (for Hegel this is a more capacious term than that used it in this book—anything identified by the subject as outside of itself—including other people—can be an object).

Hegel called the process of this ongoing working and reworking of consciousness the "dialectic." The term derives from the Greek word for "debate" (it is etymologically related to the word "dialogue," as well). This metaphor tells us something about the dialectic as a concept—a debate is a conversation or verbal contest that aims to change the viewpoints of an audience or an opponent. It presumes that there is a process or action of transformation through discourse. Hegel's understanding of the dialectic is more abstract than this, the subject and object are not speaking contestants but abstractions of the self and its "other," but Hegel did believe that the dialectic could help explain the realities of historical change. As the subject gains knowledge of the world, the "dialectical movement" alters the nature of this consciousness—this is what Hegel says we call "experience": the creation of new knowledge through an unceasing process of change. This view was implicated significantly in Atlantic slavery during the nineteenth century as it defined who could be a "subject" and who was an "object." Hegel's other writings on the "master-slave" dialectic make clear that he viewed slavery as an innate part of human society. While couched as an intellectual exercise, it is important to note that this theory, in practice, violently sustained and promoted the Atlantic slave trade that was still active during Hegel's lifetime. Denying the subjectivity of a person could also justify an economic system that treated slaves as objects to be sold and used within the human machine of production.

Hegel's writings are notoriously difficult, and arguably the reason we continue to grapple with their complexities is one of Hegel's most famous readers: Karl Marx. The young Marx, studying philosophy in Berlin, was immersed not only in his own reading of the famous Hegel, but also knew the analyses of his writings that were taking place in the scholarly culture throughout universities in Germany. Friedrich Feuerbach, for instance, used the work of Hegel to argue for a return to Christian principles. His *Essence of Christianity* was an act of "transformational criticism" that was of "epochal importance" to readers of Hegel in this period, the modern editor of Marx's writings has argued (Tucker xxiii). Marx would take up his own consequential reinterpretation of Hegel following on these efforts. One of the key concepts in Hegel's dialectic was alienation. Whenever consciousness gains knowledge it becomes something new, but this change also leaves the subject momentarily alienated from itself. Although abstract, there is also something intuitive about this description of experience: when college seniors think back on who they were as first-year students they may feel the sense of alienation from the former self that Hegel describes. In order to gain knowledge, consciousness as it develops must continually become strange to itself. But this is what constitutes the ultimate goal of consciousness. Hegel writes, "In pressing on to its true form of existence, consciousness will reach a point at which it will lay aside its semblance of being burdened with something alien that is only for it, or as an other, that is, where appearance becomes equal to essence, the presentation of consciousness consequently coinciding at this very point with the true Science of Spirit" (160). Hegel argues that the development of consciousness, and of history more generally, is *teleological*, it has an aim or goal (*telos*=Greek "target").

Like a believer interpreting the cryptic words of a prophet, Marx found in Hegel a "hidden" meaning that became the basis for his own formulation of the dialectic (Tucker xxiv). For Hegel, the development of consciousness into Spirit was a process of alienation from the self. For Marx, this view of the world was insightful in theory but wrong in its particulars. The dialectic, for Marx, was not driven by the consciousness or spirit, but the material circumstances created by capitalism. In one of his earliest writings, *The German Ideology*, Marx argues for this practical view of human history: "Thus it is quite obvious from the start that there exists a materialistic connection of humans with one another, which is determined by their needs and their mode of production, and which is as old as humanity itself. This connection is ever taking on new forms, and thus presents a 'history'…" (157).[1] Marx goes on to use the language of Hegel to refute his notion of "consciousness" and "spirit": "…humanity also possesses 'consciousness,' but, even so, not inherent, not 'pure' consciousness. From the start the spirit is afflicted with the curse of being burdened with 'matter'" (158). In a telling note from the manuscript in this section Marx elaborates: "Humans have history because they must *produce* their life, and because they must produce it moreover in a *certain* way: this is determined by their physical organization: their consciousness is determined in just the same way" (158 n. 4, author's emphasis).

Marx's materialism differed from that of Descartes and the other scientifically minded scholars of his time. He did not see the material world as independent of the human world—his was not a "mechanistic" materialism. Rather, as the passages above from *The German Ideology* point out, humans played a significant role in shaping their material circumstances. Even if the "modes of production," to use Marx's famous terminology, had come to determine the fate of humanity, the revolutionary beliefs he held rested on a belief in the dialectic, on the possibility that humans could ultimately (and permanently) alter their material circumstances. Even scholars who might feel lukewarm about the political agenda of Marx have been influenced by this view of history and the relationship between humans and the material world. The writings of Marx and his collaborator Friedrich Engels would form the basis of what came to be known as "historical materialism," a view of the interrelated nature of subject and object.

---

[1] I have chosen to alter the gender-specific language of Tucker's translations of Marx. The German "Mensch" or "Menschen" from the original may accurately be rendered with the more inclusive "human," "humanity," or "people."

Fetish

Hegel's view of History (a word he would have capitalized) followed his beliefs about subjectivity. Societies, even continents, have a "Spirit" with a historical trajectory. In the West, this Spirit began its development in Jerusalem with Christ; Hegel saw the centuries that had passed since then as a long upward progression toward the enlightened philosophical ideals that he espoused. By contrast in Africa (and Hegel problematically treats the continent as though it were a monolithic society) the Spirit of History had hardly begun to stir. African consciousness, Hegel argued, had not developed to a point where it saw anything outside of itself—the objective world, God, nature—as "other." "Religion begins," Hegel wrote, "with the consciousness that there is something higher than man" (93). Yet in the African religions that Hegel imagines (he never had first-hand experience himself with the people he writes of) the individual asserts a misbegotten magical power over nature. Hegel calls them "sorcerers." As such, they were still bystanders on the path of History and had not achieved subjectivity.

One of the examples Hegel draws upon to illustrate this mystical relationship between humans and objects is the "fetish," a word that had only recently come into widespread use among Europeans through contact with sub-Saharan Africa during the first decades of the slave trade. The word comes from Portuguese, and refers to the small objects that these Europeans observed the indigenous people of Guinea using in their religious worship. According to the *OED*, "feitiço" (or its variations) was the word that the Portuguese used to describe these objects—it meant "amulet" or "sorcery" (Hegel says the term denotes "magic"). The ultimate root of the word is the Latin "*facticuius*," denoting something manufactured or handmade. But the etymology of "fetish" is complex—the anthropologist William Pietz calls it "a novel word responsive to an unprecedented type of situation" (6). Pietz emphasizes that the term, as well as our concepts of the fetish, emerged from the cross-cultural spaces and contacts that took place during this early period of interaction between cultures. In looking at the history of this keyword, that is, we should take a more nuanced approach that reaches beyond this story of origins. For following its propagation in Europe in the nineteenth and twentieth centuries (and beyond) the fetish has come to represent a broad spectrum of concepts and beliefs. It is a keyword that provides a microcosm of the complex work language sometimes must carry out in representing human-object relationships.

As will be discussed in Chap. 7, Marx used the term "fetish" to describe a relationship that is peculiar to capitalism. Unlike Hegel, who left the fetish in Africa, Marx applied the concept to the production and consumption of commodities in Europe. The commodity becomes a fetish, Marx argued, through the division of labor that the capitalist society necessitates. Because my shirt is sewn by laborers in Bangladesh, from cotton farmed in India, and sold by workers in the United States, I come to view it as a kind of mystical object, Marx argues. Since I can no longer see the work of human labor that goes into making my goods, I come to view the objects in my life as magical entities not unlike the fetishes Marx had read about from the Guinean coast (for further discussion see Chap. 7). Interestingly Marx generalizes the fetish to religious belief more broadly. It is not just a part of African religions, he suggests, but "mist-enveloped regions of the religious world" more broadly (321). Through the nineteenth century the term became assimilated into the European lexicon. It surely retained some of its exoticism (note Marx's "mist-enveloped regions"), but the fetish also had come to be indicative of a key dimension of *modern* life.

After Marx, the fetish became a significant part of another discourse of modernity, psychoanalysis. Perhaps the most famous use of the word comes from Sigmund Freud, for whom the fetish served as a useful term to describe his psychosexual theory. Freud believed that a young boy's discovery that women do not have a penis (or "phallus"—the Greek term that psychoanalyst critics sometimes use) generated a "castration anxiety." With the realization that it is possible not to have a phallus, Freud argued, the masculine subconscious must also assume that it can have its manhood negated. Moreover, this fear confirms that the boy's natural sexual desire for his mother (what Freud famously called the "Oedipus Complex") is a danger to him. In the boy's mind, the father, the child's chief antagonist in his pursuit of his mother's love, might castrate the boy to punish his desire. The fetish then becomes for the boy an object or even part of the body that can lessen his anxiety. "It remains a token of triumph over the threat of castration and a protection against it" (Leitch 954). Thus, the fetish represents a natural tendency to sexualize the object as a replacement phallus—a symbolic restitution to the fear of castration that permeates (as Freud sees it) the human male psyche. Taken to an extreme, the fixation on such an object can become a form of neurotic sexual desire—Freud says that fetishists "praise the way in which it eases their erotic life" (Leitch 952–53). The fetish—Freud uses the examples of a piece of underwear, a shoe, a nose—can stand in for sexual attraction, and therefore replaces normative human desire.

Although most of Freud's theories have been dismissed by contemporary psychologists, we are still left with the notion that "fetish" describes an eccentric sexual desire. The sense that this desire is somehow linked to an object or material is also still present, too, even in our everyday lexicon. Such an attachment may be understood as sexual, but a fetish can describe a desire more generally. When I say I have a "sneaker fetish" I am probably not talking about sexual desire (although that is still an available meaning); rather, I want to say something about an excessive, maybe irrational impulse I have to collect as many Air Jordans as possible. Our contemporary usage therefore blends the meanings of Marx and Freud—of the commodity and the carnal—even as it retains something of the exotic resonance of the original Portuguese term.

This brief history of the word "fetish" reveals that words, like objects, may sometimes need to be decolonized (see the discussion of collections in Chap. 5). As Pietz observes, "The discourse of the fetish has always been a critical discourse about the false objective values of a culture from which the speaker is personally distanced" (14). The Portuguese merchant had no more understanding of what he saw in the worship practices of the peoples on the western coast of Africa than Hegel did—in the most significant ways they were both "personally distanced" from the language and beliefs of those cultures. The use of "fetish" as both word and concept has been "hegemonic" to use a term from Marxist theory—it reveals the structures of power that have persisted between Europeans and the people that they enslaved. Yet the word also shows some resilience to the burdens that Hegel placed on its meaning. In preserving a record, however incomplete, of this early encounter, the word "fetish" may re-energize dialogue around the dialectical relationship between European and African modes of thought. This is the argument of anthropologist L. Lorand Matory, who sees in the discourse of the fetish an opportunity "…to create the common terms of a value-neutral comparison and of a mutually respectful and reciprocally enlightening conversation among the inhabitants of culturally divergent worlds" (43).

Animals and Objects in the Environment—Affordances

Imagine walking into a building. As you pass through the doorway you see in front of you a large, inclined surface with a series of small tiers that lead to another flat surface about 3–4 meters above you. We call this a stairway in everyday language, and it is the kind of structure in our environment that we normally think very little about. In fact, if you were in the building described and wanted to walk up to the second floor, you would likely do so with barely a thought about your actions. Even a crawling baby or a small toddler understands what one does with a set of stairs (although they might also figure out a way to turn it into a place for a game). The structure itself seems to invite the behavior of climbing: each step is spaced at a distance that most ambulatory humans will find comfortable to climb, and the steps themselves are roughly the width of a human foot (maybe a little longer), allowing for easy placement when you step onto it. Unlike elevators or lifts, stairways typically allow you to see where you are going. They provide visual clues that help you ascend or descend to your destination. Most stairways have other mechanisms and features that further enhance their use: grip tape or rough material on the steps to help with foot traction; a railing placed at about waist level that can be held by the hand for balance; a gentle slope to reduce strain in climbing.

In the influential language of famed environmental psychologist James J. Gibson, the stairway is an "affordance": something found in our environment that is complementary to the lives and survival of humans and other animals. Gibson coined the term to capture this relationship of utility between animals and their environment. "The *affordances* of the environment are what it *offers* to animal, what it *provides* or *furnishes*, either for good or ill" (127, author's emphasis). Animals perceive stairs to be ascend-able, Gibson would argue, because of the many physical characteristics described above that enable this behavior. A wheelchair ramp next to the stairway has a similar set of affordances for vehicles and walkers alike: they provide visual evidence that allows us to perceive how we can use the structure. Importantly these features are "relative to the animal" (127). The perception of a stairway's use for climbing is relative to walking humans (or similarly sized animals); stairways do not afford climbing for mice, say, in the same way.

For Gibson, therefore, the environment determines the basic relationships between humans and objects: the materials and physical rules of the earth structure our capacity to interact with it. "We all fit into the substructures of the environment in our various ways, for we were all, in fact, formed by them. We were created by the world we live in" (Gibson 130). Yet humans are also able to alter the environment to "change what affords" them: they create objects to make life easier and aid in survival. A hand-sized rock can be used to break open a mollusk shell to provide food, it also can be launched from the hand as a projectile for self-defense (or to play a game). Gibson argues that we perceive objects based on their affordances, rather than on other qualities or properties that they have (color, size, shape, etc.). That is, affordances define the primary relationship between human subject and object. Gibson calls on child psychology for his evidence: "The affordance of an object is what the infant begins by noticing. The meaning is observed before the substance and surface, the color and form, are seen as such" (134). We can illustrate this by returning to the stairway example: a crawling baby understands that the stairway is ascend-able before she knows that it is made of stone, is especially wide, or even that it falls into the class of architectural objects that we call "stairways."

Gibson's work has been influential on a growing body of psychological and neuropsychological inquiry that explores how our brains interact with real objects in our lived environments. His original project to understand the way our brains and bodies perceive objects has inspired a number of studies that have expanded our understanding of the unique way we as humans use and understand objects. Indeed, for cognitive psychologists and neuroscientists, the idea that our minds couple with the world around us in creating thought is now uncontroversial. Here are just a few of the studies and conclusions that have been drawn by these scholars:

- Developmental psychologists have found that infants look at objects differently than they do two-dimensional images or representations (Gerhardt)
- Objects we can touch and hold make us more attentive and allow us better focus in our environment (Gomez)
- Experiencing food as a real object rather than an image has been shown to influence decisions that consumers make: we are willing to pay more and have a stronger sense of a food's nutritional qualities when we encounter it in actuality as compared to a 2D image (Romero et al.)
- Students in a series of studies found that it was easier to concentrate on reading in a physical book or document, had better recall of plot points in physical books, and that they experienced more enjoyment from reading in a book as compared to on an e-reader or computer (Baron; Mangen et al.)

This behavioral research is now being tested by neuroscientists who are looking for evidence within the functioning of the brain for a better understanding of human perception and its relationship to objects. According to one of these studies, evidence is growing that "real-world objects elicit stronger and more prolonged neural responses in action-related visuo-motor networks than images do"; those areas of our brain that respond to and control our interactions with the environment (the "visuo-motor networks") engage differently (and "stronger") when we observe or hold something real (Marini et al. 12). Such studies are changing the way we understand the working of the brain in our environment.

In his account of subject and object, Gibson observes a state of interrelation that he argued had not been observed in either psychology or philosophy. As described in the previous discussion of *dualism*, the relationship between subject and object imagined by Descartes and others placed the human subject at the center. In *historical materialism*, Marx argued for the importance of the dialectic, a relationship that gave more importance to the object but nonetheless saw a separate status for each. In Gibson's environmental view of subjectivity and the affordance, the concepts of subject and object become "inadequate." An affordance, he argues, "…is neither an objective property nor a subjective property; or it is both if you like. An affordance cuts across the dichotomy of subjective-objective and helps us to understand its inadequacy. It is equally a fact of the environment and a fact of behavior. It is both physical and psychical, yet neither" (129). Gibson's ideas, and the research they have inspired, thus seek to establish a new paradigm for a very old problem.

Radical Thingness: Object-Oriented Approaches

In the twenty-first century there has been considerable new energy in philosophy and other disciplines directed toward theorizing the material world. This chapter has already traced some of the trends that have driven this interest, but the turn toward "object-oriented" theories in this period follows a new set of interests: a move away from expressly humanistic (and thus anthropocentric) scholarship, and an embrace of objects as important representatives of the "non-human" or "posthuman" world, as well as a wider critique of Western thought and its responsibility for crises such as global climate change and ecological catastrophe. "Object-oriented" serves as a broad label that encompasses a range of theories that seek to undo the classic dualistic and dialectical philosophies of prior centuries. Timothy Morton, one of the leading voices in this field, has succinctly described the impact of this shift: "We've become so used to hearing 'object' in relation to 'subject' that it takes some time to acclimatize to a view in which there are only objects, one of which is ourselves" (165).

The sociologist Bruno Latour's "Actor Network Theory" (ANT), for instance, argues that objects need to be reasserted as part of the definition of the "social." He observes that in language we tacitly acknowledge the role of objects as actors: knives "cut" bread, kettles "boil" water, security cameras "see" or "monitor" our doorsteps and homes. For Latour these verbs are not merely personification, nor do they reflect some mystical idea about objects having souls. Rather, this language amounts to a real acknowledgment of how objects work within our environment as co-actors to carry out the business of our lives. "ANT is not the empty claim that objects do things 'instead' of human actors: it simply says that no science of the social can even begin if the question of who and what participates in the action is not first of all thoroughly explored, even though it might mean letting elements in which, for lack of a better term, we would call *non-humans*" (Latour 72). Latour's response to the subject-object divide originated by Descartes is to reject the very notion of that separation. Rather, for Latour, humans and non-humans need to be observed as unique actors within the social system. Latour uses the behavior of the "couch potato" to illustrate his point: does the behavior of a binge-watching couple make any sense if we ignore technologies and objects that make it possible? Without the development of infrared transmission that allows the remote control to "communicate" with a streaming device, the widespread social behavior is impossible. Anyone who has lost their remote knows this well. This situation that plays out daily for millions around the world is, for Latour, an illustration of the deeply enmeshed networks of humans and non-humans that constitute the realm of the social.

To understand the stakes of another object-oriented theory, think for a moment of the disastrous nuclear meltdown at the Fukushima Daiichi power plant in 2011. Damaged by a massive earthquake and subsequent tsunami, the nuclear reactors at this station used to produce electricity in northern Japan began spewing radioactive gas into the atmosphere to prevent further catastrophic meltdown within their nuclear cores. As an ocean surge caused by the tsunami flooded the plant, radioactive materials also leaked out into the Sea of Japan and into groundwater in the surrounding area. Radioactive molecules of caesium—between 17,500 and 20,500 "terabecquerels"—spread over thousands of miles throughout Japan and around the world by air and sea. One becquerel is the measurement of one radioactive molecule degrading in a second, thus 20,000 terabecquerels equals 20,000,000,000,000,000 (that's twenty quadrillion) of these events of molecular decay ("Radioactive Caesium" 137). With a half-life of about 30 years, the caesium emitted by the Fukushima reactors will be circulating in streams, the atmosphere, and the soft tissue of animal bodies until at least 2071. The plutonium in the now deactivated cores of the reactors will decay gradually over the next 4.6 million years.

If you find the numbers and scale of this disaster hard to grasp, perhaps it is because they are unimaginable, quite literally: the effects of a large-scale nuclear catastrophe like Fukushima's are only comprehensible by machines with computational power many orders beyond the capabilities of the human brain. Timothy Morton uses the term "hyperobjects" to describe objects like these radioactive caesium isotopes, the effects of global warming, or any phenomena that exist on such an enormous scale. Hyperobjects are "objects massively distributed in time and space that make us redefine what an object is" (Morton 167). That redefinition, for Morton, is a new way of understanding subject-object relations that he and others call "object-oriented ontology" or simply "OOO" (triple-O). The concept of hyperobjects offers helpful grounding for this complex philosophy: at the core of OOO is a belief in the proposition that objects exist and interact independently of human understanding or consciousness. The material effects of Fukushima are real but "withdrawn," according to Morton: with our basic human faculties we can't see or touch isotopic decay and even if we can (with the help of a powerful microscope, for instance) there will forever be some aspect of this object that is beyond our observation and understanding. To describe this "withdrawn" character of objects, Morton also uses the phrase "strange stranger": non-human objects, like human beings, share a quality of being "radically unpredictable" and not fully knowable. In just the same way we can't fully understand the massive hyperobject of global warming, individual objects will eternally remain strange and obscure to us.

Morton aligns on this point with Graham Harman, a theorist who has published extensively on OOO, and who likewise questions the underlying philosophies of traditional metaphysics: "object-oriented philosophy is a useful antidote wherever the idea prevails that things can be defined in purely relational terms rather than as autonomous realities in their own right" (Harman 197). Skeptical of the dialectical account of Hegel and Marx, or of any idealist view of metaphysics, Harman and OOO theorists persistently argue for the "autonomous realities" of objects. In this, Harman, Morton, and other OOO theorists follow the writings of Martin Heidegger, a German philosopher whose "phenomenological" approach to metaphysics has been significant to a wide range of contemporary theory. (It also bears mentioning that Heidegger remains a controversial figure due to his membership in the Nazi party; reassessments of his ideas in this light are ongoing.) For phenomenologists the debate about subjects and objects staged by Hegel and Marx (for example) may be avoided by focusing in on the consciousness and how it shapes and encounters objects in the world. More to the point, for phenomenologists the *only* objects that exist are those that are in our awareness: "phenomena" (a word that comes from the Greek, "appearing to show"). Heidegger had his own reading of the metaphysics of objects that began with phenomenology, but ultimately argued for the independent "strangeness" of objects (to use Morton's term). Imagine a tool that you use every day: your smartphone, for instance, or a vehicle you use for transportation. You probably don't think much about the operation of these complex objects, even though they are an essential part of your lived experience. Your awareness of these "phenomena" is mainly in the background or latent to your consciousness. But what if your car breaks down, your smartphone screen cracks, or your train is late due to maintenance? The object-ness of these tools is then thrust to the foreground of your awareness by their malfunctions. Does this mean that these tools as objects did not exist for you before they were broken? Heidegger says no, their status as objects remains even as they are not recognized or engaged by the consciousness as "phenomena". He intuited, therefore, that there is always something hidden from us about the object.

Not only are objects profoundly hidden from humans, but importantly they are independent of and obscure to each other: "Objects encounter each other as operationally closed systems that can only (mis)translate one another... An object is profoundly 'withdrawn'—we can never see the whole of it, and nothing else can either" (Morton 165). This radical insight is a key to understanding the metaphysics of OOO. The things that surround us will always withhold some essential part of their meaning to us; but they also exist alone within "closed systems" that remain remote and distinct from one another. There is an ontological complexity to objects that not only goes beyond our human understanding, but that also emphasizes a fundamental self-contained integrity within these objects. Material causality, an idea as important to Marx as it was to Descartes or Newton, becomes "vicarious" within OOO, as Harman puts it—the nature of object interaction is forever "strange" or "weird" (Harman, "Vicarous" 187). To return to the Fukushima disaster for illustration, the effects of those long-circulating hyperobjects are both profoundly material (pollution, altered weather, physical disease) but also made up of a series of "strange" encounters between radioactive isotopes, ecosystems, air, and animal biomes. OOO forces us as humans to reexamine our idealizing tendencies and accept an altered place within a world where objects operate beyond our control or understanding.

Despite the complexity of this theory, Harman poses what I would argue are the three key concepts of OOO. Here they are by way of summary:

Objects are irreducible to mere matter. Tables and towels are not the same because they share atomic similarity. As objects they will always retain separate identities that are "non-relational," that is, we shouldn't compare a table to a towel (or to a human being) in order to define its being. A more significant example is a work of art: Harman (and others) argue that we will never understand the *Mona Lisa* or a coffee cup by reducing it to its molecular components.

Objects may not be the same, but they are ontologically equal. This idea, referred to as "ontological flatness," argues that all objects exist within an equal ("flat") relationship to one another. A common trope within OOO writings is to give readers lists of disparate objects to prove this point: a sycamore, a sphinx, the idea I hold in my mind of a hippogryph, and a phalanx of Roman soldiers may all be different kinds of objects, but they share a fundamental object-ness. Note the departure of this idea from Descartes, for instance, or Hegel, both of whom championed the thinking qualities of the mind. There are no hierarchies between or among objects, and since there are no subjects (only human objects) many believers in OOO maintain that we should shift our understandings of ethics to reflect an inherent vitality within objects.

Philosophy must be re-envisioned as non-human. The skepticism within OOO of "relationalism," or "coorelationalism," the insistence of seeing objects as having meaning only in relation to other objects, may be understood as part and parcel of the theory's rejection of human-centered inquiry. To dispatch with the notion of the subject is to critique the very foundations of modern philosophy. That important move is also a critique of anthropocentrism (from the Greek meaning "human centered") and reveals a wider interest in OOO in uncovering the story of the "Anthropocene," the period of global history that encompasses *homo sapiens* and the effects the species has had on the environment. This is straightforwardly Timothy Morton's project, who, for instance, finds OOO as a key underpinning of his "ecological criticism." As the political theorist Jane Bennett puts it in her important book *Vibrant Matter*: "…the image of dead or thoroughly instrumentalized matter feeds human hubris and our earth destroying fantasies of conquest and consumption. It does so by preventing us from detecting (seeing, hearing, smelling, tasting, feeling) a fuller range of nonhuman powers circulating around and within human bodies" (x). To become object-oriented is thus political as well as ecological for these theorists, an attempt at undoing not just the thoughts but actions of a destructive humanity.

Conclusion

"How many angels can stand on the head of a pin?" This question is a centuries-old parody of overly complex and esoteric philosophical thinking, a rhetorical question meant to lampoon the seriousness of theologians who pursued agendas that would be of little interest to most people. To the beginner the discussions of object theory may sometimes look like a version of this problem: how many things can you fit on the head of that pin? But underlying and intertwined with the abstract thinking of these theorists are momentous questions about what it means to be human (or non-human). How we answer that question has had serious consequences throughout history and remains pressing within current crises. Hegel's view of history can be read as a justification for centuries of white supremacy, a philosophical accompaniment to a powerful racist ideology. Contrast that with Marx's view of the dialectic, where human labor is seen as the defining attribute of the subject, something that capitalism exploits but that can be reclaimed by revolutionary action. In contemporary times the dialectical thinking of Marx has given way to more radical views of materiality that seek to create new pathways for understanding ecological crisis. The way we theorize objects today, or in the past, presents a deeper look into what we value and the problems or opportunities that stand before us.

As important as these theories are to the study of material culture, this book argues for approaching Object Studies as a practice (or a series of practices). Ironically, the study of things has often been treated with abstraction, problems to be thought through rather than objects that are worked on. While it is therefore important to understand the history of ideas that stands behind some of the questions raised in this book, if you find yourself confused and overwhelmed by hyperobjects, the dialectic, and the etymology of "fetish," it may be helpful to ground some of this theoretical language in experiences that you hold with a firmer grasp. Do you find that any of the ideas discussed here elucidate the research you have done on an object of personal or communal significance? Does an artifact from your personal collection challenge Descartes's notion of dualism? How do Marx's ideas hold up against the research you have done on an object (like a coffee cup) produced hundreds of years ago? If the discussions of subjects and objects in this section help stoke your curiosity about larger theoretical debates you may want to pursue these investigations further (and there are some suggestions at the end of this chapter on how to do so). But in the remainder of the book, we will return to hands-on work with objects, albeit now with an understanding of how these practices fit within a much larger philosophical framework.

Procedures and Methods

This chapter offered an overview of some of the more important theories related to objects since the time of Descartes. It can also be a model for pursuing further investigations into other theoretical areas not covered here. In several places in this chapter, I focused on a particular word or phrase as a means of opening theoretical discussion. This method is inspired by the work of Raymond Williams, whose *Keywords* (1976, 1983, 2015) is one of the touchstones of twentieth-century theory. As Williams puts it, the goal of such a project as this is to construct a living vocabulary: "a vocabulary to use, to find our own ways in, to change as we find it necessary to change it, as we go on making our own language and history" (22). In object studies this methodology has been especially important as a means of uncovering the variability in meaning of materiality over time. Martin Heidegger, for instance, engaged in an extensive analysis of the etymology of "thing" vs. "object" as part of his philosophical ruminations on the topic (Heidegger, "What is a Thing?"). The keywords and concepts presented in this chapter are not meant to be exhaustive, and I encourage those who use this book to expand upon it with other words that fill out the theoretical story by connecting with other fields of study.

Words are a kind of thing themselves, and by looking deeply into a particular expression or phrase we can find a foothold on even the more complex schools of thought. Beginning with a shared vocabulary of concepts is important—entering into a theoretical conversation can be daunting for those new to this mode of thought. Moreover, creating this vocabulary is an excellent way to avoid the trap of over-abstraction. In a course you may find it useful to keep a running list of these words in a shared document or on an editable wiki page. With the resources suggested below, as well as with other articles, books, and resources provided by your instructor, that annotated list can provide theoretical background for the specific object studies you are carrying out in your class.

Resources and Research

As demonstrated in several of the words used in this chapter, the *Oxford English Dictionary* (especially the online version) can be an excellent starting place for research into the words and concepts of Object Studies. This is especially true in the case of vocabulary from everyday life: "relic," "stuff," "hoard," or even "subject" and "object" each preserve a long history of changing meaning and adapted ideas. When it comes to the jargon of a field or technical language of philosophy ("affordances" or "object-oriented ontology," for instance in this chapter) the *OED* is unlikely to provide the information you need, however. Your professor may introduce you to key theoretical texts within particular fields of study that provide further resources for studying concepts that are important to your course. You may also find that textbooks such as the *Norton Anthology of Criticism and Theory* or the expansive web resource *The Stanford Encyclopedia of Philosophy* can offer basic to intermediate treatments of the theories that are relevant to your course of study. These resources can also point you in the direction of primary sources—writings by the philosophers or thinkers themselves—that allow you to make your own interpretations of these theories.

Acknowledgment Sincere thanks to my research assistant Nicole Short for her help compiling the sources in this chapter.

Work Cited

Baron, Naomi S. "Redefining Reading: The Impact of Digital Communication Media." *PMLA*, vol. 128, no. 1, Jan. 2013, pp. 193–200. https://doi.org/10.1632/pmla.2013.128.1.193.

Bennett, Jane. *Vibrant Matter: A Political Ecology of Things*. Duke UP, 2010.

Bloom, Paul. *Descartes' Baby: How the Science of Child Development Explains What Makes Us Human*. Basic Books, 2005.

Descartes, René. *Meditations on First Philosophy: In Which the Existence of God and the Distinction of the Soul from the Body Are Demonstrated*. Hackett Publishing, 1993.

Gerhard, Theresa M., et al. "Distinct Visual Processing of Real Objects and Pictures of Those Objects in 7- to 9-Month-Old Infants." *Frontiers in Psychology*, vol. 7, 2016, https://doi.org/10.3389/fpsyg.2016.00827.

Gibson, James J. *The Ecological Approach to Visual Perception*. Psychology Press, 1986.

Gomez, Michael A., et al. "Graspable Objects Grab Attention More Than Images Do." *Psychological Science*, vol. 29, no. 2, Feb. 1, 2018, pp. 206–18. https://doi.org/10.1177/0956797617730599.

Harman, Graham. "On Vicarious Causation." *Collapse*, vol. II, Mar. 2007, pp. 187–221.

———. "An Outline of Object-Oriented Philosophy." *Science Progress*, vol. 96, no. 2, June 1, 2013, pp. 187–99. https://doi.org/10.3184/003685013X13691199842803.

Hegel, Georg Wilhelm Friedrich. *Hegel Selections*. Edited by M. J. Inwood, Macmillan, 1989.

Heidegger, Martin. *What Is a Thing?* H. Regnery, 1967.

Latour, Bruno. *Reassembling the Social an Introduction to Actor-Network-Theory*. Clarendon Lectures in Management Studies, Oxford UP, 2005.

Leitch, Vincent B., et al. *The Norton Anthology of Theory and Criticism*. Norton, 2001.

Mangen, Anne, Bente R. Walgermo, and Kolbjørn Brønnick. "Reading Linear Texts on Paper versus Computer Screen: Effects on Reading Comprehension." *International Journal of Educational Research*, vol. 58, Jan. 1, 2013, pp. 61–68. https://doi.org/10.1016/j.ijer.2012.12.002.

Marini, Francesco, et al. "Distinct Visuo-Motor Brain Dynamics for Real-World Objects versus Planar Images." *NeuroImage*, vol. 195, July 15, 2019, pp. 232–42. https://doi.org/10.1016/j.neuroimage.2019.02.026.

Marx, Karl, and Friedrich Engels. *The Marx-Engels Reader*. Edited by Robert C. Tucker, 2nd ed., Norton, 1978.

Matory, J. Lorand. *The Fetish Revisited: Marx, Freud, and the Gods Black People Make*. Duke UP, 2018.

Morton, Timothy. "Here Comes Everything: The Promise of Object-Oriented Ontology." *Qui Parle*, vol.19, no. 2, 2011, pp. 163–90. https://doi-org.libdatabase.newpaltz.edu/10.5250/quiparle.19.2.0163.

Pietz, William. "The Problem of the Fetish, I." *Res: Anthropology and Aesthetics*, vol. 9, Mar. 1, 1985, pp. 5–17. https://doi.org/10.1086/RESv9n1ms20166719.

———. "The Problem of the Fetish, II: The Origin of the Fetish." *Res: Anthropology and Aesthetics*, vol. 13, Mar. 1, 1987, pp. 23–45. https://doi.org/10.1086/RESv13n1ms20166762.

"Radioactive Cesium-137 Released from Fukushima 1.5 Times Tepco Estimate." *The Japan Times*, May 10, 2014, https://www.japantimes.co.jp/news/2014/05/10/national/radioactive-cesium-137-released-from-fukushima-1-5-times-tepco-estimate-study/.

"relic, n." *Oxford English Dictionary Online*, Oxford UP, www.oed.com/view/Entry/161910.

Riekki, Tapani, et al. "Conceptions about the Mind-Body Problem and Their Relations to Afterlife Beliefs, Paranormal Beliefs, Religiosity, and Ontological Confusions." *Advances in Cognitive Psychology*, vol. 9, no. 3, 2013, pp. 112–20. https://doi.org/10.2478/v10053-008-0138-5.

Romero, Carissa A., et al. "The Real Deal: Willingness-to-Pay and Satiety Expectations Are Greater for Real Foods versus Their Images." *Cortex*, Special Issue in Memory of Professor Glyn Humphreys, vol. 107, October 1, 2018. pp. 78–91. https://doi.org/10.1016/j.cortex.2017.11.010.

The Stanford Encyclopedia of Philosophy. Edited by Edward N. Zalta, Spring 2021 ed., https://plato.stanford.edu.

Tucker, Robert C.. "Introduction." *The Marx-Engels Reader*. Edited by Robert C. Tucker, 2nd ed., Norton, 1978.

Williams, Raymond. *Keywords: A Vocabulary of Culture and Society*. Oxford UP, 2014.

Chapter 5

Collecting Things: The Psychology of Accumulation, from Museums to Hoarders

Students will describe and analyze a collection of objects, seeking the ways in which objects come to be redefined by the act of collecting and curating, through the methods of individual and institutional collectors, and by viewers of collections, who bring their own acts of interpretation to bear upon these assemblies of objects.

Overview

"Collectors are the physiognomists of the world of objects," Walter Benjamin observes in his essay "Unpacking my Library." His metaphor is clever: physiognomists are face readers, people who claim the ability to see into the character of a person, or even view into their future, by interpreting facial features. It is a mystical practice with ancient roots still used around the world today. Collectors, similarly, "read" objects and try to project their value. They see the object's history through its features, or even imagine what the object's future place in a collection might be. Throughout his essay Benjamin uses similar occult language in describing how a collector relates to their objects: "The most profound enchantment for the collector is the locking of individual items within a magic circle in which they are fixed as the final thrill, the thrill of acquisition, passes over them" (60). It is a remarkably spiritual turn for Benjamin, a well-known Marxist theoretician who is nevertheless religious, even, in the way he writes about books as objects: "One has only to watch a collector handle the objects in his glass case," he writes; "As he holds them in his hands, he seems to be seeing through them into their distant past as though inspired" (61).

If you have ever been a collector, of if you have a collection now, then perhaps you relate to the transcendent language Benjamin uses in this portrait of the collector. I certainly can: like many Americans my age, I had a brief period as a baseball card collector as a child. Thinking back on it now, I remember the thrill of the ritual

© The Author(s), under exclusive license to Springer Nature Switzerland AG 2023
C. Mulready, *Object Studies*, https://doi.org/10.1007/978-3-031-09027-1_5

involved in opening wax or foil packs filled with cards, flipping through them in search of a rare find. There was also a pleasure for me, too, in sorting them into various categories (position, team, year) so they could be filed away for future reference (perhaps an early sign of my future as a scholar). Sports cards in the age before the internet were also a source of useful information: player statistics, hometowns, minor league seasons, and factoids about player likes and interests. I spent many hours poring over these details and squirreling them away for debates with friends about the merits of one second baseman over another. I'm embarrassed at how much of this trivial knowledge I have retained over the years: Mark McGuire's 49 home runs as a rookie, Dave Winfield's hometown (St. Paul, Minn.), Don Mattingly's 0.356 average in 1986 when he won the batting title…I'll stop. As I became a more invested and engaged collector, I sought out card shops and "shows" held in dimly lit social halls where I could make trades for cards I wanted or purchase others. I can still remember paying the princely sum of $28 for my favorite player's rookie card. Although my collection never grew to be especially large or valuable (I had the misfortune of collecting during a time when overproduction of cards decreased their investment value dramatically), I still had a strong psychological, and yes, even spiritual connection to those thin pieces of cardboard. When I was in college a fire did extensive damage to my family home, destroying my neatly organized collection of baseball cards. Fortunately no one in my family was hurt in the fire, but even many years after the event the loss of that childhood collection is painful to me. The psychic investment I have in that small library of baseball cards remains substantial.

Any study of objects must also include consideration of how they typically present themselves to us: not as individual pieces but as part of a collection. To return to Benjamin's metaphor, if objects are individual faces then the collection is the community that develops through the assembling of various parts. And as in any community, the relationship between individual members and the collective is fascinating to observe. There are times when the identities of particular objects are subsumed under the more expansive features of the collection. A sculpture in a museum of modern art, for instance, is one example alongside many that represents some idea of modernity. Yet an individual item can also stand out in such a way that it can transcend its place in a collection: DaVinci's *Mona Lisa*, Michelangelo's *David*, Lindberg's *Spirit of St. Louis*, the Elgin Marbles, or my Don Mattingly rookie card. All these are treasures that, although part of a collection, seem to stand on their own as objects of adoration. As within human communities, placing individual objects together also leads us naturally to the process of categorization. We may better understand objects in seeing them through these groupings (fine art, craft, objects of the 1960s, technology) but categories can also create controversy: the labeling of African American art as "folk art" or the creation of the category of the "oriental" are examples of categories that have reflected the same kinds of bias and prejudice that attend to the categories of human society. Sometimes objects, like people, demand that we see in them both similarity and diversity, the features that can align them within collections but also distinguish them from one another.

Yet the definition of a collection or a collector is not as easy to articulate as that of an object. Collections can be formal and heavily curated (museums, homes, libraries) or they may be more chaotic and disorganized. They can be large, encompassing warehouses of storage space (think of the Smithsonian, familiarly called "America's Attic"), or they can be small enough to fit in a phone booth (see the Warley Museum in west Yorkshire, housed in a decommissioned phone booth). Even defining what it means to be a collector can be more difficult than it seems at first glance. They might be a person with a hobby or with more serious intentions for the things they acquire. A sheet music collector, for instance, may be a musician with an interest in a particular genre or period of musical taste, or she may just enjoy the artwork printed on the cover. A wine collector probably enjoys drinking wine, but he also might see the cases in his collection as a financial investment. And a historical society or museum (such as Historic Huguenot Street, profiled in Chap. 2) might view the things they collect primarily for their capacity to tell stories about the past that reveal something about the community.

As it has been argued by a generation of scholars in the fields of museology, anthropology, and archeology, the contexts in which we experience objects—the webs of connections that exist between items in a group—can define how we understand the things before us. As the range of possibilities for collector behavior detailed above might suggest, however, the challenge in approaching collections from a critical point of view is that there is a wide diversity of opinion within the scholarship about how to interpret collections. Does it even make sense, for instance, to call both my baseball cards and a museum like the 9/11 Memorial & Museum in New York "collections"? These questions all return, inevitably, to the objects held in the collections themselves: what is historical, what is art, what is junk, what has mere sentimental value and what has larger cultural or monetary worth? In many cases it is hard to ask those questions without understanding an object as part of a collection. Doesn't the coffee cup I discussed in a previous chapter seem more important if we encounter it in a display case at the British Museum alongside other examples of Safavid arts and crafts? Does its value increase because it is part of this collection?

These questions often center on the presumed viewer of a collection as much as the collector or curator of the objects. The interpretation of collections is therefore similar to the work of reading a novel or a film: each of these forms can work as a narrative that we piece together as we attempt to understand their signs and language. Museums themselves can be organized by such storytelling building blocks as historical development, thematic relationships, character development (author or creator-focused exhibitions), and places or settings (the photography of the American South). These features make the critical tools often associated with literary or historical interpretation equally important to the understanding of object collections.

The goal of this chapter is to approach the interpretation of collecting by looking at several examples. Through these I will illustrate some of the key cultural, theoretical, and psychological ideas surrounding collections that have developed in recent scholarship and museum practices. The analyses I carry out will then illustrate how these approaches can help us better interpret the meanings of these collections, as well as the objects they hold.

Model Essays

1. "It's like a time machine to me": Hobbyist Collecting and "Retrocomputing"

Do you remember the first computer you used? Depending on when you were born the textures of that memory may differ: the size of the screen, the color of the text, the place (school, work, home), or even the smells and sounds of the machine. For most of us computers are objects that have been both a ubiquitous and changing feature of our environments. They have been a part of human society for decades yet the devices we use today are probably quite different from those that we used when we first sat down at a keyboard. I have an early memory of using an Apple II computer that was bolted to a cart so it could be transported from room to room of my elementary school. It was the only computer in the building. Before you turned on the computer you were directed to rub your thumb against a metal plate on the back of the CPU; apparently there was a fear that a static electric spark from a child's finger might fry the delicate circuitry. I can still remember the feel of the cool metal on my thumb as I ran it back and forth over that shiny spot on the back of the machine, a little anxious at the thought of breaking the school's computer if I didn't take this crucial step. The reward was a cherished 20 minutes with a favorite game: *Oregon Trail*, *Lemonade Stand*, or an adventure through a haunted mansion whose title is lost to time. Even the relatively basic digital technology of that early Apple computer delivered to me a set of indelible experiences.

Upon reflection I see that working on a computer in those days was a fully immersive material experience: the cart getting wheeled into the classroom, being assigned a number to determine when I'd get to use it, selecting the software I wanted to play, even booting up the computer. In recent years a group of hobbyists have begun collecting machines and parts from prior decades of computing technology. Interested in recapturing their formative experiences with these technologies, they repair and rebuild their retro machines to bring them back to life. "You get into this mind-set of what it must've been like to be someone in the late '70s," Clint Basinger, a retrocomputer collector with his own YouTube channel told the *New York Times*, "it's like a time machine to me" (Key). Some ingenious collectors have even managed to retrofit earlier computers with programs that allow them to do contemporary activities like check email or post to active discussion boards while using these decades-old interfaces.

Those of us who lack the know-how and budget to acquire and revive these machines can visit any number of computer museums around the world: The National Museum of Computing in Bletchley Park includes a working Colossus, the computer used during WWII to break encrypted Nazi communication; Silicon Valley's Computer History Museum includes labs where you can see machines like the one-ton PDP-1 "microcomputer" from 1959 demonstrate the early videogame *SpaceWar!*; and at the Nexon Computer Museum in South Korea you can see one of the holy grails of early computing, the Apple 1. These are the most high-profile museums, but there are countless other regional and local institutions that speak to collector fascination with these artifacts of the early digital age.

Collectors and collections rose alongside the creation of consumer society—this is the influential thesis of Russell Belk, who argues in *Collecting in a Consumer Society* and elsewhere that collections and collecting must always be understood as essentially part of the capitalist economy. This is not to say, however, that collecting is the blind activity of individuals who are locked into the habits of capitalistic consumption. Rather, Belk describes how collecting personalizes and transforms objects from being part of a mass market to something more individualized. In fact, Belk argues that what constitutes a collection is the act itself of moving objects from their intended daily use into something that ties a consumer more closely to their possessions. "...things comprising a collection are removed from ordinary use" (66), Belk argues. Salt and pepper shakers, for instance, if they are part of a collection, are not likely to be placed on a table; rare stamps aren't, of course, used for sending mail. Collecting therefore is a different form of consumption that ties a collector more intimately to the objects in question. "As a result collectors tend to feel attached to their collections in ways that may seem irrational if viewed in terms of the normal functions of the things collected" (66). Retrocomputing is an apt illustration of this concept: even though we have available to us machines that are otherwise faster, more efficient, and capable of carrying out many more functions, the collector of computers from the 1980s finds a more "irrational" connection to these objects. Another way of saying this is that they are more spiritually connected. Their relationship to these objects goes beyond mere use. Belk calls collecting a process by which objects are "sacralized": he argues that "collecting epitomizes the sacralization of consumption in the contemporary world. Although the locus may have changed, the need for something that is transcendent, numinous, or magical in our lives remains" (94).

If you read around discussion boards and Reddit threads on retrocomputing you'll find collectors who express a reverence for their old machines that sounds religious. In the popular 68kMLA forum, a user named falen5 described in detail their discovery of a Lear Siegler ADM 3+ terminal: "Picked this up in Dublin...It's from Trinity College...Am seriously thinking a major retro fit! But then I don't like altering old machines. Prefer to just try to restore them." The user's desire to keep the machines as intact as possible comes up several times in the thread: "looks like one of the early machines. All the more reason not to destroy any part of it...I don't even like cleaning off all the 'age'." And elsewhere falen5 is almost rhapsodic about the experience with the machine: "Oh the smell from this! I swear, if I could bottle it. The smell of the electronic revolution's birth!!" Other collectors express the feelings of nostalgia generated by their retro machines:

> When I was mowing lawns in my junior year of HS, one of my customers had [an Apple] //c. I gushed over it, and so he made me a deal: If I cut his lawns enough times, I'd get the //c instead of the usual payment. After gladly accepting, really looked forward to getting that machine. Alas, I'd signed up for the Army Reserve and had to ship off to Basic Training before I could close the deal, and the fellow just paid me what he owed. So, here I am—retired from the Army with time and some money (though less than I'd hoped) on my hands—so getting this machine will be a long wish fulfilled.

Reading around in these online communities of avid retrocomputer collectors, I see the pleasure these hobbyists derive from the search for these objects. Discussions about the best places to get old machines (estate sales and Craigslist are best, avoid eBay), what kinds of components to use, what the best monitors and other peripherals are, how to find software. Like many collectors, retrocomputer enthusiasts frame their hobby as a quest (or series of quests) for their computers: "a long wish fulfilled" as the purchaser of the Apple //c described above.

The collector's quest for the objects of their collection is yet another dimension of what Belk calls sacralization. In describing the rare Apple 1 I have already used a reference to the Holy Grail, the mythical cup of Christ from the last supper that became the central plot focus for a series of stories beginning in the Middle Ages. In the Grail Quest narrative, interestingly, the knights who sought out the cup did not always achieve their goal—in fact, some of the stories were left incomplete by their authors. The structure of these narratives emphasizes the path and process rather than the achievement of the goal. The grail is the object that sits forever beyond the reach of the quester; it is the adventure that drives both the story and characters who pursue their goal.

Thinking of the collector in the grand narrative of the questing knight puts a different perspective on their activity of accumulation. This is Belk's point: although collecting is closely aligned with consumer culture, it is not identical to consumption. Rather, the process of obtaining parts, machines, new software, and other components is the core of the experience. It may not lead to something as transcendent as the grail, but part of the lesson of those stories is that the object of desire becomes individualized: just as the quest expresses something different for one knight than another, what is "magical" about a collection of outmoded computers may not be the same for everyone. For one person a set of operational 386 PCs brings back nostalgia for their early experiences with computing in college, while for another bringing old Commodores back to life is a way of better understanding how computer systems worked. We can witness the range of interests within a community, but it is through their acts of collecting and curating, of determining what has value, that the individual defines herself and what it means to own these objects.

2. **Colonizing Collections, Decolonizing Objects: Avery Brundage and the San Francisco Asian Art Museum**

In the interior of Thailand, not far from the modern-day border with Cambodia, sits one of many ancient temples that can still be found throughout southeast Asia. Today the Prasat Khao Lon Temple is part of the Ta Phraya National Park, and it is accessible by foot with a small hike up a rocky hill. Built in the tenth century CE as part of the Khmer Empire, the temple was first sacred to believers of Hinduism and was later converted into a Buddhist shrine. Its original builders decorated the temple with various adornments and carvings to honor their gods, including large relief sculptures carved out of sandstone that spanned the tops of the temple's doorways. One of these distinctive "lintels," as they are known, is a 1500-pound rectangular piece of brown-orange sandstone roughly 64" wide and 22" high. Its ornate carvings depict, in the center, a monstrous face with a faceless deity riding it. As the description of this magnificent object reads, there are ornate naturalistic depictions of leaves and vines: "The foliage and other motifs of this lintel are particularly deeply cut, giving a strong sense of light and shadow" ("Lintel"). This intricately crafted lintel sat atop its temple doorway in Thailand for almost 1000 years, where countless worshippers passed beneath it as they entered the structure for worship. But sometime in the 1960s it was removed illegally from its temple doorway and later acquired by an antiquities dealer based in Paris. The lintel would eventually join thousands of items in the world's largest collection of Asian art and artifacts, held in San Francisco by the Asian Art Museum (Fig. 5.1).

There are collections around the world that include items that, like this Thai lintel, were secured through unethical means. These same collections may have been assembled by people whose quests for objects were far from noble. Avery Brundage, the man who purchased this ancient Thai artifact in 1968, was a collector who had both an insatiable taste for Asian art and a limited concern about the ethics of purchasing stolen artifacts. We know that shortly after he purchased the lintel, Brundage was contacted by the Thai government and asked to return an artifact it viewed as stolen property. He reached out to his dealer in Paris for advice but never attempted to return the object. By 1968, he had assembled one of the world's largest collections of art and objects from China, Japan, and other regions of Asia. On his death

Fig. 5.1 Thai Lintel from the San Francisco Asian Art Museum. (Image from *United States v. Lintels*)

in 1975, in a front-page obituary the *New York Times* described the 7000 piece collection as "the finest individually owned one in the world" (Litsky 40). In 1959 Brundage entered into an agreement with San Francisco to donate his collection to create the Asian Art Museum; its estimated value in 1966 was $30 million (roughly $500 million in 2021 dollars). Brundage knowingly purchased some of these items even when, as with the Thai lintel described above, he had been warned about their shady provenance. Earlier he had acquired a similar lintel from a dealer in London with whom he exchanged letters documenting that it had been illegally taken from Thailand. He took no action to return any objects that were suspected of being stolen and some of these still remain in the collections of the Asian Art Museum.

Brundage built his collection through an unsparing and relentless pursuit: "High quality, low prices" was the purchasing motto he often boasted of in his lifetime. Even when he wasn't obtaining artifacts that he knew to be stolen, he used his powerful position with the International Olympic Committee as leverage in negotiations with local dealers and politicians in China, Japan, and other places with art he coveted. "Abroad he would seek advice on where bargains might be obtained from his host officials, and they in turn would invariably be anxious to please the president—often presenting, in *Godfather* fashion, 'an offer he couldn't refuse'" (Meyer 330). *The New Yorker* reported in a 1960 profile of Brundage that on a trip he took to Japan, presumably in the lead up to the 1964 games that were held in Tokyo, he was greeted at the airport by two members of the Japanese Olympic delegation and two art experts. "It was great fun," Brundage commented on this trip that intermingled his two passions, "and when I saw the Emperor afterward and told him what a service I had done for Japan, he agreed" (Shaplen 70). I see in that statement the barely hidden suggestion of a quid pro quo: we don't know what treasures he left Japan with during this visit, whether he added to his collection of thousands of *netsuke*, or Japanese porcelains, or screen paintings, but his position in negotiations with the Japanese must have been strong. As an American responsible for the decision to bring the Olympic games and all the "services" that came along with it, Brundage surely would have been at an advantage in any negotiation.

In his own lifetime he was a marginally controversial figure—he was called out in the 1960s as "Slavery Avery" for his punishment of black athletes who protested during the Olympics. But his reputation as a philanthropist and collector remained largely unsullied, despite his long record of racism and sexism. As a member of the International Olympic Committee (and later its chair) he was involved in the decision to have America participate in the 1936 games in Berlin (the event where the track start Jesse Owens famously won gold medals in front of Hitler). Brundage was an unapologetic Nazi sympathizer at the time. As a member of the American Olympic Committee in the 1930s, he was sent to Germany to investigate accusations of anti-Jewish discrimination. He concluded that there was none, and as he told the *New York Times*: "The fact that no Jews have been named so far to compete for Germany doesn't necessarily mean that they have been discriminated against on that score. In forty years of Olympic history, I doubt if the number of Jewish athletes competing from all nations totaled 1 per cent of all those in the games" ("Racist IOC President"). After the 1936 games he concluded that America could "learn much from Germany" and gave voice to the need for "An intelligent, beneficent dictatorship" like the one established by Hitler. He actively opposed women who wanted to participate in athletics. He thought, for instance, that distance running was "too strenuous for most of the opposite sex."

We may now judge Brundage's beliefs as reprehensible, his actions as a collector to be unethical, and attitudes as part of another time. But how do these judgments shape our understanding of his collections? Furthermore, what is the responsibility of the institution and the City of San Francisco, which owns the museum, to address this legacy? After all, one of the reasons Brundage donated the majority of his collection to San Francisco (and not his hometown of Chicago) was the significant presence of an Asian American community there. Is it possible to have a collection that reflects imperialist or colonial attitudes still be a source of good within a community? These are the questions that the Asian Art Museum and the people of San Francisco have been grappling with since 2020, when public awareness of Brundage's character and views emerged as part of a larger American conversation about the continuing legacies of racism. Dr. Jay Xu, the museum's director, addressed Brundage's connection to the institution in a public letter:

> If we pride ourselves as guardians of a historical art collection, we must contend with the very history of how our museum came to be. Avery Brundage, whose collection forms the nucleus of this institution, espoused racist and anti-Semitic views. We have removed his name from museum initiatives but have yet to address this history in a fully open and transparent way. Only by publicly condemning Brundage's racism and examining the foundation of our museum can we become an even greater source of healing and connection. (Asian Art Museum)

Yet disentangling the institution from the history of its acquisitions is difficult, a lesson demonstrated by the story of the Thai lintels with which I began this section.

A Thai official first saw the stolen lintels on display at the San Francisco Asian Art Museum in 2016, and shortly after began proceedings with the United States Department of Homeland Security to reclaim them as stolen property (*United States v. Lintels*). For several years the museum and city denied that the objects were stolen property. It was only after the US government brought a lawsuit against the city that the museum agreed to return the items to Thailand, in early 2021 (the case was named, extraordinarily, "US v. Two One-Thousand-Five-Hundred-Pound, Hand-Carved Lintels Removed from Religious Temples in Thailand"). Even in returning the artifacts, the museum claimed that the Thai government was confusing the objects with a third lintel, which Brundage had (they contended) returned in 1970: "The artifacts left Thailand 'under circumstances that are very unclear'," Robert Mintz, the museum's deputy director told a newspaper reporter (Dazio). But the research carried out by the US Department of Homeland Security showed that the two lintels were, in fact, acquired by Brundage and the museum illegally in the 1960s. Perhaps because of the changing tide in public opinion, and a desire to stand behind the values espoused by Dr. Zu in his 2020 letter, the museum negotiated the return of the sacred lintels to Thailand.

The lintels and the Brundage Collection raise the question of whether there are some objects that shouldn't be in collections, or, if they are, how museums and collections held in public or private institutions should handle their colonial histories. I have used this particular case to illustrate a wider, centuries-old practice of objects being collected and used as an expression of cultural or political hegemony: The Elgin Marbles in the British Museum, Nigerian bronzes in the New York Metropolitan Museum, objects held in French museums from its former colonies, paintings seized from Jewish families by the Nazis throughout Europe. Museums that are tied to these histories have been, at times, reluctant to acknowledge the legacies of their objects and institutions. Yet a growing number of scholars, curators, and museum directors have been calling for "decolonizing" collecting practices: de-acquisitioning objects that can be documented as having been stolen or looted, organizing exhibitions that acknowledge the origins of their collections, and engaging more forthrightly with the public about the connections between collecting and colonialism. As the organizers of a special colloquium held at the British Museum wrote in expressing this view, "Museums are obliged to proactively research their collections in order to understand, present and interpret collecting histories, the colonial past, and the legacies of the empires of the colonial period for the postcolonial present" (Giblin et al. 486). Object Studies can be a fundamental part of this project, for it is through a recognition of the specific material character and history of an object that we can understand it as something more than the collection of which it is a part. Such was the case for the Thai lintels formerly in the Brundage Collection and now in the Bangkok National Museum: a public repatriation ceremony for the lintels was held in Los Angeles in May 2021, presided over by Thai and American officials. The objects' return was celebrated with ceremonial dances and prayers.

3. **Empowering Objects: Collecting for Social Change**

Breast pumps, diaphragms, tampons: these are objects that rarely receive cultural or scholarly attention. Instead, society ignores or shrouds the materiality of women's health and reproduction in euphemisms like "unmentionables" or "feminine products." An exhibition curated to challenge these taboos, "Designing Motherhood: Things that Make and Break Our Births," gathered together a collection of objects to give voice to the history of this essential part of womanhood. "These objects are often used by people who have not had the power to write history, make decisions or frame material culture," Michelle Millar Fisher, one of the exhibit co-creators explained. "They have just not been part of the conversation, out loud, until recently" (Ryzik). The remarkable exhibition presented a range of objects designed for women's bodies that, in various ways, constitute the material conditions that support (or restrict) motherhood.

Equally remarkable were the collaborative partnerships that brought the project to the public: a coalition of scholars, museums, a non-profit health group, and a private arts and culture foundation. The "Designing Motherhood" exhibition represents yet another kind of collection, one that tells a story designed to expand awareness of a pressing social issue, educate the public about these problems, or give voice and representation to people who have been marginalized in society. Such projects often form around community coalitions and interdisciplinary work between scholars, institutions, and organizations with wider social missions. This approach has been called museum and collections "activism," a practice, as described by the museologists Robert Janes and Richard Sendell, "shaped out of ethically-informed values, that is intended to bring about political, social and environmental change" (2). In response to the traditions of collecting represented by figures like Avery Brundage, museum professionals, librarians, scholars, and even individual collectors have sought in recent years to use collections of objects as a powerful demonstration of societal problems or to promote new narratives about lives, places, and histories that receive little attention.

Following the global migration crises that arose in the early 2010s, for instance, several institutions in the UK and Europe developed exhibitions to address the history of immigration and the lives of those affected by wide-scale population shifts. In 2016 the Museum of German History in Berlin assembled a collection of stickers that spoke both to that historical moment as well as the longer history of immigration and xenophobia in twentieth-century Germany. *"Angezettelt"* ("Sticky Messages"), presented a collection of anti-Semitic and racist messages placed on stickers, as well as anti-racist counter-messaging that resisted these ideas. On the surface this looks like a very different kind of collection and exhibition than the Designing Motherhood project, but each represents an attempt at assembling a narrative from the fractured pieces of material culture that might otherwise go unnoticed. The power of both exhibitions derives from the accumulation of objects and the point of view of the curators and their acts of interpretation. In everyday life we might encounter a sticker on a lamppost or on a car bumper that conveys an individual message ("Go Home" or "There's No More Room"), but when dozens of such objects are brought together the collection conveys a story that is more than just the sum of its parts. Particularly for German history, where the memory and impact of anti-Semitism is so powerful, an alignment of Nazi-era speech with more recent examples gives a new texture to that history. Collected together, the objects in the exhibition document "a social practice of misanthropic prejudices and recounts at the same time the history of fighting against antisemitic and racist stereotypes," as described in the promotional materials.

Refugee Week in the UK, an annual celebration held in June, has inspired many exhibitions and collections that likewise address the experience of refugees and migrants forced from their homes by war. In 2020–2021, London's Imperial War Museum created a series of exhibits, "Refugee," that used various forms of visual media to tell these stories. "Forced to Flee" walks viewers through a series of rooms meant to trace the migrant's path from home to war to relocation. "Could you leave everything behind," is the question the exhibition poses, a proposition that sets up the viewer's experiences with various objects that have belonged to displaced people over the past 100 years: sheet music, a teddy bear, a postcard. The exhibit uses these objects, collectively, to evoke the emotions of loss and displacement in the viewer that have been experienced by the migrants who had to leave these things behind. These objects are accompanied by photographs, brief narratives, and (in another part of the exhibit) an immersive video experience that places the viewer in a panoramic video displaying the refugee camp in Lesbos. Activism in collecting can use the affective power of even these everyday objects to engage the viewer sense of justice and promote change.

Following an activist paradigm, older collections might be reconfigured or reinterpreted to bring out their associations with histories that would otherwise be unseen. One of the Victoria and Albert Museum's contributions to Refugee Week in 2021, for instance, was a special tour designed for children and families that revealed migrant stories within six objects in their collection. An architectural piece of archway from a Spanish synagogue illustrated the comingling of Jewish and Muslim cultures in medieval Spain, while a plate from nineteenth century Mumbai inscribed with the word "welcome" written in Farsi was used to tell the story of Persian immigration into India. Interpretive questions asked children to consider: "What do you think this dish was used for? Perhaps it was made as a present for somebody to feel welcome after arriving in a new place? Can you think of a way to make someone who is new to your school or community feel welcome?"

Activist collecting can also involve curating collections that expose material histories of racism, bias, and oppression. Like the exhibit of stickers advertising Nazi propaganda in Germany, the Jim Crow Museum of Racist Memorabilia at Ferris State University in Detroit recodes objects from the long history of America's racist past: they "use items of intolerance to teach tolerance" (Pilgrim). These "items of intolerance" also play an important role in demonstrating how the ideology of racism and white supremacy was propped up by a set of material objects that reinforced its values. As David Pilgrim, the museum's founder, writes:

> Jim Crow laws and etiquette were aided by millions of material objects that portrayed blacks as laughable, detestable inferiors. The Coon caricature, for example, depicted black men as lazy, easily frightened, chronically idle, inarticulate, physically ugly idiots. This distorted representation of black men found its way onto postcards, sheet music, children's games, and many other material objects.

It seems counterintuitive that assembling a collection of such objects could be an act of resistance to such racist ideals. But this is yet another dimension of activist collecting. By preserving and presenting those materials of the past that make us feel uncomfortable, they validate continued efforts to achieve equality and even material reparation. It may be harder to regard racism as something in the past when you are faced with hundreds of artifacts that preserve a history of racial degradation.

4. "I Collect a Lot of Stuff": Hoarding and Extreme Collecting

The American television show *Hoarders* represents a popular sub-genre of reality television. There are various versions of this show found around the world, but they all follow a similar pattern. We see a person living in squalid conditions apparently of their own making: massive volumes of objects, trash, and unsorted goods overwhelm their living spaces, yards, and garages. We witness bereaved family members who intervene in the life of the hoarder with the help of mental health experts and organizational coaches. Sometimes the story wraps up with a newly cleaned and organized home, other times the recalcitrant hoarder is left with still more piles of stuff. It does not make for happy viewing, as the shows tend to emphasize that hoarding is a mental illness. The title screen that opens *Hoarders* establishes this: "Compulsive Hoarding is a mental disorder marked by an obsessive need to acquire and keep things, even if the items are worthless, hazardous, or unsanitary." *Britain's Hidden Hoarders* similarly establishes the pathology of its subjects, and notes that as many as three million people in the UK suffer from compulsive hoarding. Even the soundtracks for these shows, heavy on strings and spare piano music, evoke genres of horror or tragic melodrama.

All these shows provide a fascinating window into a particular dimension of Object Studies, the relationship between people and their things gone to an extreme. Hoarding is especially interesting to consider in the topic of collecting because it is a behavior that is defined not so much by a relationship with an individual object, but with many objects. The *Oxford English Dictionary* shows this meaning in its first definition of "hoard," "An *accumulation or collection* of anything valuable hidden away or laid by for preservation or future use" (Def. 1.a., emphasis added). The examples offered by the *OED* for the word date back over 1000 years and typically speak of treasure, food, or money. Through human history, the collecting and preserving of valuable materials has been a practice tied to survival—preparations during days of plenty for times of scarcity. The *OED* does not register, exactly, the shift in meaning the word has taken during more recent years, when "hoarding" has now come to suggest something pathological (as seen in the previously mentioned television shows). While some of the language of hoarding in previous centuries implies moral hazard—the book of Proverbs warns in an early English translation "Who so hoardeth up his corne, shall be cursed amonge the people"—the problem in these cases is covetousness or greed. Historically it has not been the hoard that is the problem, but the hoarder's unwillingness to share her treasures with the community. Now in contemporary discourse, hoarding is a psychological or behavioral affliction that is a sign of a lack of personal control and an excess of desire for things that leads to mental, physical, and social harm.

In 1996 "Hoarding Disorder" was first described in psychological literature as follows:

1. The acquisition of and failure to discard a large number of possessions that seem to be useless or of limited value.
2. Living spaces sufficiently cluttered so as to preclude activities for which those spaces were designed.
3. Significant distress or impairment in functioning caused by hoarding. (Nordsletten and Mataix-Cols 167)

The American Psychological Association has since formally recognized hoarding as a disorder in its *Diagnostic and Statistical Manual of Mental Disorders*, the guidebook mental health professionals use to assess patient behavior. How did this practice, once associated positively with saving treasure and storing up grain for lean harvests, come to indicate disease? The answer to that question is complicated, but there is evidence to suggest that the rise of consumer capitalism over the past 100 years or so has been a deciding factor. The linguistic record provided by the *OED* here is again helpful: the kinds of materials associated with hoarding in generations prior to the twentieth century were raw materials or money. Figuratively the meaning of hoard extended to feelings and ideas that have strong metaphorical weight: health, sin, love. These could be hoarded up in one's heart much as the corn in the granary. Moreover, for the purposes of object study, is there a relationship between excessive forms of collecting and the hoarding behaviors outlined in the *DSM*? This is a question of special importance: is collecting like casual alcohol and drug use, fine in moderation but dangerous when taken to excess? Or do collecting and hoarding have less in common than might appear on the surface? Are hoarders motivated by different things than the more common collector? These are some of the questions that motivated a team of psychologists in a recent study, "Hoarding versus Collecting," where they did a wide-scale secondary analysis of available data on hoarding and collecting to determine where the behaviors overlapped and differed. "In a society that is arguably driven by consumption, understanding where that dividing line should be drawn represents a challenge. In the context of Hoarding Disorder, then, the question becomes: do the proposed diagnostic criteria offer an acceptable framework for establishing this line?" (Nordsletten and Mataix-Cols 166).

After my own study of an episode of *Hoarders*, it is hard to deny that the subject of the episode, a woman named Cindy, suffers from a mental illness. Although she begins the episode joking ironically, "I collect a lot of stuff," it quickly becomes apparent that her life has been overtaken and devalued by the things she owns. By the conclusion of the episode the professional cleaning team that works with her hauls away from her four-acre property 50,000 pounds of trash, 20,000 pounds of scrap metal, and several more cars and vehicles. Matt Paxton, the "extreme cleaning expert" featured in the episode, estimates that there remained twice that much stuff left on the property after they left. "I was pretty much smacked by the volume of stuff," Paxton says at one point in the episode. These programs are hard to watch because they feel so intrusive into the intimate details and spaces of people's lives. But I also find the pathologizing around object possession discomfiting: "I don't want you to focus on stuff," a daughter-in-law says to Cindy," I want you to focus on family." That logic of pitting people vs. their things crops up throughout the episode.

Is Cindy a collector or a hoarder? What is the difference between these two labels? Part of the distinction, I would argue, is based on class. Cindy, like many of the people I saw featured in my watching of these shows, was a member of the lower class. Her speech, home, hair, and clothing (just some of the material characteristics we use to mark and recognize social class) were all notably different from the professionals who came on the show to intervene in her life. Cindy lived in a rural area of Mississippi and although she had gained some wealth through marriage that allowed her to accumulate her hoards, the brief biography that opened the show explained that she had little education and that after her husband died she was forced to live a life of apparent destitution. *Hoarders* and shows of its kind fall into the category of "poverty porn," a term used by the sociologist Tracey Jensen to describe television that gives us a voyeur's view into the lives of the impoverished. While I wouldn't deny there are underlying mental and emotional explanations for Cindy's behavior, I also think hoarding could be a diagnosis (like many others) that targets and stigmatizes the poor disproportionately. Do we make the same kinds of judgments of people who collect those things that are judged by society to have monetary or cultural value? Did anyone ever think they had to intervene in Avery Brundage's life as he spent millions of dollars collecting his artifacts?

Nordsletten and Mataix-Cols come to a suggestive conclusion about the overlap between these behaviors. "Extreme collectors," they suggest, "appear closer to the hoarding population than their normative collector counterparts. More research is clearly needed on this topic but it cannot be fully ruled out that some of these 'extreme' collectors may actually meet criteria for either Hoarding Disorder or other mental disorders known to cause hoarding symptoms (e.g. ASD)" (174). These authors lend credence to the argument that what separates hoarding from certain forms of collecting is cultural rather than psychological.

We also see this difference in cultural judgment play out when we look at large museums and institutional collections, where practices of collecting can look more like hoarding on a larger scale. Most museums display only a small portion of their holdings and keep in place stringent policies against deaccessioning, or selling off parts of their collection. The Metropolitan Museum in New York came under scrutiny in 2020 when it announced that it was laying off and otherwise reducing its paid staff by 20%. This action was taken despite its multi-billion dollar endowment and priceless collection of objects. There is a lively debate to be had about the pros and cons of deaccessioning collections, but museums like the Met provide examples of what we might think of as socially sanctioned hoarding. As one artist, David Ayala-Alfonso, has pointedly argued, "In the past four decades it has become increasingly apparent that museums do not only hoard art, but also financial capital, real estate, bodies…" (19). If we reclassify museums as hoards, does that make us think differently about the people we see on television? I would guess not, but perhaps it should. At the very least, it might make us approach the subject with more critical thought and compassion.

5. "Last Seen on 102nd Floor of WTC I": The 9/11 Memorial and the Materials of Memory

Even before you know its subject matter, the photograph is haunting. It is a 5 × 7 glossy print depicting a dense city streetscape. The buildings in the foreground are clearly defined, but as your eye follows the avenues up toward the top of the photo the urban mass blurs into a barely distinguishable haze. The faint outlines of two bodies of water sit at the shoulders of the image. At the center a faintly recognizable spire reaches skyward, but the effect of the low clouds alters it, too, in a fuzzy outline. The mist and muted colors of the photo give it the feel of memory, something real-seeming that falls just beyond complete recollection. I took this photograph in early January 1999, from the 103rd floor of the World Trade Center's North Tower (WTC 1) in lower Manhattan. The presence of the Twin Towers is like a ghost in the photograph: a thing you can't see but you know it is there. Less than three years later a hijacked jet plane crashed into the building, just a few floors below where I took

Fig. 5.2 Photograph of Manhattan, 1999. (Photograph by the author)

this photo. The view I captured that day shows the exact approach the American Airlines Boeing 767 would take as it flew toward the building's north facade on the morning of September 11, 2001 (Fig. 5.2).

The events of that day have defined my generation. Many of us who were alive at the time are only a few degrees of separation from a person whose life was impacted by 9/11, either from the attacks or from the wars and other repercussions that followed. This is especially true in the region where I live in New York, only about 90 miles (150 km) from Manhattan. There are small memorials in almost every community here that commemorate those who died that day. The photograph I own is my small connection to the story of the 9/11 attacks. My cousin Gregg worked in IT for the bond-trading firm Cantor Fitzgerald. Over the Christmas holidays in 1998–1999, my wife and I were visiting him and our family in New Jersey, and he took us up to his office to show us around and share the spectacular views. I snapped this photo that day with a cheap 35 mm camera. Even without the photograph I remember the day well. Standing 100 floors above Manhattan had an unreal, even magical quality to it. The immense windows of the towers amplified that effect—you felt as though you were in the clouds. My cousin survived the 1993 World Trade Center bombing and, fortunately for my family, he had left his firm just months before the attacks in 2001. Cantor Fitzgerald occupied the 101st–105th floors of WTC 1. When the plane hit the building between floors 93–99, it cut off all escape routes for anyone above the impact zone: 658 people from Cantor Fitzgerald died on 9/11, many of them were my cousin's colleagues and friends.

Object collections are also bulwarks of memory; they protect the most valuable and delicate experiences that define our histories. Museums that, for instance, commemorate the Holocaust, the Slave Trade, and War Memorials all stand to preserve the memories of people who were lost in these tragedies. Their collections create a material record that can serve to educate the public and create an archive through which future generations can understand the past. At the same time, these histories are not neutral: it is important to remember when studying such collections that their narratives of the past are shaped by the materials that others use to reconstruct them. The 9/11 Museum and Memorial in New York stands as an apt demonstration of this close interaction between memory and material present. When we put a critical light to the location of the memorials, the objects that constitute the museum's collection, and the construction of the physical space, it highlights the importance of these components in constructing both a record and experience of the past.

Today the site has several memorials to the events of 9/11. The largest features are the two "memory pools" that occupy the sites where the two towers formerly stood. Water cascades along the edges of the pools into deep cavities that fill with water. Surrounding each at waist-level is a dark metallic railing that records the more than 1300 names of each victim of the attacks on the World Trade Center, the Pentagon, and the hijacked United Airlines flight that crashed in rural Pennsylvania after it was re-commandeered by its passengers. When I visited the museum the experience was powerful, even transformative. The memorial site has the feeling of a peaceful park, but when you stand beside the immense crevices where the towers once stood the feeling of absence is overwhelming. The Freedom Tower, completed in 2011 and looming just to the north of the site, amplifies the effect as you sense its monolithic presence in contrast to the voids in the earth marked out by the pools. The sound of the water crashing into the pools was both calming and unsettling—a subtle reminder of the towers' collapse. The most poignant part of the experience, though, came from being at the place itself, "Ground Zero" as it came to be known in the aftermath of the attack. As the site where the Twin Towers and other buildings in the World Trade Center complex collapsed, Ground Zero was recognized immediately by many as a sacred space of memory. It would be the final place of rest for many of those who died in the catastrophes, as the physical remains of more than 1100 people have never been found.

The 9/11 Museum sits below the memorial plaza and therefore evokes the feelings of a tomb or burial chamber, which it is. The remains of an untold number of 9/11 victims sit behind an immense wall bearing an epitaph from Virgil's *Aeneid*: "NO DAY SHALL ERASE YOU FROM THE MEMORY OF TIME." The architectural features of the museum and memorial create an evocative backdrop, but it is the collection of objects that brings life to the memories housed on the site. The 9/11 museum is now home to thousands of artifacts that tell multiple dimensions of the story: the attacks, the victims, those involved in rescue and recovery, and ultimately the rebuilding of the site. Preserving the memory of 9/11 through objects began almost immediately within the New York City community. Jan Seidler Ramirez, the museum's first chief curator, tells a story of receiving a dust-covered mask on the afternoon of 9/11 from a friend who had walked out of lower Manhattan through the vast cloud of debris that formed after the towers' collapse. Knowing she was a museum professional, he gave her the item: "there, you have your first artifact."

This story illuminates collecting as a behavior we engage with intention during times that we know hold significance. It is not only something we do retrospectively, but also in the present as a way of anticipating a future need for remembrance. Perhaps when we fear the inevitability of forgetting we are even more aware of the need to hold on to those things that will attach us to the past. Shortly after 9/11 makeshift memorials and shrines sprang up all around the boroughs of New York City, New Jersey, and Connecticut. For me, some of the most poignant collections of 9/11 remembrance come from these sites. The 9/11 Museum has hundreds of missing person fliers, small posters that family members posted at hospitals and recovery centers around the city in hopes of finding their lost loved ones: "We Need Your Help," "Last seen on 102nd Floor of WTC I (E-Speed/Cantor-Fitzgerald)," "MISSING One World Trade Center," "DESAPARECIDO" (Wall Panel). A digital projector shows a rotating collection of these images on one of the walls as you descend into the exhibition space. Each sign is a material connection to these families, the photographs a reminder of their loss. At support centers like the Pier 94 Office of Emergency Management site, these posters papered walls everywhere. As the days passed and hopes for recovery waned, the walls and posters themselves transformed into memorials. Tributes, prayers, expressions of love and loss filled in the gaps between the images of the missing. An eight-foot section of this wall is now a permanent part of the 9/11 Museum exhibit, a collection within a collection that presents a visceral memory of anguish and loss in those earliest days of the tragedy.

How do we tell stories of the past, particularly those that have as many complexities and twisted paths through them as the 9/11 attacks and their aftermath? What is the history we wish to preserve? Do we include photographs and biographies of the hijackers? Do we document the war in Afghanistan launched in retaliation to the attacks? Do we commemorate the dead and celebrate the community that rallied around the survivors? Like many of the features of our material culture, we may take this memory-creating function of our collections for granted. But objects can also be destroyed: buried, burned, or hidden away by anyone who wishes to conceal memories that are painful or unflattering. How we construct the past is a choice that has consequences for the legacies we wish to preserve.

Procedures and Methods

In the course of this chapter there are several different kinds of collections that suggest a wide range of possibilities for analysis of these object networks. Many collections come seemingly pre-defined: they are a part of an institution with a clear mission or set of principles that establish the logic of their categories. Other collections might require you to engage your own acts of interpretation to define their parameters—is a hoarder's home a collection? In your analysis of a collection begin by establishing these definitions and then proceed through the following suggested steps. It may the case that through the process of analyzing the group of objects you have selected you come to see their identity as a part of a collection more clearly.

1. *Collection History:* Give a description of the history of the collection. What are the notable events in the collection's history? Who or what were its founders? From where did it receive its initial donations and funding, and how does it receive funding today?
2. *Collection Organization and Physical Space:* What are its collection principles? What are the boundaries and guidelines of the collection? Describe its physical environment, building, architecture, layout. How are objects arranged? Give a comprehensive overview of details such as these and how they matter to the characteristics of the collection.
3. *Parts of the Collection:* Choose 2–3 objects that you think best represent the collection. These can either be famous objects for which the collection is known or be more obscure items that nonetheless represent something that you see as the core of the collection. Give a rich and detailed description of the object, including its physical features and history. How did the collection come to hold this object? Who has owned it previously? Also, explain why you think this object fits in this collection, how the object has changed meaning from its origins now that it is a part of the collection, and (if you can) describe how the object is displayed in the current collection.
4. *Experiencing the Collection:* If you are able to visit the collection in person give an account of the experience of encountering it physically. Are there any emotional responses to the pieces that you had (or witnessed others having)? In addition to the visual cues you see around the physical space, pay attention to lighting, smell, temperature, and other experiential dimensions of the collection that create the atmosphere in which the objects are situated.

Resources and Research

Most museums and collections maintain a worldwide presence through webpages, social media accounts, and other forms of digital outreach. These are all invaluable in understanding a collection, as are catalogues for special exhibitions and other literature often published by larger institutions. But the digital world has also created opportunities for studying other lesser-known collections (like the retrocomputing communities discussed in the first model essay of this chapter). Discussion boards, hobbyist websites, and other user-created forums can be an invaluable source of research for collections of these kinds.

Analyzing collections builds on the skills of research and writing developed earlier in this book, but also introduces a new conceptual framework for Object Studies—psychology. The psychology of collecting operates for both collector and viewer. Looking at collections as not merely networks of objects but as curated and shaped by an individual collector opens the interesting but difficult question of intent. Many of the ethical problems that arise from collections (like Avery Brundage's trove of Asian Art) return to the intentions and actions of the collector. Looking at the choices of a collector may also be the key to understanding what the collection may have meant at the point of its assembly. The famous Barnes Foundation in Philadelphia, the product of an idiosyncratic collector, Albert Barnes, preserves the vision he had for modern art in the early twentieth century. But the psychology of collecting need not be an effect of only the collector. How we as viewers interpret and engage with the pieces of a collection can be equally important and interesting. As one scholar has found, a significant portion of the museum-going public desires a "numinous" experience with these objects, a "holistic uniting of intellect and affect" (Latham). Considering how a collection may or may not achieve this kind of transcendent experience in its viewers can also be an important dimension to understanding how we interact with objects in these spaces.

Further Applications

Object Studies, in its orientation toward material specificity and close observer interaction, can be a tool for new methods of decolonized readings. This is the argument the anthropologist Christina Hodge makes in describing a pedagogical framework she has developed called ESP: "Experiential Observation + Synesthetic Analysis + Polysemous Interpretation" (151). This process integrates an interdisciplinary approach to collection interpretation that involves rich descriptions of the material characteristics of artifacts (Experimental Observation), a consideration of "possible affordances, meanings, and significances, as well as the possible intentions of its creators and users in the past and present" (Synesthetic Analysis), and finally a "Polysemous Interpretation" or consideration of how these material qualities might instruct us about the place of the object within its original networks of meaning. Work like Hodge's demonstrates how pedagogical practices might be reimagined with the changing imperatives of collecting practices around the world.

Works Cited

Asian Art Museum [@asianartmuseum]. "Black Lives Matter. A Letter from Museum Director Jay Xu." *Twitter*, 4 June 2020, https://twitter.com/asianartmuseum/status/1268692217528553477/photo/1.

Ayala-Alfonso, David. "Glamorous Hoarding." *Institutional Garbage*, 2018. https://www.academia.edu/37973545/Glamorous_Hoarding.

Belk, Russell W. *Collecting in a Consumer Society*. Routledge, 2013.

Benjamin, Walter. "Unpacking My Library." *Illuminations: Essays and Reflections*, edited by Hannah Arendt, translated by Harry Zohn, Shocken Books, 2007, pp. 59–67.

Works Cited

Giblin, John, et al. "Dismantling the Master's House." *Third Text*, vol. 33, no. 4–5, Sept. 2019, pp. 471–86. *Taylor and Francis+NEJM*, https://doi.org/10.1080/09528822.2019.1653065.

Hazel Plush. "The 'world's Smallest Museum' Opens inside a Yorkshire Phone Box." *The Telegraph*, https://www.telegraph.co.uk/travel/destinations/europe/united-kingdom/england/articles/worlds-smallest-museum-opens-in-rural-phone-box-warley-museum/.

"Hoarders." *Cindy*, 128, A&E, 31 Aug. 2020.

Hodge, Christina J. "Decolonizing Collections-Based Learning: Experiential Observation as an Interdisciplinary Framework for Object Study." *Museum Anthropology*, vol. 41, no. 2, 2018, pp. 142–58. *Wiley Online Library*, https://doi.org/10.1111/muan.12180.

Janes, Robert, and Richard Sandell. *Museum Activism*. Routledge, 2019.

Jensen, Tracey. "Welfare Commonsense, Poverty Porn and Doxosophy." *Sociological Research Online*, vol. 19, no. 3, Sept. 2014, pp. 277–83. *SAGE Journals*, https://doi.org/10.5153/sro.3441.

Key, Kim. "The Impractical but Indisputable Rise of Retrocomputing." *The New York Times*, 8 Jan. 2021, https://www.nytimes.com/2021/01/08/style/retrocomputing.html.

Kinsella, Eileen. "'Shameful and Misguided': Former Met Staff and Others Say the Museum Would Set a Dangerous Precedent by Selling Art to Cover Costs." *Artnet News*, 8 Feb. 2021, https://news.artnet.com/art-world/news-of-potential-met-deaccessions-1942367.

Lintel. Asian Art Museum, San Francisco.

Latham, Kiersten. "Numinous Experiences With Museum Objects." *Visitor Studies*, vol. 16, no. 1, Jan. 2013, pp. 3–20. *Taylor and Francis+NEJM*, https://doi.org/10.1080/10645578.2013.767728.

Litsky, Frank. "AVERY BRUNDAGE OF OLYMPICS DIES." *The New York Times*, 9 May 1975, pp. 1, 40.

Message, Kylie. *Museums and Social Activism: Engaged Protest*. Routledge, 2013.

Meyer, Karl, and Shareen Blair Brysac. *The China Collectors: America's Century-Long Hunt for Asian Art Treasures*. St. Martin's Publishing, 2015.

Wall Panel [IL.2012.18.4]. National September 11th Memorial & Museum Collection, New York, https://collection.911memorial.org/Detail/objects/114296.

Nordsletten, Ashley, and David Mataix-Cols. "Hoarding versus Collecting: Where Does Pathology Diverge from Play?" *Clinical Psychology Review*, vol. 32, no. 3, Apr. 2012, pp. 165–76. *ScienceDirect*, https://doi.org/10.1016/j.cpr.2011.12.003.

Ryzik, Melena. "Menstrual Cups in Museums? It's Time." *The New York Times*, 10 June 2021, https://www.nytimes.com/2021/06/10/arts/design/menstrual-cups-designing-motherhood-mutter-museum.html.

Shaplen, Robert. "Amateur." *The New Yorker*, July 1960, pp. 28–71.

United States of America v. Two One-Thousand-Five-Hundred-Pound, Hand-Carved Lintels Removed from Religious Temples in Thailand. Oct. 27, 2020. US District Court Northern District of California San Francisco Division, https://www.justice.gov/usao-ndca/press-release/file/1366266/download.

Zirin, Dave, and Jules Boykoff. "Racist IOC President Avery Brundage Loses His Place of Honor." *The Nation*, June 2020, https://www.thenation.com/article/society/avery-brundage/.

Chapter 6
The Things We Read

This chapter demonstrates an application of Object Studies to a work of fiction. Students apply the skills of close description they have cultivated through their attention to objects to note examples of material culture in a novel, poem, or other literary text. They then connect their research on the object they choose to a broader theme or idea central to the scholarly discussion of that work.

Overview

In the summer of 2020, a British auction house sold a lock of hair for £320 (Allitt). The purchasers were the John Hampden society, a group dedicated to preserving the somewhat obscure legacy of the seventeenth-century politician and war hero. Tucked into a gilt locket set in a display case against a black velvet background, the brown strands of hair curl into concentric circles. It is believed that the hair clipping may have been Hampden's, although it is more likely that it was taken from an anonymous corpse believed to be his in 1828. That year one of his descendants, Lord Nugent, exhumed a body from an unmarked grave in the Great Hampden church where Hampden was buried following his death in 1643 (Russell). We know now that Nugent was probably wrong in identifying the body, but at least two locks of its hair still survive (including this one) and are now in possession of the John Hampden society. You may be able to see one of them on display at the historical society in Thame, near the site of Hampden's death.

Remembrances of John Hampden can be found all around the UK and the world: statues in St. Stephen's Hall at Westminster Palace and in the Aylesbury town square; a boot spur in Oxford's Ashmolean Museum; a necklace that may have been on his body when he died in the collection of the Bodleian Library; an obelisk in Buckinghamshire marking the field where he received his fatal wound. Even in the

New World there is testimony to his legacy: Hampden-Sydney College in Virginia bears his name, as does Hampden County in Massachusetts. These remnants and monuments of Hampden's life preserve centuries of fascination with his story. Many were erected long after Hampden died and, like the lock of hair that someone was willing to buy for 300 pounds, raise the question of why this person's legacy has been and remains so important.

To answer that question, this chapter turns to another material trace of Hampden's life, an unexpected and little-noted mention of him in Mary Shelley's 1818 novel *Frankenstein*. *Frankenstein* is today the most frequently taught novel in the canon of English literature (according to the Open Syllabus Project) and one of the more widely adapted and recognizable pieces of English literature. With such widely read works, it can be a challenge for students and professors to bring new critical insights to bear in their readings. In this chapter, I demonstrate how an interpretation of a work of fiction can be richly illuminated when we pay attention to details provided by objects and material culture in the narrative. *Frankenstein* offers an intriguing case study not only because of its popularity, but also because it has become for us the definitive novel of *ideas*. Students are encouraged to read for themes of identity, existence, creation, fate, science, and so on. As important and relevant as these ideas are, thematic readings (as literature professors will attest) do not typically produce the most critically thought-provoking work from our students. Object Studies can offer a different, more critically engaging methodology for interpreting works of fiction.

This chapter, for instance, focuses on an intriguing moment in the text in which Victor Frankenstein reports stopping in his travels at the Oxford tomb and battlefield memorial for John Hampden, a republican hero of the English Revolution. In the voluminous scholarship on *Frankenstein,* there has been remarkably little written about the presence and significance of these objects in the text. But the reference to the place and circumstances of Hampden's death raises important questions about Victor's political agenda and his troubled relationship with his creation, the creature. I use the reference to this shrine as a starting place for exploring the political significance of *Frankenstein*, its treatment of liberty, and Mary Shelley's own interest in radical politics. The episode also opens a window to Shelley's writing process and a late addition she made to the manuscript of her novel. This chapter therefore models how close attention to an author's description and placement of an object in a narrative can open insights to the larger ideas we want to bring to our readings and interpretations.

Books themselves are objects, and the stories they contain intersect with materiality in ways that are both complex and compelling: from the technologies of writing used by the author to the modes of production that brought the book to light; from evidence of the material culture that exists within the world of the fiction to the status of the book as a commodity. In this chapter's main essay, I will demonstrate how an attention to these various dimensions of material culture can open avenues of cultural, literary, and historical interpretation. My goal is to model the process of discovery (and excitement) that can come from researching deeper levels of meaning within the novel. Too often in the study of literature we promote readings that retread over well-worn terrain: madness in *Hamlet*, satire in *The Adventures of Huck Finn*, or the dangers of technology in *Frankenstein*. Traditional close reading or language-based analysis of texts, which has an unquestioned place in literary study, tends to advantage those who have a significant base of knowledge and experience with the author or literary period. That form of knowledge places the professor or the expert at the center of inquiry. But the work of material analysis rewards curiosity, observation, and a beginner's mindset that allows overlooked details to come to the surface.

Model Essay

Publication History

Frankenstein; or, the Modern Prometheus was first published in 1818, anonymously, by a small press in London. The edition ran to only 500 copies, and Mary Shelley earned no royalties from the novel's modest sales (Robinson, "*Frankenstein*" 15). The circumstances of *Frankenstein's* publication are well-known to modern scholars because of the survival of advertisements and reviews as well as letters and diaries written by Mary Shelley and her husband, Percy Bysshe Shelley, which document the process through which the book came to be printed. Percy Shelley served as what today would be called a literary agent: he approached publishing houses with the manuscript he said was written by a young friend. The largest publishers in London rejected the manuscript, and so it fell to an "undistinguished" press, Lackington's, that was mainly known for publishing work by "hack writers" according to Charlotte Gordon, a biographer and editor of Mary Shelley's works (*Romantic Outlaws* 244). It wasn't until the significantly revised edition of *Frankenstein* in 1831, published under Shelley's name, that the novel found a wider readership. This later edition, a novel that is "darker and even more dystopian," in Gordon's words, is the version of the story that has most typically been read since the nineteenth century (Gordon, Introduction xix). The 1818 edition remains an important point of comparison for scholars who are interested in the evolution of the novel and Shelley's vision of the story.

Though these facts of publication are well established, there remain many questions and areas of inquiry for scholars who are interested in studying the genesis of *Frankenstein*. First and foremost, what is the relationship between the 1818 edition and later revisions? What can we understand about the story by looking at the changes that Shelley made in her revisions? How have other adaptations of the story (plays, films, comic books) contributed to the story's mass appeal? And what particulars of her material cultural world—what objects, places, and technologies—did Mary Shelley weave into her story? Any of these questions can help us to understand and better interpret the novel and its remarkable history and cultural impact over the past 200 years.

The starting point for this study is a little-known story from the novel's publication that sheds new light on an important political subtext within *Frankenstein*. Within the period just before the book's publication, Mary Shelley made an important addition to her novel. The inspiration seems to have been a road trip to Oxford in October 1817. Shelley briefly recorded this trip with her father William

Godwin in her diary: "On Monday go to Hamden in a gig with Papa—see Hamdens [sic] monument—The gig breaks down—The scenery between Hamden & the Harrow is very beautiful" (181–82). Shelley had been working on *Frankenstein* for over a year, and it was now finally being printed. Along with her husband and other members of her circle, Shelley had begun revising "proofs," the first printed pages of the text that fall. The novel had also just been advertised in a London journal as a forthcoming "work of imagination" that was "in the press," the announcement further promised. But while at Oxford, Shelley's visit to "Hampden's monument," as she calls it in her diary, apparently made her reconsider part of the novel's third volume. After returning home from the trip, Percy contacted the publisher on his wife's behalf and asked if she could revise a section of the novel where her titular character, Dr. Victor Frankenstein, takes a similar voyage to Oxford to visit the tomb of "illustrious Hampden." According to Charles Robinson, a scholar who has carefully reconstructed the details of *Frankenstein's* publication, the evidence for this change comes from a letter that Percy wrote to the Lackington publishers shortly after the trip to Oxford, where he described "considerable alterations" that were being made to the novel: "But the alterations will be found of the last importance to the interest of the tale," Shelley promised (Robinson, *Frankenstein Notebooks* XC). I take it Shelley here means "last" as in "greatest in degree" (OED "Last," adj., def 6.), similar to the sense that his contemporary Walter Scott uses it when he writes of Napoleon: "Territory of the last and most important consequence." Since the printed proofs and manuscript additions no longer exist, we can only speculate about the additions that came in at this late stage. Robinson finds the coincidence of the Oxford trip and the differences between the existing manuscript draft and the printed version of the 1818 text convincing: there is no mention of Oxford in the manuscript, yet it appears in the novel: "the dramatic differences between the Draft and *1818* together with the evidence for [22] October and for 28 October 1817 make this a very likely cause and effect" (*Frankenstein Notebooks* XC). Readers today who are interested in the manuscript can view digital images of it online through the Bodleian Library website; the early chapters of volume three are not included in the draft manuscript (Digital *Frankenstein*).

Why would a visit to a tomb provoke Shelley to take such an extraordinary action and make this late revision to her finished novel? The detail might surprise modern readers, who have come to think of *Frankenstein* as a treatise on the dangers of scientific inquiry, an exploration of the human condition, a story about creation by a remarkable female writer, or a horror story. It is all of these things, of course, a novel that through its many editions and retellings has found one of the largest audiences in the canon of English literature. More rarely, though, do we think about it as a political novel, and a radical one at that. The Oxford section that Shelley revised in October of 1817 suggests that a belief in revolutionary government change may have held special significance for her vision of the story. John Hampden was important in expressing this commitment: "For Mary Shelley, as for her father and husband, Hampden was the supreme English model of political leadership," Fred Randel argues; "he is *Frankenstein's* ideal male revolutionary" (478, 479). Read this way, Mary Shelley's writing of Hampden into her novel was a "political act," according to Randel, an inclusion that readers in her time would have understood immediately. Who was this person whose mere name could conjure such strong historical resonances? And what exactly did Shelley see on her trip?

Hampden's Monument and Nineteenth-Century Political Radicalism

Hampden was a prominent member of Parliament during the early years of the English Revolution, the period from 1642–1649 when members of Parliament challenged the power of King Charles I and eventually overthrew the monarchy. Hampden became famous for resisting a crown policy known as "Ship Money," a strategy that the government used to raise revenue for the navy by placing levies on landowners. These taxes had been justified for many centuries by the premise that the navy provided defense for towns and lands along the coast which, therefore, should pay extra for the protection. But in the 1640s the cash-strapped Charles I attempted to extend the collection of this duty to inland communities (Russell).[1] Hampden, who represented the district in Buckinghamshire that was his family's seat, led the opposition to what he saw as an unfair burden and government overreach. The crown singled out Hampden and brought him to court over this refusal to pay the Ship Money. That trial and the court's subsequent verdict against him turned Hampden into a hero. In legal defeat he found political victory: rather than stamp down the revolt against the king, the decision inspired others to withhold ship money. As a modern biographer notes, "Hampden was campaigning for the principles of rule of law and taxation by consent, not for an arbitrary right to refuse any tax he did not like" (Russell 979).

Hampden was thus at the center of the subsequent conflicts that precipitated the English civil war; the king impeached him along with four of his fellow parliamentarians in 1642 and attempted to arrest them in the House of Commons. The group became known to history as the "Parliamentary Five," celebrated by republicans for their willingness to resist arbitrary authority. The standoff they staged at the House of Commons against the king's forces is one of the most famous moments in parliamentary history. Having drafted a warrant for the arrest of Hampden and other

---

[1] The specifics of this dispute are complicated and not especially relevant to this discussion. Nonetheless it may be important to note that the opposition to Ship Money was more than a resistance to taxes. Even more offensive to Parliament and his subjects, the king hid this tax under the guise of military conscription—instead of calling it a tax for a general naval fund, the crown demanded funds from subjects such as Hampden that it said would pay for a particular ship in a particular place (a galleon in Portsmouth, for instance). In fact, the bills that were issued to landholders went into the king's general naval budget. This kind of misrepresentation was seen as not just bad faith, but an illegal form of hidden taxation. Thus, Ship Money became one of the fundamental causes of the rift between Parliament and the king in the lead-up to civil war.

leaders of Parliament, the king brought his armed forces to the Commons chambers and demanded entry to execute their warrant and arrest the leaders. The members of Parliament barred the doors of the chamber and refused the soldiers and officials access while Hampden escaped with the rest of the wanted men. To this day, each year the opening of Parliament includes a sanitized reenactment of this conflict, with the members of the Commons slamming the door on the royal procession in a symbolic statement of parliamentary independence.

After open war broke out between members of Parliament and the crown in 1642, Hampden became a military leader, as well, and served as a colonel for the parliamentary army. His military activity, however, was much shorter than his political career. In the early summer of 1643, he led forces in a siege on Oxford, where King Charles had moved his court to escape the parliamentary stronghold of London. In a field at Chalgrove, Hampden was wounded in the shoulder by a gunshot. He died six days later, on 24 June, at a home in Thame that had once been a tavern known as the Greyhound. Today, a plaque to commemorate the place of his death marks the spot where that building stood: "With great courage and consummate abilities he began a noble opposition in an arbitrary court in defence of the liberties of his country…Mortally wounded at Chalgrove Field he died in this house a few days later." He was buried in a tomb at Great Hampden church, the place that Mary Shelley would visit with her father over 150 years later. Portraits of Hampden, widely printed in the eighteenth and nineteenth centuries, often depict the scene of his mortal wounding at the battle along with his image. Some also include a scroll marked "Magna Charta," connecting Hampden with another moment of uprising against the monarchy. When Hampden died in 1643, he left money to erect a monument in his name at the church of St. Mary Magdalene in Great Hampden. It wasn't until over 100 years later that a monument to him was finally commissioned by his great grandson, who in 1756 erected the memorial that Shelley and her father saw and that still stands there today.

St. Mary Magdalene's in Great Hampden is a small, picturesque country church that hasn't changed much since the early nineteenth century. It remains an active congregation and still stands as a shrine to the "Patriot" who shares the village's name. There are several memorials to Hampden at the church, including a stained-glass window crafted in the twentieth century that depicts the local hero. The grandest monument sits on a northern wall of the chancery (near the altar) and commemorates several generations of the Hampden family (Fig. 6.1).

It is an imposing marble structure that occupies a large portion of the church wall. The top half of the monument is an oval panel that comprises a relief with a large tree depicting the Hampden family lineage and coats of arms. Beneath the tree in the oval is a depiction, again in sculptural relief, of the battle at Chalgrove (one of the standard visual motifs for Hampden memorials). A wounded Hampden can be seen in the center of the relief, reclined against one of his soldiers who is carrying him away from the battlefield. The bottom half of the monument includes two naked baby boys— *putti*, decorative figures typical of Renaissance and neo-Classical art— set in poses of mourning for the family. One holds a scroll marked "Magna Charta" (another motif of Hampden memorials) and the other a hat that one antiquary

Fig. 6.1 Hampden Family Memorial. (Photograph by Iain McLauchlan)

describes as "the cap of liberty." The inscription on the monument records John Hampden's death in 1643, but also establishes the lineage for his descendent, Robert, who inherited the family estate and commissioned the monument:

ROB.^T HAMPDEN
Dedicates this Monument.
With all due Veneration,
To his *GREAT-GRAND-FATHER's*
& to his *BENEFACTOR'S*
Memory.

The dramatic monument commemorates the moment of Hampden's wounding and martyrdom for the cause of liberty, but also impresses on the viewer a sense of his family's legacy. Its neo-classical styling poses the Hampdens as an august English family with deep roots in the region.

This history gives some context to the unexpected appearance of Hampden in Shelley's novel, but it remains unclear why a relatively distant figure came to be a part of *Frankenstein*. What did Hampden mean to readers in the early nineteenth century? While few advocated for outright civil war during that period, there was a significant movement to reform English government. Mary Shelley, her father William Godwin, her mother Mary Wollstonecraft, and her husband, Percy Bysshe Shelley, were all seriously engaged in these efforts. Percy was sent down from Oxford in 1811 for his espousal of radical beliefs. His political agitations did not end there. In a remarkable letter dated from March 1817, Mary Shelley reported to Percy's friend Leigh Hunt that her husband had a plan to be Hampden's "successor" in refusing to pay taxes that he saw as "illegally imposed" (Bennett 23). "As a prelude to this," she wrote to Hunt, "you must be reminded that Hamden [sic] was of Bucks [Buckinghamshire] and our two worthies [Percy and his friend Thomas Love Peacock] want to be his successors for which reason they intend to refuse to pay the taxes as illegally imposed" (Bennett 23). Although Shelley writes to Hunt with some anxiety—"What effect will this have & ought they to do it is the question? Pray let me know your opinion" (Bennett 23)—the point of the letter suggests that Hampden was not a remote historical figure to Mary and Percy. He was a precedent for real political action, particularly because of the geographic proximity of the Shelleys' home in Marlow: "Our house is very political as well as poetical," Mary writes to Hunt in the same letter, "and I hope you will acquire a fresh spirit for both when you come here" (Bennett 23).

In the Shelleys' home in 1817, both politics and poetry were a continual occupation. At the time that Shelley wrote her letter to Leigh Hunt, she was in the midst of completing *Frankenstein*. Also in early 1817, Percy published an essay in a pamphlet advocating for reform in British Parliament. Signed "the Hermit of Marlow," "A Proposal for Putting Reform to the Vote Throughout the Kingdom" called for a general referendum that would allow the people to vote for government reform (Scrivener 114). By twenty-first century standards many of these reforms seem modest, even incomplete—the freedom for people to gather and assemble, enforcement of habeas corpus laws, scheduled annual meetings of Parliament, and the right for all men to vote—but they were such a challenge to the political order that advocates faced legal consequences for endorsing such changes. John Thelwall, for instance, one of the most vocal proponents of reform and the expansion of individual rights was imprisoned and tried under sedition charges in 1794. Although William Godwin and Thelwall found themselves in different factions of the republican debates, they both admired John Hampden. Thelwall signaled his commitments to radical politics by naming his two sons after Hampden and another hero from an English revolutionary past, Algernon Sidney. By 1817 a series of "Hampden Clubs" sprung up around England, locales where like-minded political allies could meet to debate their ideas and even collect signatures to petition government reforms.

It is in this moment that Shelley took her trip with her father to visit Hampden's tomb. It appears from Godwin's journals recording the trip that they were accompanied by Percy and his friend Peacock (his fellow tax-evader). Mary Shelley doesn't record what her thoughts were on seeing Hampden's monument; I suspect she might have been disappointed. The memorial, while bearing signs that acknowledge Hampden's history, is more subdued as a monument to radical politics. The family tree and coat of arms that dominate it seem to strike a more conservative note, emphasizing as they do the lineage of Hampdens through many generations on the Buckinghamshire soil that gives the family tree its life. Its grandeur tames the political narrative of John Hampden's life, placing it as secondary to the genealogical story. But directly facing this monument, on the south wall, there is another Hampden memorial in the church, and I wonder if it is this one that aligned more closely to Mary's sentiments and interests in Hampden. John Hampden himself had it erected in memory of his wife, Elizabeth, who preceded him in death in 1634. It is a much simpler memorial, a tall framed stone slab engraved with an inscription that reads, in part:

> To the eternal memory
> of the truly
> vertuous and pious
> Elizabeth Hampden wife of John
> Hampden of Great Hampden Esquier,
> …
> …the tender mother
> of an happy offspring in 9
> hopeful children
> In her Pilgrimage
> The stay and Comfort of her neighbours
> The love and glory of a well ordered family
> The delight and happiness of tender Parents
> But a Crowne of blessings to a husband
> …
> John Hampden her sorrowfull
> husband in perpetuall testimony
> of his conjugall love hath
> dedicated this
> monument

While the monument mostly predates Hampden's career as a politician and war hero, it is this Hampden that I find more closely represents Mary Shelley's vision of domestic love, poetry, and national politics: a member of a house that is "very political and very poetical." There are several images of such a fusion of domesticity, art, and politics in the novel: the De Lacey family that the creature spies on in the woods are a group of political outcasts who share time together reading aloud; Victor's plans for his marriage to Elizabeth Lavenza seem to be organized around his hopes for creating a family legacy; even the letters of Robert Walton to his sister, Margaret

Saville, which frame the novel, bear witness to a close bond organized around storytelling (and readers have long noted that Margaret Walton Saville shares Mary Shelley's initials (MWS));

The spaces in which the dead are remembered—churches, public monuments and places of remembrance, cemeteries—can create powerful emotional responses in visitors just by their material presence. Death and the deceased are "spacialized," according to anthropologists Elizabeth Hallam and Jenny Hockney: "...through fleeting or permanent association with the dead, [these sites] can evoke profound emotion by acting as potent reminders of particular persons and the condition of human mortality. Through the embodied experience of such spaces, one out of a range of possible meanings is produced" (83). Mary Shelley herself frequently sought out the "embodied experiences" found at her mother's gravesite. She would often visit her mother's, Mary Wollstonecraft's, grave, and even brought Percy there to profess her love to him in the presence of her mother's remains (Gordon, *Romantic Outlaws* 80). For Shelley, the experience of various grave sites is embodied and therefore does "evoke profound emotion." But author biography is not the only evidence of the affective power of gravesites. In volume three, Victor lets forth an emotive flood when he visits the tomb that holds William, Elizabeth, and his father. In this passage his grief is expressed in remarkably physical terms, as he kneels on the ground and kisses the earth while promising to seek vengeance for their deaths:

> The deep grief which this scene had at first excited quickly gave way to rage and despair. They were dead, and I lived; their murderer also lived, and to destroy him I must drag out my weary existence. I knelt on the grass, and kissed the earth, and with quivering lips exclaimed, "By the sacred earth on which I kneel, by the shades that wander near me, by the deep and eternal grief that I feel, I swear...to pursue the daemon, who caused this misery, until he or I shall perish in mortal conflict. (196)

Victor Frankenstein and Republicanism

What might Mary Shelley's visit to St. Mary Magdalene's church and this understanding of John Hampden's significance to nineteenth-century radicalism reveal about *Frankenstein*? The details of Victor's visit to Oxford—the section she added at the last possible moment to the story—are woven into the third and final volume of her novel, which begins shortly after Frankenstein's creation, the "fiend" as he calls him, has confronted him, demanding explanation for his existence. The creature further insists that Victor create a companion for him, a female counterpart who might ease the pain of his loneliness. Victor finds that the task is not so easy to carry out—he views the thought of a second creature with "repugnance" but also admits that he "could not compose a female without again devoting several months to profound study and laborious disquisition" (145). His solution is a trip from his home in Geneva, Switzerland to England, where he "had heard of some discoveries having been made by an English philosopher" that would aid in the new venture (145).

With his friend, Henry Clerval, Victor travels the length of Britain, from London to Perth, spending several months in study, recreation, and sightseeing. Their journey takes them to Oxford, where they "passed a considerable period." We might expect that the university would be Victor's destination—after all he set out on a mission of scientific research—but the main attraction for him is the city's political history:

> As we entered this city, our minds were filled with the remembrance of the events that had been transacted there more than a century and a half before. It was here that Charles I. had collected his forces. This city had remained faithful to him, after the whole nation had forsaken his cause to join the standard of parliament and liberty. The memory of that unfortunate king, and his companions, the amiable Falkland, the insolent Gower, his queen, and son, gave a peculiar interest to every part of the city, which they might be supposed to have inhabited. The spirit of elder days found a dwelling here, and we delighted to trace its footsteps. (154–55)

In the seventeenth century the court of Charles I moved to Oxford during the revolution, and it is this history that excites Victor and Clerval. They venture outside the walls of Oxford, "endeavouring to identify every spot which might relate to the most animating epoch of English history" (155). Their ventures take them to cites that had become tourist destinations following the revolution—the same stops Mary Shelley would make in 1817: "We visited the tomb of the illustrious Hampden, and the field on which that patriot fell. For a moment my soul was elevated from its debasing and miserable fears, to contemplate the divine ideas of liberty and self-sacrifice, of which these sights were the monuments and the remembrancers" (155).

Although Victor is inspired by these "sights," the burden of his duty to his creation overwhelms him. "For an instant I dared to shake off my chains, and look around me with a free and lofty spirit; but the iron had eaten into my flesh, and I sank again, trembling and hopeless, into my miserable self" (155). The language that Victor employs here—of freedom, liberty, chains, and misery—carries various layers of meaning in this context: it refers to his spiritual state and the psychic burden of meeting his creation. But Victor also casts this struggle in political terms: rather than viewing his actions as self-directed (a consequence of his own dabbling in science) he feels the task as an external burden not unlike that of a tyrannous ruler. Some critics have noted that Shelley, who held abolitionist beliefs, may have been reflecting on the trauma of enslavement in these passages. At the conclusion of the chapter he describes the labor—"a filthy process; the most detestable occupation"—in these terms: "I looked towards the completion with a tremulous and eager hope, which I dared not trust myself to question, but which was intermixed with obscure forebodings of evil, that made my heart sicken in my bosom" (159). The visit to Hampden's tomb, like his extended sojourn in Britain, allows Victor to express this profound ambivalence about his work. Just as it elevates his thoughts, it reminds him of the danger and cloudy moral position in which he finds himself.

Reading through these materials that Mary Shelley added late to the novel, I am struck by the complexity with which she treats Victor's stay in Oxford and his visit to the Hampden memorials. In one way it follows a pattern set forth earlier in the novel, as it presents the Frankenstein family as exemplars of a European republican tradition. The first sentence of Victor's narration establishes him as the descendent of a "distinguished" family of the Geneva "republic." "My ancestors had been for many years councellors and syndics; and my father had filled several public situations with honour and reputation" (23). Victor thus roots himself not just in a city known for its democracy, but identifies his lineage with some of the leaders of the government—the "syndics" he mentions here. His own father was so dedicated to public service, Victor says, that "it was not until the decline of life that he thought of marrying, and bestowing on the state sons who might carry his virtues and his name down to posterity" (23). It is intriguing how Shelley uses the language of inheritance—Victor's father "bestowed" his sons to the "state." He makes the Genevan republic his inheritor and leaves Victor with the legacy of "his virtues." It is not land, title, and property that define Frankenstein (or not just those things) but a dedication to democratic virtues. In Mary Shelley's England, this characterization would have struck readers as a subtle but clear political statement. As Stuart Curran notes, "the fact that the first sentence of the novel as it presents itself ends with so defiant, if understated, an assertion of liberal political values indicates the presence of a submerged political viewpoint that observant readers will be able to detect throughout the novel" ("Republic").

Yet Victor and Clerval's arrival in Oxford strikes a more nostalgic image of the royalist government of Charles I than one might expect, given that political backdrop: "This city had remained faithful to him, after the whole nation had forsaken his cause to join the standard of parliament and liberty." Victor remembers Charles as "that unfortunate king," names his doomed confederates "the amiable Falkland, the insolent Gower, his queen, and son," and concludes with a wistful sentence: "The spirit of elder days found a dwelling here, and we delighted to trace its footsteps." By walking the streets of Oxford, Victor recedes into the past and away from his own troubled mind. Frankenstein finds himself instead enamored of the treasures from Oxford's revolutionary history: "Our little voyages of discovery were often prolonged by the successive objects that presented themselves" (155). The metaphor Shelley uses here to describe Victor and Clerval's travels is telling—they are conquistadores on "voyages of discovery" who accumulate knowledge and sights around the English countryside. These include the tomb of "illustrious" Hampden and the field at Chalgrove where he died. These activities are a release that free Victor only momentarily before he "sank again, trembling and hopeless, into my miserable self" (155). Even with his deep-seated political beliefs, Victor is unable to find escape.

Contrast this account of Victor's experience with history, then, with that of Frankenstein's creature, who earlier in the novel describes how he came to know about European civilization from the *Ruins of Empire*, a book he hears the rustic De Lacey family reading from while he hides out in the forest:

> Through this work I obtained a cursory knowledge of history, and a view of the several empires at present existing in the world; it gave me an insight into the manners, governments, and religions of the different nations of the earth....I heard of the discovery of the American hemisphere, and wept with Safie over the hapless fate of its original inhabitants. (110).

Immediately the creature finds empathy for the vanquished, the original inhabitants of the Americas. Unlike Victor, who unselfconsciously models his sightseeing tour after European explorers, the creature reflects with horror (and "wonder") on the actors in this story:

> These wonderful narrations inspired me with strange feelings. Was man, indeed, at once so powerful, so virtuous, and magnificent, yet so vicious and base? He appeared at one time a mere scion of the evil principle, and another as all that can be conceived of noble and god-like. (110)

The creature expresses disbelief about the ideals of history's supposed great men. They may be capable of high morality, but that capability is also undermined by the evil of their motivations and consequences of their actions. It makes him question the core principles of human civilization: "For a long time. I could not conceive how one man could go forth to murder his fellow, or even why there were laws and governments; but when I heard details of vice and bloodshed, my wonder ceased, and I turned away with disgust and loathing" (110).

In reading the creature's reflections on "how one man could go forth and murder his fellow," I see the specter of revolution and civil war; the French and American Revolutions, as well as the earlier English wars in the seventeenth century, continued to loom large for Shelley and her readers in 1818. These tumultuous events were the dark shadow that always lay behind republican ideals in the period. I also think about Hampden's famous death at the hands of royalists, the event that cemented his fame through the generations. "Hampden" was a name that came to represent uncomplicated patriotism or resistance to authority, in much the same way that Gandhi, George Washington, or Toussaint Louverture might today. In America, several counties, cities, and even a college bear the name Hampden, a reflection of the revolutionary significance of his name in the early republic. Hampden the "patriot" certainly resonated with Mary Shelley's account, but he could also be remade into a particular kind of Romantic patriot: an avatar of good humanity whose sense of familial responsibility also extended to the nation as a whole. Percy Shelley himself later began writing a play about the English Revolution (never finished) featuring Hampden as one of its protagonists.

He may have been the kind of sympathetic revolutionary who could ease the pain of the monster, who finds himself on the outside of the harsh structures of human economy:

> I learned that the possessions most esteemed by your fellow-creatures were, high and unsullied descent united with riches…And what was I? Of my creation and creator I was absolutely ignorant; but I knew that I possessed no money, no friends, no kind of property. I was, besides, endowed with a figure hideously deformed and loathsome; I was not even of the same nature as man. (110–11)

Shelley wrote and inserted the Hampden section after she had composed the creature's ruminations on "vice and bloodshed." Perhaps she did this to soften the feelings that Frankenstein's creation gives voice to here: the "disgust and loathing" in response to human history. Hampden may have been someone who could restore the creature's faith in humanity. But the opposite may also be true: the creature's understanding of the *Ruins of Empires* could be read as a warning to the radical readers that would include Shelley's husband and father. Hampden in that case, especially as seen through the eyes of Victor, is a false idol. On viewing his tomb Frankenstein says that "my soul was elevated from its debasing and miserable fears to contemplate the divine ideas of liberty and self-sacrifice," but that is "for a moment." Even in the patriotic shadow of Hampden, he cannot escape his "miserable self." The monuments of the past do not erase the evil of the present.

There is yet another possibility for understanding this Oxford episode, one that returns us back to St. Mary Magdalene's church and the visit that brought Shelley and her father William Godwin there in 1817. Mary Shelley's biographer Charlotte Gordon has recently argued that *Frankenstein* is a novel dominantly concerned with family connections: Mary dedicated it to her father, perhaps in an attempt to patch up a relationship that had been severed by Mary's scandalous relationship with Percy (who was already married when they met). According to Gordon, the story also expresses yearning for the absence of Mary Wollstonecraft, Mary's mother who died shortly after giving birth to her. "Mary was sure that if Wollstonecraft had lived, she would never have severed their relationship as Godwin had, and as Frankenstein had with his creature" (*Romantic Outlaws* 213). Gordon sees the severed bond between Frankenstein and the creature as an expression, in part, of the estrangement between Godwin and Mary Shelley: "Like Mary, the creature has only a father, and his father fails him, leading the creature to seek murderous revenge. In a world without mothers, she suggests, havoc reigns and evil triumphs" (213).

While I have to admit skepticism about such psychological readings, the shrines to the Hampden family offer support for Gordon's assessment that has not been recognized by other scholars. As discussed above, the monuments to Hampden at the church are really memorials to his family and their lasting legacy in Buckinghamshire. I think Mary would have noted, especially in the presence of her father, the warm and loving memorial John Hampden left for his wife, the mother of his nine children and, as Hampden's plaque for his wife reads: "The love and glory of a well ordered family." Of all the revolutionary heroes Mary Shelley could have chosen (including Hampden's more famous cousin, Oliver Cromwell), it seems appropriate to *Frankenstein* that she turned to a martyr who was also remembered as a family man. The added sections of the novel proceed from Victor's own desire to marry into an "ordered family" with his cousin, Elizabeth. At the beginning of volume three, Frankenstein's father proposes the match, much to Victor's excitement: "My future hopes and prospects are entirely bound up in the expectation of our union," he exclaims to his father (146). But before he would marry, Victor recognizes that he will find security only if he fulfills his promise to the creature by making *him* a companion. He will never feel safe until he knows that he has met the desires of his creation.

The trip that Victor and Clerval make to England is therefore premised upon the establishment of family: both Victor's future with his beloved Elizabeth and the creature's hope for a family outside of human society. This narrative detail might shed further light on the nostalgic tone Victor uses when recalling King Charles I and the revolution. "The memory of that unfortunate king, and his companions, the amiable Falkland, the insolent Gower, his queen, and son, gave a peculiar interest to every part of the city, which they might be supposed to have inhabited" (155). In Victor's eyes Oxford was not just the site of the wartime government, but a domestic space: the home of King Charles, Henrietta Maria, and their son, the heir to the throne (later Charles II). It is unsurprising that the daughter of two of England's most famous political thinkers, the same woman who proclaimed her home with Percy to be "very political as well as poetical," would cast Oxford as a place that also melded these spheres. John Hampden's final resting place in his family church at Great Hampden also bears witness to this connection between the domestic and political. The church and its relics of the past had a powerful effect on the final shape of the novel.

Yet those thoughts and emotions are lost to time. What remains for us is the complicated narrative of the novel and the material traces of Hampden's legacy to read and ponder. The complexity of Hampden's tomb as an artifact and metaphor is another reminder of the brilliance of Shelley's novel. We read *Frankenstein* 200 years later because it doesn't yield easy answers to our inquiries. As radical as Shelley's and her family's politics may have been, she knew that literature doesn't survive if it is simple propaganda or a direct representation of the author's life. I wrote previously about the "profound emotions" that the anthropologists Hallam and Hockey observe come along with the embodied spaces of memory and grief. In looking at the different perspectives on revolution and society expressed by Victor Frankenstein and his creature, I wonder, in conclusion, if Shelley's novel teaches us about the different qualities of experiences elicited by different sorts of objects. The creature tells us that what moves him about *Ruins of Empire* is the reading of it Felix delivers: "I should not have understood the purport of this book, had not Felix, in reading it, given very minute explanations. He had chosen this work, he said, because the declamatory style was framed in imitation of the eastern authors" (110). In looking through Mary Shelley's diaries, one is struck by the amount of reading aloud that took place in her household—the endless evenings that Mary, Percy, and their friends spent reading plays, histories, poetry, news, and other various texts aloud to one another. There is a particular kind of understanding that comes from this sort of encounter with history, she seems to suggest in the voice of Frankenstein's creature, as you hear the words and the explanations that they generate. But standing in front of Hampden's tomb, or on the field where he died, is yet another material experience with its own effects and consequences. It provides less of the cognitive stimulation than the reading, but is more experiential, embodied, and therefore emotional. It is debatable which of these perspectives the novel prioritizes—the intellectual or the affective—but in looking at these differing modes of political and historical discourse it is clear that Mary Shelley understood how objects frame our experience. In a novel structured around various material forms of storytelling—letters, books, oral reports, diaries—Shelley also shows a keen understanding of how objects form their own stories.

Procedures and Methods

Of all the objects considered in this study, books are perhaps the most complex and varied. I say that not merely because they are the things that I as a professor of literature. The objects we call books have a wide-ranging multinational history, a peculiar way that they encode material culture in their creation, and come in various forms (printed text, eBook, Audiobook, etc.). Furthermore, books are by their nature multilayered because unlike most objects they also have a linguistic or representational component to them. Yet those words and images can only exist when housed in some kind of physical object, a medium through which we can read the text. For this reason, Jerome McGann, a prominent scholar of book history, calls books a "double-helix": like a strand of DNA they are encoded with both linguistic signification and physical meaning.

Materialist readings of fiction and poetry begin with a simple yet rich idea: any text we read today was created during a specific historical time and under a particular set of social and historical circumstances. That time could be last year and that culture might be recognizable to us; it could also be that the world of the text is distant to us both in time and in cultural familiarity. "Only as texts are realized materially are they accessible," the book history scholar David Scott Kastan argues, "Only then can they delight and mean. The work of the imagination is unable to constitute itself; it is always dependent upon imperfect physical supports for it to be presented to its readers…" (4). The work of materialist scholarship then is to understand how these "physical supports" emerged in various ways through history and how they influence our reading today. What traces or evidence does the book offer us to the conditions of its creation? Taking on this point of view in approaching books as objects, too, we look to the actors who were involved in their creation including, but also beyond, its author. Was there an editor who was actively involved in the process of preparing the final text? Can we see those changes in a manuscript or copyedited text? How did the publisher, the business owner who decided to produce and sell the book, shape the text as we know it? What marketing strategies did they employ? We might even ask questions about the mechanical operations of the printing house: how were books in a given period made, how much involvement did the author have in that moment of creation, and what effect did that have on the presentation of the text?

Any combination of these approaches can orient us to the story of a book and its relationship with the story *in* the book. As we saw in the narrative of Sojourner Truth, the enslaved woman whose autobiography provided evidence of life in colonial America, a book can provide witness to other dimensions of material culture. In the same way that a film or television show from the 1970s might give us a sense of the fashions and objects that defined that time (telephones with cords!), narratives within books can provide details of particular objects and their place in the world of the story. Since books are media themselves—they are material that represent the world—it is important to recognize how objects within books are mediated through language and the physical representation of the book. Sojourner Truth's story was in fact her first-hand oral account as told by the Boston publisher who produced her autobiography. When we read about the dank conditions of her upbringing, we can see this as a narrative choice, a beginning of a story arcs towards Truth's triumphant escape to freedom. But it is also a piece of historical record and, when taken together with other material evidence from eighteenth-century colonial America, it provides a personal insight to the cruelties of slavery at that time.

When we approach books from the point of view of Object Studies, there are many types of research questions that might motivate our inquiry:

- What were the circumstances of the book's publication, what Robert Darnton has influentially called the "Circuit of Communication": who were the various actors who were responsible for bringing the text from the hand of the author to eyes or ears of readers?
- How does the physical presentation of a text affect the way we read it? How is the experience of reading a play different when it includes stage directions, act and scene divisions, or a list of the cast (the "persons of the play")? Does our reading of a novel on a Kindle or eReader differ from a reading of the same book in print?
- Does the mention of a physical object, place, architectural space, clothing, or other element of material culture within a narrative elucidate something about the culture or society of the book's creation?
- How does a printed book, or electronic text, or even a manuscript fit within a larger history of media—how have narrative forms changed over time (oral, print, digital) and how do those alterations affect storytelling.

In addition to the specifics of textuality suggested by the prompts above, a materialist reading of the kind carried out in this chapter may also proceed from that which is found or referenced *within* the text itself: an object mentioned or suggested in the novel, an item of clothing, a location, or some other physical thing that comes up in the course of the story. The essential critical move with these approaches— whether in interpreting the material history of the text itself or reading into the materiality suggested within the story—is to elucidate the history of the object as related to the author's time. Strive to provide some interpretive insight about the novel as a whole through your reading of the object and its relevance to the story.

Resources and Research

For those new to literary studies, there are several very accessible resources and types of reference work that can be helpful in assisting this kind of research:

Digital Repositories

Many canonical texts and authors have a host of online resources to aid critical work. These can include digitized texts of the author's major works (even multiple editions of those works), commentaries, diaries, and other primary resources for the study of these works. In the case of *Frankenstein* such materials can be found through the *Romantic Circles* project, a wide-ranging digital resource for the study of the period's literature and culture. Newer or lesser-known texts may not have the same digital apparatus available, but it is worth seeking out these kinds of projects as you begin your work.

Textual Companions

One of the main challenges in literary research is getting a handle on the large bodies of scholarship that have been produced about many books, poetry, and plays (particularly well-known works like *Frankenstein*). Textual or authorial "companion" volumes, such as the series produced by Cambridge University Press or the "Sourcebook" texts from Routledge, can give readers useful summaries of the major interpretive and critical discussions that have been taking place in both recent and older scholarship. As you engage your object study with a broader interpretive thesis, these books can offer a good starting place for finding those discourses that have been most important to the text.

Scholarly Editions and Essays

One great entry point for research into a moment in a text is a scholarly edition—a version of the novel, poem, or play that includes notes created by scholarly reader(s) of the text. Some of these (like the Arden Shakespeare Series) can be expansive and include multiple points of view on a given passage. The Broadview edition of *Frankenstein* is especially comprehensive in its annotations of the novel. Others might be more limited but can give you a sense of what other readers have noticed (or have overlooked) within a story. Most scholarly editions will also include a thorough discussion of the publication history of a book, so these can be excellent reference resources for the exploration of your book's textual history.

Once you have oriented yourself to the essentials provided by the above sources, you may need to delve more deeply into the scholarship. In literary studies this means expanding your research through the MLA International Bibliography or other databases to find what scholarship has been produced on your topic. But don't be discouraged if you find that there is little available work on a topic related to your object. It may be that you have discovered a detail about the text that has not been widely studied.

Further Applications

The work carried out in this chapter could be done on a smaller scale to produce a collaborative annotated edition of a novel or poem that focuses upon the material dimensions of the text. Annotation software such as Hypothes.is allows students in a course (or across various courses) to create notes within a text. If the novel that you are working with is in the public domain (as *Frankenstein* is) then this project would be easy to carry out with the use of a freely available full text edition through Project Gutenberg or other sources. This is an especially exciting option if you are working with a text that does not have a scholarly edition already in print or has limited scholarship more broadly. A class might aspire to use its collective research and readerly insight to produce an open-source annotated edition of the text you are studying.

Works Cited

Allitt, Frances. "John Hampden Society Buys Lock of Hair Believed to Belong to the Famous Parliamentarian." *Antiques Trade Gazette*, July 2020, https://www.antiquestradegazette.com/print-edition/2020/july/2451/news/john-hampden-society-buys-lock-of-hair-believed-to-belong-to-the-famous-parliamentarian/.

Curran, Stewart. "Republic." *Romantic Circles*, Oct. 2012, https://romantic-circles.org/editions/frankenstein/V1notes/republic.

Frankenstein: Digital Bodleian. https://iiif.bodleian.ox.ac.uk/iiif/viewer/53fd0f29-d482-46e1-aa9d-37829b49987d#?c=0&m=0&s=0&cv=0&r=0&xywh=-5032%2C-395%2C15141%2C7893.

Gordon, Charlotte. *Romantic Outlaws: The Extraordinary Lives of Mary Wollstonecraft and Mary Shelley*. Random House, 2016.

———. Introduction. *Frankenstein: The 1818 Text*. Penguin, 2018.

Hallam, Elizabeth, and Jenny Hockey. *Death, Memory and Material Culture*. Routledge, 2020.

Kastan, David Scott. *Shakespeare and the Book*. Cambridge UP, 2001.

Open Syllabus. https://opensyllabus.org/.

Randel, Fred. "The Political Geography of Horror in Mary Shelley's *Frankenstein*." *ELH*, vol. 70, no. 2, 2003, pp. 465–91. https://doi.org/10.1353/elh.2003.0021.

Robinson, Charles. *The Frankenstein Notebooks*. Routledge, 2020.

———. "Frankenstein: Its Composition and Publication." *The Cambridge Companion to Frankenstein*, edited by Andrew Smith, Cambridge UP, 2016, pp. 13–25. https://doi.org/10.1017/CBO9781316091203.003.

Russell, Conrad. "John Hampden." *Oxford Dictionary of National Biography*, edited by H. C. G. Matthew and Brian Harrison, vol. 24, Oxford UP, 2004, pp. 979–84.

Scrivener, Michael Henry. *Radical Shelley: The Philosophical Anarchism and Utopian Thought of Percy Bysshe Shelley*. Princeton UP, 2014.

Shelley, Mary. *Frankenstein: The 1818 Text*. Penguin, 2018.

———. *Selected Letters of Mary Wollstonecraft Shelley*. Edited by Betty T. Bennett, Johns Hopkins UP, 1995.

Shelley, Mary Wollstonecraft, and Percy Bysshe Shelley. *The Journals of Mary Shelley, 1814–1844*. Edited by Paula Feldman and Diana Scott-Kelvert, vol. I, Clarendon Press, 1987.

Chapter 7
Consuming Objects

Where do the things we use every day come from? How are they made? What effects do these things have on people and the environment? This chapter asks you to choose an object that you purchased recently and seek out what you can about the materials, labor, transportation, packaging, and other material processes that were involved in its creation.

Overview

Much of this textbook has placed objects in a positive light: as beacons that can lead us to places of new knowledge of ourselves, our families, our communities, our histories, and our lives. There may be some doubts lingering about this methodology for many readers, however, as the phrases "material culture" and "object studies" also suggest concepts that we value negatively: materialism, objectification, and, by association, consumerism. The projects in this book have touched upon these ideas indirectly, but in order to fill out a complete study of objects, we must turn to their central role within the mass consumer culture that connects people and things around the globe today. The mass production and consumption of goods intersect with nearly every dimension of modern life. Turning to this side of Object Studies widens our purview into new disciplinary areas: economics (business, trade, manufacturing), human behavior, ecology, global sustainability, and even government and political life. The relationship between people and objects in the marketplace has also historically been important to many religious laws and tenets.

Objects have been at the center of some of the most important economic thought over the past 200 years—particularly in the Marxist analysis of capitalism. The controversies that have surrounded Karl Marx's work since its writing obscure what is, at its core, a powerful argument about objects in an exchange economy. "To discover the various uses of things," Marx wrote in *Capital*, his *magnum opus*, "is the work of history" (303). In this Marxist view of history, things must be at the heart of how we understand society. The crucial change in society that takes place with the rise of capitalism can therefore be traced in how we view those objects. It was always the case, Marx observes, that our labor combined with Earth's raw materials to create things that are useful to our everyday lives: tables, clothing, hammers, nails, and so on. In the pre-capitalist society Marx imagines, these objects bear the marks and identities of the person who made them. There is a close relationship between person and object. Equally important, these objects are products of an interdependent social circle where people know and hold a relationship to the makers of their things. Abe the carpenter supplies tables for his local economy using a hammer and nails he acquired, perhaps through barter, with Sasha the blacksmith. The wood from the local sawmill is harvested by workers who are also Abe's customers. The table Abe makes is a product of that shared labor in ways that are clear to anyone in their society. If you purchase a table from Abe, you understand its origins and also have social relationships through your own labor with the various people who contributed to its creation. Maybe you are the baker whose bread serves as the staple of the workers' diets, and whose yeast supplies your local brewer.

The capitalist market economy still relies on human labor, but because tables are now produced in massive quantities, the identity of that labor is removed. Marx actually says that the labor is "abstracted" through the process of production, by which he means it becomes a monetized form of value that can now be placed on the object. He is especially interested in the effect this change has on the worker—Marx famously says that we become "alienated" from the work produced by our muscle, bone and sinew through capitalism. Sadly, for Marx, the worker in a table factory does not have the same relationship to the table he produces as Abe, the pre-capitalist carpenter. The table is no longer an object but a "commodity"—once removed from the human labor that created it, it only has value if it can be exchanged for other goods or money. The table as it is viewed in capitalism is not a useful object for dining at or playing games on. It is an assemblage of wood, fasteners, and stain that has a calculable monetary value.

The second important argument Marx presents about objects follows from the first. Once objects are disconnected from people—once the human labor that produced them is forgotten or erased—we start to view objects as having independent qualities previously reserved for humanity: sociability, status, and even the ability to communicate. Marx says that under capitalism our human social relations become expressed *through objects*: "There is a definite social relation between men, that assumes, in their eyes, the fantastic form of a relation between things" (321). This "fantastic form" is wrongheaded, even a corrupt way of viewing the world for Marx. We explored the idea of "commodity fetishism" and its origin in Chapter 4: Marx takes the word "fetish" from his understanding of religious practices from anthropologists of the time (incomplete and biased, as it is): "…to find an analogy, we must have recourse to the mist-enveloped regions of the religious world. In that world the productions of the human brain appear as independent beings endowed with life and entering into relation both with one another and the human race" (321). Animism is the belief that things have souls, even a kind of personhood, and it is to this religious belief that Marx alludes to here. Therefore, if someone becomes confused about the power of a commodity, mistaking it for an idol rather than an item with use, it is because of the capitalist system that creates it. Once removed from their connections to humans, commodities take on a "mystical" quality, Marx says at one point. As such they gain meaning and significance beyond their material usefulness to us.

For all the difficulty presented by reading *Capital,* this single idea is worth dwelling on for its implications for the study of things in our world. Marx has a point that in a capitalist economy, relationships between people are replaced by relationships between objects. I understand who I am by the things I own and therefore my things, according to Marx, become a "social hieroglyphic," a kind of "language" that expresses my identity. We can recognize this effect in clothing, electronics, cars, and various objects of everyday use—our commodities speak for us whether we are aware of it or not. Yet here is where I find a point of disagreement with Marx, who says that the "social" life of a pen or piece of clothing as a commodity exists independent of me as a purchaser of that object. Seen from the systemic view of capitalism, where objects circulate in abstract exchanges in the digital columns of spreadsheets, Marx's argument makes some sense. But at the ground level I am more skeptical. Isn't it possible, I would ask Marx if he were here before me, that I can have a genuine relationship with an object I purchase, and honor the conditions of its creation, even if it is the product of a chain of capitalist manufacture?

The project of this chapter is to test that possibility. Through the work of research and scholarship, can we restore the humanity that is behind the story of our commodities? Is it possible to be more humane and ethical in our consumption of goods? The things we purchase today are a product of multiple sites of labor around the world, and in the nineteenth century when Marx wrote it may have been difficult if not impossible to obtain the stories behind each of these components. We have so much more information available to us today through the internet and social media. Using these tools, we can find out more about the people and places that create the things we use. For this project, then, I chose a seemingly uncomplicated object: a ballpoint pen. I wanted to take seriously my pen's history for what it can teach me about our consumer culture and hoped to gain a better understanding of how the object was made, the materials that went into its creation, and the impact it has on the economy and the environment, as well as my role as a consumer within this system. In the following sections, I look at several pieces in the multi-part chain of production for a Pilot pen: the mining operation that produces the tungsten-carbide rollerball, the product engineers in Japan who created the pen's design, and the operations workers in Jacksonville who assemble and prepare these pens for distribution.

Model Essay

I have a specific material memory of the time I began writing with a rollerball pen. I was in my second year of high school and had just purchased a box of Bic pens that I found when shopping for supplies at a large office supply store. This came at a time when I was becoming more serious about my academic work, and making a conscious choice about the tools I was using to write felt like way of demonstrating that dedication. I had joined the debate team, a group of students known for pen pickiness. They even had a special way of spinning the pen around on their fingers, a fidgety habit that served as a shibboleth within the debating community. My new pens weren't the basic writing utensils issued by my school district to students in English classes, the blue ballpoint pens with flimsy white shafts that were required for theme writing. Rather, this pen had a wider circumference, a gold-colored metal clip, and a grip with a soft, matted feel. Most importantly, instead of the gummy blue line that I was used to a pen producing, it made a slick, perfectly black mark that flowed easily from the tip. The feel of that pen crossing the paper was a revelation: the friction of the point on the surface, the absorption of the black ink into the weave of the paper, the bold impression my words left on the page. Writing with those pens as a teenager wasn't just a way of performing some idea of intellectualism (although I have to admit that it was that, too). The tactile experience of using a rollerball pen created in me, literally, a different feeling about my writing. If I allow myself to be conscious of those sense cues today—the touch of the pen in my hand, the movement of it over the paper, even the sound of the nib scratching the surface—I can still summon that feeling when writing with a rollerball now.

After those black Bic pens, I quickly moved on to a thinner model favored by a friend of mine and many of the debaters in my school circuit: the black Uniball Micro. It had a silver clip with a ridged design on the cap that made it easier to pull off and on. This action also came with a satisfying click. I used this pen almost exclusively for the rest of high school and through college, even though it ruined many pieces of clothing. Rollerball pens are deadly to cotton fabric—if you are unfortunate enough to have one come uncapped in a pocket (or forget to cap it) the tip will dispense the full contents of the thin ink into the fabric without mercy. The effect is even more catastrophic if the pen winds up in the laundry.

While I am no longer as unyielding about my use of rollerball pens, I still prefer to use them for writing. The physical clarity of the pen marks translates, ever so subtly, into a sense of sharpness about what it is that I am writing (we will explore this connection between writing and objects in Chap. 8). At this point, too, I can admit to having a certain level of psychic connection to these pens that goes beyond what they do for my writing. I have a sentimental attachment to them—they remind me of my student days and the importance I put on what I wrote. On the debate team, they connected me to a community formed through a shared material language. I also find writing with them pleasurable. I like the way they look in my hand and the way the writing they produce looks on the page. Writing with a well-chosen pen is an aesthetic experience for me.

I know that I am not alone. The internet and social media platforms are full of blogs, discussion boards, and articles where pen enthusiasts proclaim devotion to their favorite brands and styles: "The 100 Best Pens, As Tested by Strategist Editors *Gels, ballpoints, rollerballs, felt-tips, and fountain pens—we tried them all* (*New York Magazine*);" "The Rollerball Pen Guide (*Gentleman's Gazette*)." The hashtags

#pens and #penaddict have hundreds of thousands of Instagram posts. There's even a *Pen Addict* podcast. *Hackaday*, a website popular among "engineers and engineering enthusiasts" includes an article about ballpoint pen technologies that has generated dozens of comments like this one: "You might like the Pilot Precise V5 Extra Fine Rolling Ball, I switched from the G2 and I'm never going back."

Even in our digital world, pens are a big business. For all its challengers—computers, smartphones, digital pens—the ink pen remains a prevalent technology. Rollerball pens like my Pilot V5 are generally considered part of the "luxury pen" market, a segment that has become especially popular in recent years ("Luxury Pen Market"). It may be the case that people are writing less by hand, but they are more willing to spend money on writing tools that work well or that are more stylish. Thus my connection to the rollerball pen as an object is also that of a consumer—this is a commodity that has been meticulously created and marketed to appeal to my desires as a buyer. In the same way that I enjoy buying a new shirt or a new book, I also like buying pens. And I have to give it to the pen industry for their effectiveness in finding me as a consumer; I am as aware of pen brands and features as I am of clothing, cars, computers, and other items that are more obviously a part of our commercial culture. Before this project, I never thought about a pen in this way. Yet their status as commodity has been sitting in plain sight: I recognize that there are different brands and styles, and I am even vaguely aware of advertisements I have seen over the years for these objects. I know that I pay more for a premium pen than I do for a basic ballpoint, that like other commodities there are various price points for writing instruments.

The pen I have taken to using in recent years is the Pilot Begreen Precise V5 Extra Fine Rolling Ball pen. Even this fairly simple object, upon closer analysis, is astounding in its complexity. My pen is made of hard plastic that is smooth to the touch and has a glossy lacquer-like shine. The cap has a long silver clip on it embossed with the Pilot brand. The end of the cap is slightly beveled, giving the pen a more designed look, and the end of the pen shaft (visible when the pen is capped) is a scalloped clear stopper. Aside from these design flourishes, most of the surface of the pen is black, with the exception of a printed green area that shows the Pilot name and logo and the branding details for this particular pen. It is just less than 5.5″ when capped (13.5 cm) and 6″ when the cap is removed and placed on the back of the pen for writing (a little more than 15 cm). With the cap removed you can see the clear plastic at the tip, ridged to provide a better grip, and the patented pen tip. Pilot uses a distinctive 4 mm needle-like nib for this model of pen, and upon closer inspection I can see several impossibly small divots near the rollerball. Pilot calls this the "Hi Tecpoint" that gives this pen a particularly smooth writing feel.

The many steps in the process of creating and delivering this pen to me involves people from around the world: the miners who unearthed its raw materials, the recycling plant manager who oversaw the production of its plastic, the Japanese inventors who innovated its designs, the warehouse worker who packaged the pens for shipment to my campus. It is the product of multiple technologies that date back centuries and arrives in my hand only after a long chain of production and transportation. Even this small object contains a dizzying array of raw materials (likely beyond what can be enumerated here): plastics (petroleum-based/recycled), metal alloy clip, tungsten-carbide roller, stainless steel nib, ink (carbon black, water, various solvents and chemicals). When I begin to view the multiple layers of history, labor, and knowledge that went into the creation of my pen, I sit in awe, once again, of how much I continue to take for granted about the material world around me.

An American Pen in Japan

In 1945, the Gimbel Brothers department store placed a full-page ad in New York City newspapers advertising a new product for the "atomic era"—a ballpoint pen: "Fantastic...miraculous" the ad declared (Panos). At $12.50 apiece (just under $200 today), the item would have been a luxury for most shoppers at the time. But the pen, made by the Reynolds Company in Chicago, caused a panicked binge of buying like those seen during the holiday shopping season today. "Thousands of people all but trampled one another last week to spend $12.50 each for a...pen," as *Time* magazine reported. The scene is hard for us to imagine today; the ballpoint pen is a ubiquitous part of our daily lives, a technology we take for granted. In fact, we have probably lost sight of it as a technology. Such is the fate of objects whose uses we have assimilated into our daily lives. Yet early advertisements for the Reynolds ballpoint put that technology front and center: "No tricks, no magic—just scientific principle...This pen is the first of those long-predicted inventions of the post-war atomic world planned to make living as smooth as velvet" (Panos). Buyers were promised the ability to write at high altitudes, in exotic locations, and even under water. Unlike traditional fountain pens, which are prone to leaks, need frequent refilling, and require some dexterity to produce a clear line, the ballpoint offered writers flexibility and ease of use.

My Pilot rollerball pen was manufactured in Japan, as indicated by the small mark on both its hard plastic case and the replaceable ink cartridge insert. According to the Pilot website, manufacture of its rollerball components take place at its Isesaki factory outside of Tokyo. How did the pen go from an American export to a Japanese import? The ballpoint pen found its way to Japan during American occupation after World War II. The technology became especially useful for the large military bureaucracy that developed over the course of the global war. It could be used on planes, boats, and in varying temperatures and climates around the world. When American GIs brought their ballpoints with them overseas, the object became both a useful advance over messy fountain pens and a part of the rage for American goods and culture of all kinds in postwar Japan. The Pilot company had begun making both high end and mass-market fountain pens in the 1920s, but adapted to demand for these newer objects in the 1960s. Pilot made its first rollerball pens in 1976 (the technology was developed in Japan in the 1960s by the OHTO company, one of Pilot's competitors).

Rollerball pens differ from traditional ballpoint pens not in their nibs—both use a small metal ball that transfers ink from the pen's cartridge to the writing surface—but in the kinds of ink they use. Rollerballs have a water-based ink that creates its signature flow and dark line that absorbs more readily into the fiber of the paper. Traditional ballpoint pens employ an oil-based ink that is more viscous and therefore produces a line that can be less smooth and, at times, prone to leaving sticky blotches on the paper. This ink also allows for a slimmer ballpoint, the "extra fine" or "micro" sized nibs that rollerballs are known for. Manufacturing these micro-scale components is itself a technological feat: Pilot produces its own tungsten-carbide ball bearings for these pens with a patented manufacturing process. As I learn about the history and production of the rollerball pen, my everyday writing instrument comes into focus for me as a high-tech object for the first time. Even the ink inside of it is the product of trade secrets closely guarded by the company. The pen's name—Pilot Precise V5—sounds more like a sports car or laser-guided missile than a writing instrument. I think it is no coincidence that this pen originated in Japan, the same country that produced cutting edge electronics, video games, automobiles, and revolutionized factory production methods from the decades of the 1970s to 1990s.

The Pilot company has filed thousands of patents related to its products and pens. Browsing through the Google Patents database I see recognizable images of pen component parts (clips, cartridges, nibs, bodies) representing the technologies that underlie the range of products the company produces. The array of patent images presented on screen is dizzying, as is the legal language used in describing the various inventions created for Pilot's pens: "The water-based ballpoint pen comprises an aqueous ink and an ink follower directly filled in the ink container thereof, and is so designed that the ink follower follows the ink with the consumption of ink therein and prevents the ink from leaking out from the back end of the ink container." It probably doesn't help that the text is translated from Japanese. What is addressed in this brief text, though, is a technical problem that had never occurred to me: how does the ink flow continuously through the ballpoint as it is used without leaking out of the back of the cartridge? The answer is presence of a "follower," a thicker substance (typically a resin or oil) positioned behind the water-based ink that stops the ink from leaking out the back. On the Pilot V5 cartridge this substance is yellow and clearly visible at the back of the ink cartridge. I would guess that this small pen has at least a dozen such technological innovations that have led to its creation.

It is easy to think of technology as a disembodied force in our world, but each one of the inventions that led to the creation of my pen came from the mind and labor of many people. In the case of Pilot, there is one name that comes up regularly in the patent database: Masashi Ando. He is responsible, alone or working with other engineers, for over 200 patents filed by the Pilot Corporation. I am unable to find out much about this inventor, beyond the products he has created, but his name is the closest I can come to finding an individual creator for the object. That desire to find an author for this product of manufacturing is admittedly naïve; it ignores the complicated web of labor and development I have been describing in this chapter. Yet similarly we credit Steve Jobs with the creation of the iPhone: a statement that has truth to it but is ultimately a fiction required by the complexities of our capitalist world. Nonetheless, my desire to give a name to the ingenuity of a particular

Japanese inventor works as a remedy to the alienating tendencies Marx described within capitalism. I imagine that Ando and his team take great pride in the various advancements they have made in pen design, even if it is hidden behind the Pilot corporate façade.

The more I understand about the creation of my pen, and the more I appreciate its scientific feats, I also come to see the technology itself as an important part of the object's appeal. I learn that, historically speaking, the success of Pilot (as of many of its competitors) is closely tied to the innovations of Ando and others who develop new products for the company. The Pilot Corporation subsidiary in America was one of the first to recognize how technology can help sell pens. As described by its former President, Ron Shaw, the company began marketing its "Razor Point" pens in the 1970s to engineers, architects, and other professionals who needed instruments that could produce its fine lines (the felt-tip pens are still a part of the Pilot line). It was a niche product meant for a small market. Shaw began small campaigns to widen the visibility of these seemingly technical pens to a more general consumer. On the strength of these efforts, the US sales of Pilot's pens climbed from about $1 M in 1975 to $49 M by 1986 (Shaw 50). It wasn't long after that when I picked up a rollerball pen for the first time, awed by a set of modern design advancements that as a teenager I couldn't possibly perceive or understand.

The active development of new technologies that Pilot pursues at considerable expense gives some insight to the surprising success of pen brands in the twentieth century. Even as computers and smartphones have become omnipresent in our lives, the pen remains as a technology of resilience. In the college classroom I have witnessed various technologies that have vied with pen and paper over the years—laptops, tablets with digital pens, voice recorders—but pen and paper is still the dominant writing technology for note taking. It is also a growth industry: Pilot itself doubled its revenues in the twenty-first century, and by 2020 had a net income of nearly $1B. The success of the pen in recent years may be tied to increased rates of literacy around the world, as well, with a global market growing due to new readers and expanded education. Credit must also be given to special pen designs, inks, nibs, and grips that make these objects so desirable. But perhaps it is the simple yet profound innovation of the pen itself as a writing technology that is its greatest asset. My smartphone is a wonder, but can't perform the same functions as well. And its various distractions prove counterproductive—many times I have picked up my phone to write a note to myself only to see a message, respond to it, and then forget the reason I had the phone in my hand. If I want to write in a book, give a personalized touch to a thank you note, or write out a grocery list, the pen still remains my best option. It has really only been since the invention of the ballpoint pen that this kind of writing was possible. Writers of previous eras were tied to their desks, beholden to ink wells, writing surfaces, blotters, typewriters, and other clunky technologies. I understand why those first purchasers of the Reynold's ballpoint were willing to stand in line for a $200 pen.

The Precise V5 is less than $2 today when purchased in bulk, still rather expensive for a plastic pen. But what are the other costs associated with producing this consumer object? For that part of the story I turn from Japan to China, where perhaps the most important part of the rollerball originates.

Tungsten-Carbide

The tiny ball on the tip of my pen is another of its many innovations. Perfectly spherical, it glides the ink from my pen onto paper flawlessly. It is exceptionally resistant to the nicks and bumps a pen takes with day-to-day use, as well. If I drop it on the floor the impact will not dent the rollerball. The material that gives rollerball pens their strength, distinctive feel, and clear line is tungsten-carbide. As Pilot advertises on their website, "This alloy is one of the secrets of PILOT's quality. It effectively resists deformations caused by shocks or being dropped. The ball retains its round shape and the line remains precise, regular and without blotches or leaks" (Pilot). Tungsten-carbide is one of the hardest materials known, an alloy that can scratch and cut diamond. In addition to pen rollerballs, it is used to make armor piercing bullets (and other military technologies), airplane engine and rocket parts, oil-drilling equipment, and machine tools that manufacture an untold number of modern products. For nearly 100 years it has been the material used to make filaments in lightbulbs (although that use is dying away with the global transition to energy efficient LED bulbs). Like plastic, it is a material technology that has been silently integrated into much of modern life.

Germany innovated the use of tungsten-carbide in weapons manufacture (and other industrial applications) during World War I. The periodic table symbol for tungsten signifies this Germanic origin: W, for *Wolfram,* a word that translates into English as "wolf dirt" (the word "tungsten" comes from a Sweden, another early site of its mining). In the Middle Ages, German miners found the thin, hard strands of the metal mingled with tin ore, an annoyance that reduced their tin production: thus the material was like a wolf that devoured more desirable metals. Only later did German industrialists find ways of using this "wolf dirt" to produce an incredibly strong alloy that they would use, eventually, to make bullets and artillery rounds (Desjardins).

Today, 80% of the world supply of tungsten comes from China, where it is mined primarily from mountains in the southeastern province of Jiangxi ("Tungsten Production"). Mining it requires workers to dig thousands of feet underground to ore deposits. This is incredibly perilous work. In January of 2021, 22 miners were trapped in a gold mine in the northeastern Chinese province of Shandong. Two weeks of intense rescue operations saved 11 of these workers (one of whom died shortly after from a head injury) but the other 10 died deep underground ("Ten China Goldminers"). In 2010, eight tungsten miners died in a deep shaft in Hunan Province from exposure to poisonous gases produced from their operation ("Eight Killed"). Mining is one of the world's most dangerous professions. In 2020, over 500 miners in China died. That represented a decrease from the previous year, too. Government safety interventions have helped to reduce fatalities, but the mining industry in China is largely unregulated. Demand for metals is significant; local operators are motivated by this market to open unlicensed mines with few safeguards for their workers. They sell the metals on a thriving black market. "Men and women, wearing no more than basic face masks, work in areas thick with black particles and acid fumes," describes a Chinese journalist writing about a graphite mine, "It's hell" (Pitron, *Rare Metals*). Yet industrial demand for these metals is so high that mining corporations can pay workers in rural China high wages (upwards of the equivalent of $1400 US per week, in some cases). This leads to a steady supply of workers willing to risk their lives for the well-being of their families.

There are also environmental repercussions of tungsten mining and use in widescale manufacturing. According to the US Environmental Protection Agency, tungsten contamination is common at mining sites, industrial locations where it is produced into its alloy form, and in ammunition storage locations ("Technical Fact Sheet"). In 2006, after elevated levels of tungsten were detected in soil and groundwater sites at a military facility in Massachusetts, the governor suspended the use of tungsten-nylon bullets by its National Guard. Why the concern? There have been limited studies of the human and animal effects of tungsten exposure, but the work that has been done is disconcerting: "Occupational exposure to tungsten is known to affect the eyes, skin, respiratory system and blood. Tungsten may cause irritation to eyes and skin; diffuse interstitial pulmonary fibrosis; loss of appetite; nausea; cough; and changes in the blood" ("Technical Fact Sheet" 3). In testing on rats, the compound has been found to cause death, developmental abnormalities, and fetal death in pregnant animals. In China, the environmental effects of metal mining have been devastating and will probably mark the landscape, pollute waterways, and affect food production for generations.

Tungsten-carbide is likely the smallest ingredient in the making of my pen, and I doubt that the rollerball industry accounts for a significant level of global tungsten consumption. Nonetheless, returning to the site and conditions of this particular raw material's extraction is a humbling exercise. There are still mining operations in America, Canada, the UK, Japan, and other industrialized nations, but these are tiny in comparison to those in China, Africa, Chile, and other parts of the world that are less visible to the daily lives of the developed world. The French journalist Guillaume Pitron has done extensive reporting on the conditions in metal mining in recent years, and reflects on the effects of moving most mining operations to China and elsewhere:

> What the West has done, by moving the sourcing of its rare metals to China, is to relocate its pollution. We have knowingly and patiently created a system that allows us to move our 'filth' as far away as possible, and the Chinese have welcomed the initiative. As a Canadian rare-metals industrialist said with great irony: 'We can thank them for the environmental damage they have endured to produce these metals in our place.' (Pitron, "Toxic Secrets")

I take no joy in the thought of a Chinese landscape laid to waste by mining operations that help to produce the things I buy. And while the mountains of China seem far away from my lived reality, I recognize that an environmental catastrophe in one part of the world has real consequences for everyone in the global community. But I wonder what the result would be of moving production of tungsten to Alaska, for instance, where deposits of the metal lay deep beneath the Brooks Range of mountains. For the time being those pristine peaks are part of the protected Arctic Wildlife Refuge, and so there will be no such operation there for the foreseeable future. Such preservation comes at the cost of ecological destruction elsewhere. Would Americans, Canadians, or Germans be outraged enough to change buying habits if they saw the effects of these mining operations on their own soil?

The thought of returning tungsten mining to America serves as an apt illustration of the complexities of production in our capitalist system. Such changes require government approval and oversight. The United States government, in this example, would need to open the Arctic Wildlife Refuge to mining and other industrial operations. The opening of the Arctic for such ventures has been an extremely controversial topic in America for a generation; any consideration of introducing mining to the region would quickly become political. It seems unlikely that consumer advocates would argue for risking the environmental integrity of that wilderness landscape. There might be some who would be willing to make that exchange so that we could have safer American-governed mining. But lobbyists from the mining and oil industry would likely seize an opportunity to expand their operations into this mineral and petroleum rich landscape. Congressional hearings, public debates, ad campaigns, and demonstrations would follow. Rare metals seem like an obscure topic until you begin to consider their myriad connections our lives and the various interests associated with their production.

These, indeed, are the larger political and economic factors that sit lurking in the background of all our consumer objects. We witnessed the effects of these factors during the global pandemic when "supply chains" became a part of our everyday language as production delays caused extensive shortages in a wide range of consumer goods. As an individual, it makes you feel insignificant to consider these larger forces, especially if you want to make choices that reduce the harmful effects of consumer culture. If we are concerned about the broader consequences our objects have on society and environment, what choices do we have as consumers? Can our purchases make a difference? What if we were to stop consuming? Or, at least, radically reduce our buying and use of mass-produced objects.

Minimalism and Ethical Consumption

A popular self-help movement has grown up around questions like these in the twenty-first century. It seeks to address our relationship to objects and the things we buy by encouraging us to live with less. Marie Kondo's book *The Life-Changing Magic of Tidying Up* (and a popular Netflix series it inspired) is perhaps the best known of this movement, an approach to things that tells us to find (and keep) objects that "spark joy" while getting rid of those things that do not. But there are many lifestyle gurus who preach a gospel of minimalism and simplification based on the message that we should look carefully at why we buy and own the things we have. Joshua Fields Millburn and Ryan Nicodemus, the self-proclaimed "Minimalists," capture the essence of this philosophy: "Minimalism is the thing that gets us past the things" ("About Joshua and Ryan"). Millburn and Nicodemus encourage people to engage in a methodical stripping down of their households and lifestyle to find the essence of what matters most. They tell us in their "Less is Now" challenge to start by discarding or giving away one item on the first day, two items on the second day, three on the third, and so on. After a month see what's left. Post your progress using the hashtag #lessisnow. Their writings, podcasts, and videos have millions of readers and viewers worldwide—a testimony to the interest in this attitude toward the material world.

There is nothing particularly new about the minimalist lifestyle or aesthetic. In Christianity and Buddhism, as well as in many other religious practices, followers are encouraged to give up their worldly goods to pursue a life of the spirit. Many people who live in religious orders—monks, nuns, priests—continue to choose lives of poverty and material simplicity. Literature is rich with writers who extol the virtues of nature, of leaving the trappings of society and civilization for simpler pleasures. The ancient genre of pastoral poetry, with its shepherds, lambs, and sun-ripened fruit, is itself a witness to what may be an innate desire to separate from the material world. Shakespeare's King Lear undergoes a kind of minimalist purging exercise when he gives away his kingdom and his daughters insist that he give up the 100 knights who he retained as his followers. "O, reason not the need," Lear snaps at his daughter Regan when she asks him why he requires the service of these knights, "our basest beggars / are in the poorest thing superfluous: / Allow not nature more than nature needs, /Man's life's as cheap as beast's" (2.2.453–56). Lear's statement stands as a challenge to the minimalist ethos. What separates humans from animals, Lear asks, except the material comforts that bring us beyond those things that we "need." Later in the play he ventures out into the wilderness on a stormy night and strips down to his naked skin, a sign and performance of his madness. The full play may be read as a reflection on how things help maintain our humanity.

The newer minimalism represented in Kondo, the Minimalists, and others is cast more specifically as a response to contemporary consumer culture. The movement arose in the aftermath of a global financial crisis in 2008, spurred by economic necessity as many people re-evaluated their relationships to their houses, possessions, and work. Millburn and Nicodemus talk about leaving their corporate sales jobs and finding, instead, "A life of passion unencumbered by the trappings of the chaotic world..." (*The Minimalists*). Growing concerns about environmental effects of our consumption also inspire new forms of minimalism. The minimalist movement is a fascinating topic on its own for Object Studies—what are the shared viewpoints of this far-ranging set of beliefs and practices? How do they view our relationships to objects? What are the cultural origins of the movement? For the purposes of this project, however, I want to consider the work I have done in describing the origins of one of my consumer objects as a response the ideas of minimalism.

When we view consumer culture from a larger historical point of view, we can see that many of the problems and worries around the making and buying of goods are centuries old. In his magisterial study of global consumer culture, *Empire of Things,* Frank Trentmann traces various forms of consumer culture back as far as the Ming Dynasty in China in the fourteenth century. Moral uncertainty about consumption has almost always been at the center of these cultures—from conservative thinkers in China who feared the advances of technological innovation to Puritans in England during the seventeenth century who resisted new clothing fashions.

Trentmann traces moral concerns about the environment and the waste society to the 1960s, when rising affluence in the postwar world met with manufacturing advances that made products cheaper to buy and throw out than to fix or re-use. Thus, the focus over the past decades has largely been on encouraging consumers to buy less and recycle the materials they use. The minimalist ethos fits well within this messaging.

But do these behaviors actually have an effect on global ecology? Trentmann asks us to consider the "lives" of our objects through a wider scope. "Previously, we have followed goods from the moment they are desired and acquired to the point where they end up in the bin, the garage or a landfill" (664). But the life of a thing both precedes and extends beyond those moments it is with us—Trentmann uses the metaphor of "material flow" to emphasize how objects are in fact part of a wider ecosystem.

> What we take home in our shopping bags carries with it a material past and future. And these are considerable. In a groundbreaking analysis in 1997, the World Resources Institute reckoned that, in rich industrial societies, the typical consumer would have had to carry an additional three hundred shopping bags every week, filled to the brim with all the materials that had been needed to give them the products and lifestyle they were accustomed to. Imagine carrying a large car on your back. (Trentmann 664–65)

Paying narrow attention only to the objects in our lives—asking whether they "spark joy" as Marie Kondo instructs, or "add value" as the Minimalists ask—will never bring us awareness of the larger cycles of production that Trentmann describes here. Indeed, as one critic of contemporary minimalism notes, the lifestyle promoted by this trend shares much with the capitalist spirit it seeks to critique: "Today's minimalism, with its focus on self-improvement, feels oddly dominated by a logic of accumulation. Less is always more" (Tolentino 71). Reducing our possessions is a path to personal enrichment rather than an action for global good. This critique aligns with Trentmann's concerns with the effects of a culture fixated only on reducing waste: "Recycling has been little more than a comforting distraction from the stuff that really matters" (675).

Industrial production (object creation) is a significant source of the emissions that lead to climate change (it accounts for about 20% of global output). There are also human costs: people made to work in unsafe factories and mines. But here is a rare example of how objects loom too large in our understanding of the world. If we only look at the things we have in our homes, if we only reduce the things we buy, we ignore the more significant effects of travelling, heating and air conditioning our homes, and growing the food we eat. Those three activities account for about 50% of energy consumption and output in the United States (the percentages are similar around the developed world). To reduce the harms caused by consumer culture we also need to address issues at a larger, societal scale.

Would a culture of stark frugality be the answer for those global problems? I have to admit that I am skeptical (as is likely already clear) that purging our homes of objects to create a minimalist living environment will have a great impact. Picking up an ordinary pair of scissors and asking whether it "sparks joy" in my heart might lead me to get rid of a perfectly useful object. What happens, then, when I need to cut open a package or wrap a present? Should I buy a joyful pair of scissors? In contrast, after investigating the history of my Pilot pen, I feel that I have a better understanding of both the good and the bad associated with my purchase of this item. I think about the jobs in Jacksonville, FL that are tied to distributing this pen to writers around the United States. I reflect on the many hours the inventors in Japan spent on developing the ink technologies and writing nib that make my pen work. And yes, I have to think about the plastic (90% of which is recycled) and metal that are the products of shady drilling and mining practices around the world. To me, being a knowledgeable consumer is also being an ethical consumer. Like Lear, I don't believe that we can simply strip ourselves down to the things that we "need." We will always desire to consume as our financial means allow us. But if we are more focused and discerning about the histories of the individual things we own or purchase, we might begin to make better choices. And on this the minimalists and skeptics I have cited here all agree: "There has to be a more general appreciation of the pleasures from a deeper and longer-lasting connection to fewer things" (Trentmann 689).

Procedures and Methods

As detailed in this chapter, the object you choose should be something you purchased recently or that was purchased for you. You can think expansively about this prompt: your "object" might be food that you purchased at the store or in a restaurant, an item of clothing that you own, a watch, computer, phone, or other electronic, or any other consumer good that interests you. Your goal is to find out as much as you can about the many steps that brought the object to you as a buyer. In your research, carefully break down your object into all of its component parts (at least as a thought experiment, not necessarily physically!): with clothing, for instance, you might think about its fabric, dyes, design, and so on. Make sure that you also account for packaging, transportation, labor, and all dimensions of the object's creation and conveyance to you for purchase. Where are the places your object was made? How far did it travel to get to you?

As an experiential exercise to help you select one of your consumer objects, you can take on one of the projects advocated by minimalists in this chapter. For instance, you might choose a category of objects in your household or personal living space and sort through them using the "joy test" described by Kondo: clothing or books are probably the best choices, but you can select category you'd like (just be sure you have enough of those items to make this a successful experiment). Take photographs before, during, and after to document the process. You do not actually have to give away or discard the things that you decide do not give you joy, as Kondo instructs, but at least take those items and set them aside or place them in another room so that you can better reflect on the experience. Were any of the objects that remained things that you purchased recently? What feelings or memories are associated with that object for you? Such reflections can be a good way to begin analyzing the connections that you hold to items produced within our consumer culture.

Because it combines the study of geography, materials, and human labor, this is a project that also lends itself well to alternative modes of presentation and storytelling. One of the sources of inspiration for this project was a series reported by National Public Radio's "Planet Money" program. Over the course of several weeks, the reporters traced the origins of a t-shirt from cottonseed to its delivery in the United States. The accompanying series of video essays is archived online and offers a good example of how consumer object stories can be told through various forms of media (Planet Money). Even an "Infographic" or other visual form can translates the story of a manufactured object into a visual representation replete with data and evocative imagery of the places that produced it. Consider this graphic I produced in collaboration with one of my students based on the research presented in this chapter (Fig. 7.1):

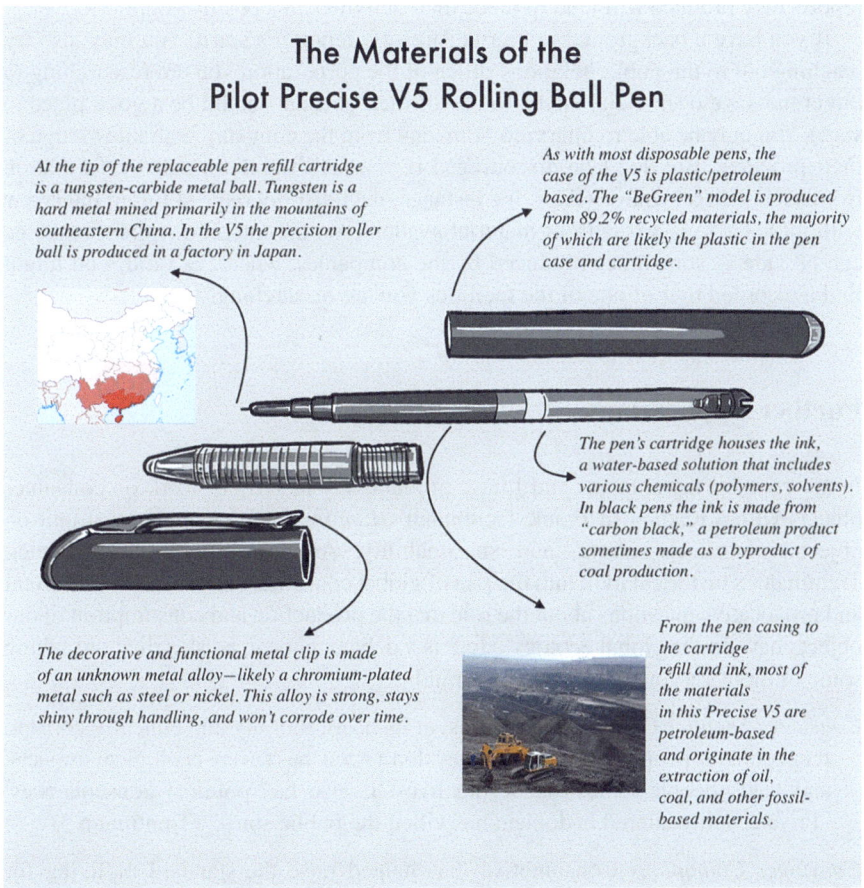

Fig. 7.1 Infographic depicting the material make-up of a Pilot pen. (Illustrations by Kimberly Blum)

Resources and Research

If your major or field of training is in the humanities or social sciences, then you may not have experience working in and interpreting research materials from businesses and corporations. Once you have narrowed your topic to a particular product or company, schedule an appointment with a research librarian who specializes in this research. They will be able to help you find sources such as corporate data and financial reports, trade magazines, press releases, executive profiles, industry surveys, and other media related to the corporation or products you are researching.

The corporations themselves can also be a good source of information, as they will typically produce reports, histories, and product profiles for investors. You should also follow the company you are researching on various social media platforms to see how they advertise their products and whether they tell the story of their supply chains. It bears saying that some of this material should be read with a critical eye—companies are in the business of making money, of course, and so the reports they produce will tend to place their activities in a positive light.

If you have a background in journalism (or a reporter's spirit) you may also try reaching out to the public relations office of the corporation you are researching (a direct message over social media to one of their accounts could be a good place to start). You may be able to interview someone from the company with knowledge of their products. But don't be discouraged if you aren't able to gather information from such a direct source (Pilot, for instance, declined my request for an interview with me). There is a wealth of material available on the internet. A great resource can be videos, sometimes produced by the companies, where, as I did, you might find a recorded tour of one of the facilities you are researching.

Further Applications

In my courses, my students and I have productively paired our work on consumer objects with a reading of Frank Trentmann's *Empire of Things* to form a unit on objects, consumer culture, and sustainability. As described in this chapter, Trentmann's historical look into the rise of global consumer culture raises important and provocative questions about the role that the production and consumption of our objects have in the global ecology. Here is a debate that can be sketched out taking some of these varying perspectives in mind:

Consumer Skeptics Consumer culture is, at its heart, morally and ethically corrupt. It encourages people to buy things they don't need, has severe ecological impacts, and leads people to less-satisfying lives. It also has political consequences: "Private, self-centered hedonism has killed the public spirit" (Trentmann 5).

Consumer Champions Consumerism has helped raise the standard of living for much of the world and gives us access to entertainment, material comfort, and basic human enjoyment at levels unprecedented in history. As the "bedrock of democracy and prosperity" it encourages choice, supports a free society, and is the source of employment for many in the world.

Where do you stand? Do you see any middle ground in this debate, a third position that might be a starting place for consensus?

Research into the environmental impacts of our consumer culture can also form the basis of a community action day, as it does in our seminar. We take part of a class period to brainstorm ideas about how our campus community might use it material resources more efficiently. These can be shared with campus administration or local governments in the form of a letter or small-scale social media campaign. For instance, here are some of the ideas generated in a recent semester:

- **Reusable Plates and Silverware.** Student clubs should pool together funds to purchase a reserve of reusable plates, silverware, cups that they can use instead of disposable products. One of our students looked into this, and the dining hall staff expressed enthusiasm for the initiative and would agree to wash them for the groups.
- **Reduce the number of single rooms in campus housing**. Trentmann writes about the rise of single-dwellings in the world and the impact this has on consumption. If possible, it would make sense for our campus to eliminate any double dormitory rooms that are currently serving as singles. Doing so encourages the sharing of refrigerators and other objects and therefore reduces the number of items students bring to campus. Would it be possible, too, we wondered, to limit the number of certain items that students can bring to a campus suite (refrigerators, microwaves, lamps, and other energy-intensive items, especially).
- **Computer Repair and Reuse.** One of our students in the School of Science and Engineering encouraged that we do more to repair computers and upgrade components rather than entire units. The campus may already do this, but he suggested that we could also sell computers to students at reduced cost rather than dispose of them.

Works Cited

"100 Best Pens: Gel, Ballpoint, Rollerball, and More, 2021." *New York Magazine*, https://nymag.com/strategist/article/best-pens-gel-ballpoint-rollerball-felt-fountain.html.

"About Joshua and Ryan." *The Minimalists*, https://www.theminimalists.com/about/.

"Tech Hidden In Plain Sight: The Ballpoint Pen." *Hackaday*, 17 Dec. 2020, https://hackaday.com/2020/12/17/tech-hidden-in-plain-sight-the-ballpoint-pen/.

PILOT Corporation. *About Us*. https://www.pilot.co.jp/company/english/corporate/history/. Accessed 31 Aug. 2021.

Desjardins, Jeff. "The History of Tungsten, the Strongest Natural Metal on Earth." *Visual Capitalist*, 1 May 2017, https://www.visualcapitalist.com/history-of-tungsten-worlds-strongest-metal/.

"Eight Killed in China Tungsten Mine, Output Unaffected." *Reuters*, 12 Mar. 2010, https://www.reuters.com/article/china-tungsten-idAFTOE62B06X20100312.

Kondō, Marie. *The Life-Changing Magic of Tidying up: The Japanese Art of Decluttering and Organizing*. Translated by Cathy Hirano, Ten Speed Press, 2014.

"Luxury Pen Market | Luxury Fountain Pen Manufacturers to Greatly Benefit During 2020–2024." *Business Wire*, 28 Oct. 2020, https://www.businesswire.com/news/home/20201028005802/en/Luxury-Pen-Market-Luxury-Fountain-Pen-Manufacturers-to-Greatly-Benefit-During-2020-2024-Technavio.

Marx, Karl, and Friedrich Engels. *The Marx-Engels Reader*. Edited by Robert C. Tucker, 2d ed., Norton, 1978.

The Minimalists: Less Is Now. Directed by Matt D'Avella, Netflix, 2021.

Monet, Pierre. "The World Is Running Low On Tungsten; Why You Should Care." *Forbes*, 14 Mar. 2012, https://www.forbes.com/sites/ciocentral/2012/03/14/the-world-is-running-low-on-tungsten-why-you-should-care/.

Panos, Kristina. "Tech Hidden in Plain Sight: The Ballpoint Pen." *Hackaday*, 20 Dec. 2020, https://hackaday.com/2020/12/17/tech-hidden-in-plain-sight-the-ballpoint-pen/.

Pitron, Guillaume. *The Rare Metals War: The Dark Side of Clean Energy and Digital Technologies*. Scribe Publications, 2020.

———. "Toxic Secrets behind Your Mobile Phone." *Daily Mail Online*, 23 Jan. 2021, https://www.dailymail.co.uk/news/article-9179751/Toxic-secrets-mobile-phone-called-green-world-depends-mining-metals.html.

Planet Money. "The Planet Money T-shirt." *NPR.org*. *https://www.npr.org/series/262481306/planet-money-t-shirt-project-series*

Shakespeare, William. *King Lear*. Edited by R. A. Foakes, The Arden Shakespeare, Third Series, Thomson, 1997.

Shapira, J. A. "The Rollerball Pen Guide." *Gentleman's Gazette*, 24 Mar. 2015, https://www.gentlemansgazette.com/the-rollerball-pen-guide/.

Shaw, Ron. "A Tale of Brashness and Japanese Boards: How a 'freewheeling Maverick' Became the Rare American to Be Elected to the Board of a Publicly Held Japanese Company." *Directors & Boards*, vol. 26, no. 3, Mar. 2002, pp. 49–50.

Takasu, Yoichi. *Water-Based Ballpoint Pen*. EP1886836B1, 18 Mar. 2009, https://patents.google.com/patent/EP1886836B1/en?inventor=Masashi+Ando&assignee=Pilot+Ink+Co+Ltd&page=2.

Technical Fact Sheet–Tungsten. Fact Sheet, EPA 505-F-14-004, Environmental Protection Agency, Jan. 2014.

"Ten China Gold Miners Confirmed Dead after Others Rescued; One Still Missing." *Reuters*, 25 Jan. 2021, https://www.reuters.com/article/us-china-accident-mine-idUSKBN29U0KC.

Tolentino, Jia. "The Pitfalls and the Potential of the New Minimalism." *The New Yorker*, Jan. 27, 2020, https://www.newyorker.com/magazine/2020/02/03/the-pitfalls-and-the-potential-of-the-new-minimalism.

Trentmann, Frank. *Empire of Things: How We Became a World of Consumers, from the Fifteenth Century to the Twenty-First*. HarperCollins, 2016.

"Tungsten Production Worldwide by Country 2020." *Statista*, https://www.statista.com/statistics/1009356/tungsten-production-worldwide-by-country/.

Chapter 8
Thinking with Things

How do objects help us think? Are they just props or tools that we use to express our ideas, or do they actually shape our thought and creative expression? To explore these questions, you will perform an experiment with an analog technology of your choice as a means of reflecting on the integral part played by physical objects in generating and producing ideas, art, and other creations of the human mind.

Overview

Introduction

So far in this book, we have considered objects from various cultural points of view: as things that humans create and collect to represent themselves and nature, share stories, dwell in and among, or trade and consume. Object Studies, from these perspectives, is an interpretive process that uses the material world as a new way of understanding human culture. As we begin to recognize this material world, we see that objects are deeply woven into our human environment—as that fabric metaphor suggests, human culture is tightly interlaced with material creations of various kinds. Material culture, once we start paying attention to it, becomes a necessary part of our "culture" in general.

But what if we shift the focus of Object Studies from the *products* of human creation to the *processes* that we use to generate ideas, works of art, and other objects? Can things also help us understand how the mind works? In this chapter, we will look into some different areas of study—psychology, neuroscience, and philosophy—that hold new possibilities for understanding the role of objects in our lives. One of the most important developments in Object Studies in the twenty-first century has focused on the human brain and how it interacts with objects. In this view, human thinking (or "cognition," as philosophers like to call it) is more than what happens between our ears—it extends out into the world through our senses, our interactions with other people, and even, of course, into our use of objects. This is a radical position. It requires us to give up at least a little of our sense of biological superiority in the world—our "brainbound" perspective, as the philosopher Andy Clark puts it. While we may feel comfortable assigning importance to objects like books, coffee cups, and architecture in historical or literary interpretation, we might find it harder to accept that objects play an essential role in how we think and create. The goal of this chapter is to engage with this very possibility, but to do so by a process of self-experimentation designed to give insight into the larger philosophical and scientific ideas that illuminate this work. To illustrate this approach, I think it is helpful to begin with an example by way of an experiment.

Like many people I enjoy playing Scrabble, the game that is based on building words using letters printed on small tiles. The purpose of the game is to score points by rearranging sets of seven randomly-selected letters into real words. In a recent game I played with my daughter (we have a long-standing Scrabble rivalry), I had this actual tray of letters:

DDWELBO

Using those letters, take a few minutes to carry out these experiments:

Experiment #1: Looking at the letters above, give yourself 30 seconds and think of as many words as you can make from them. *Just think of them, don't use a pen and paper or any other method to write them out.* Keep count of how many words you come up with.

Experiment #2: This time use a pen and paper to write out as many words as you can. Make note of how many more or less you generated compared to the first experiment. Again, you have 30 seconds.

Experiment #3: For this final experiment, write the individual letters down on squares or scraps of paper and try rearranging them using your hands. If you happen to have a physical Scrabble set handy you can use these letters and tiles. Again, give yourself thirty seconds and see how many more words you can build.

In which of the above experiments did you produce the most words? Which produced the longest or most complicated words? Which of these experiences, would you say, made it easiest for you to generate words? The work of neuroscientists and psychologists would predict that either scenario #2 or #3 would be the most productive in terms of generating more and more complicated words (Maglio, et al.). You probably also found that these experiences required less mental effort—the act of writing down words physically with a pen and paper helps us to remember the words we have already created and frees us to generate others. Manipulating tiles of letters creates a dynamic interaction between physical touch and thought and helps to generate the creative variations that our brains are uniquely capable of producing.

In my own experience with these three Scrabble experiments, I found that writing words down was the quickest way to generate a long list of options (Experiment #2). Working just with the original DDWELBO I was able to generate seven words in sixty seconds. These were mostly short words (BOW, LOB, BOL, WED). I have been writing with a pen and paper for most of my life, so it is not surprising to me that I have a quick facility with this mode of brainstorming. In experiment number three I used the same letters (on a real Scrabble tray with letters) but was still able to produce four words that I didn't come up with previously: LODE, LEWD, BODE, and BED. That process was more time consuming for me—it took me longer to move the letters around than it did to write them out (or even to visualize different arrangements in experiment one). Yet I find it interesting that three of these words are more unusual than those that I came up with in the two previous experiments. As I was shuffling letters around on the tray, I had the experience of these words coming to life in front of me, almost by a kind of mental magic. The first experiment was the most painstaking and least productive for me. I immediately recognized "ELBOW," but was able to generate only a few more short words in the given time.

"Distributed Cognition," the "Extended Mind" and a Philosophy of Things

This casual experiment raises one of the key questions of this chapter: what part do objects play in our thinking? An even more radical question: who, or what, was doing the thinking in experiments number two and three? We would all quickly agree that in experiment number one the mental processing was almost fully internal. True, I was looking at a series of tiles on a Scrabble tray (or letters on a page, in your case), and the use of sight is not trivial to our thinking. But the processes of thinking that went into generating the ideas in my head were otherwise completely internal to me. This mental/physical separation is less clear in experiments two and three. We are so accustomed to writing (or typing) that we may no longer think of it as something that is external to ourselves, but if you found experiment number two easier than number one, then you experienced that the act of writing with tools changes the nature of your thinking. This is perhaps most clear in the final experiment: interacting with Scrabble tiles (or slips of paper) is a physical exercise of manipulation, and yet it also helped me to generate new words that I didn't "think" of otherwise.

The idea that my thinking extends beyond my brain and into the objects and activities in my environment is called "distributed cognition." Since the late twentieth century, this concept has become an important field of research for not just psychologists and neuroscientists, but for philosophers as well. What is the nature of the mind? Does it operate merely as a biological or spiritual entity, as has long been the debate in philosophy, or should we understand it as an active agent and product of a wider environment, including objects. These are indeed questions of a philosophical nature, a point that becomes clear when we begin to think more carefully about some examples. If I ask you, "Do you know the time?" you will probably say "yes," by which you likely mean you have your cell phone and by looking at its automatically updated clock, you can report the time to me. Do you, therefore, know what time it is, or do you know that you have a prop which allows you to access the time? Is it your phone actually "knowing" with you, in other words, now part of a system combining technology and biology? "If this way of looking at things still strikes you as outlandish," writes Andy Clark, the preeminent philosopher of distributed cognition, "you are in good company" (*Natural Born Cyborgs* 42). It is counterintuitive for us to incorporate things like phones (or pens, typewriters, notebooks) as a natural part of our thinking apparatus. We usually think of these as unintegrated tools, things that we use but that aren't necessary to our thinking. Responding to this notion, and reflecting further on the watch-as-knowledge idea, Clark elaborates:

> Most people find such a diagnosis strange, unnecessary and (thus) unconvincing. But this reaction is unprincipled. It rests not upon any deep fact about the nature of knowledge or the preset bounds of persons but on a simple prejudice: the contemporary version, as it happens, of the old and discredited idea of the mind as a special kind of spirit-stuff. (*Natural Born Cyborgs* 43)

We should not, Clark contends, "locate the individual *thinking system* by reference to the merely *metabolic* frontiers of skin and skull" (*Natural Born Cyborgs* 43, author's emphasis). Our thinking, according to this argument, is *in things*, too. Clark and his collaborator, David Chalmers, coined the term "extended mind" to describe this concept of our cognition being a part of a widely distributed system of objects, people, and environment.

To illustrate these ideas further, consider some real-world examples of distributed cognition:

- A bartender takes an order for four drinks from her customers: a martini, a bourbon on the rocks, a pina colada, and a beer. Instead of writing down the order, to save time she lines up the four unique glasses associated with each of the drinks on her bar rail and uses these physical cues to remind her of each drink order. (Beach)
- You have a package to pick up from the mail room on campus or at the post office. It's a busy week and you worry about forgetting it, so you put a reminder in your phone that alerts you before class on Thursday to get it.
- As the first step in putting together a 1000-piece jigsaw puzzle, an expert solver divides the pieces into piles based on color and shape: edge pieces, dark pieces, red pieces, etc.

Psychologists use the metaphor of "scaffolding" to describe how people manipulate objects like those offered in these examples to promote and enhance thinking or problem solving (Berk and Winsler). In each of these examples, a person modifies an outside environmental condition as a means of carrying out a cognitive task. Notably each of these are complex problems that may be more difficult because of other environmental factors. The bartender might be able to remember four orders on a slow shift, but what about on a Saturday night when people are three deep at the bar waiting to get a drink? Under normal circumstances, remembering to pick up a package is a simple task, but what about during an exam period, or in an especially busy week at school, those times when we experience "cognitive overload"? We have all had the experience of small details like that slipping away in the whirlwind of other obligations and deadlines. Thus, an important principle in these examples is that of efficiency—our brains tend to favor solutions to problems that cost less time, less energy, and produce more accurate results. Objects, in these contexts, can be understood as tools and collaborators to our thoughts.

In a foundational essay on distributed cognition, "The Intelligent Use of Space," David Kirsh explores many of these strategies and explains how they work to increase the effectiveness of our daily activities: "To make it easier to stay in control of activity, we rely on techniques which reduce the memory load of tasks, the amount of internal computation necessary, or which simplify the visual search and categorization that is inevitably involved in performance" (65). Simplifying tasks in this way typically leads to more desirable outcomes: a bartender will take in more tips if she can make drinks quickly and accurately, so her training and practice involves doing these tasks with increasing efficiency. And the better she gets at doing this work "without thinking," as we sometimes say, the more time she will have to make conversation, check in with regular customers, and do other tasks (cleaning, organizing, inventory) that keep her bar running smoothly.

This research has important implications for how we understand the interactions between brain and object. Are we, as Descartes had it, thinking beings contained by our bodily boundary of skin and bones, or do our cognitive abilities need to be understood in terms of these environmental conditions, as well? Consider another thought experiment that Andy Clark uses to illustrate the concept of the extended mind. Otto enjoys going to the Museum of Modern Art (MoMA) in New York City and visits there regularly. He is afflicted, however, with a brain condition that makes it impossible for him to remember the location of the museum. He therefore carries a notebook in his pocket that lists the address of MoMA, on 53rd St. in Manhattan. How is Otto different from a neurotypical person who enjoys going to the museum but has memorized its address? His "memory" in this case is extended, it is an appendage to his body rather than within the body. But doesn't it *function* in the same way as my memory? And if so, then doesn't that change the way that we understand memory, belief, and knowledge? As Clark and David Chalmers say in their essay, "The Extended Mind," "The information in Otto's notebook...is a central part of his identity as a cognitive agent. What this comes to is that Otto *himself* is best regarded as an extended system, a coupling of biological organism and external resources" (232). In the example, Otto's "external resources," his notebook in particular, come to be understood as a part of his cognitive system—not the same as his brain, exactly, but a nonetheless integral element that interacts with his thinking.

These examples of the extended mind, while significant, also do not capture what we might imagine to be higher levels of expression and cognitive activity. Playing Scrabble is an activity that requires thinking, of course, but some people might see it as a more trivial example than writing an essay, creating a piece of art, or even communicating with a friend or family member. What about the tools we use to shape and influence one of my most important daily tasks—writing?

Model Essay: Being Analog in a Digital World

Introduction

To test the ideas of Clark and other theorists of the "extended mind" hypothesis, in this chapter we will carry out our own experiments in thinking with things. These experiments will be conducted on yourself, as you examine the experience of working with an unfamiliar tool that heightens your awareness of how you think or experience using the products of your environment. I call this an "analog experience" to highlight a key binary that has developed within our material world—the difference between things that incorporate digital technology (smartphones, personal computers, tablets, etc.) and those that do not. We don't typically think of these devices as objects, but as portals through which we experience millions of bytes of data—in the form of music, images, text, and video—as they "stream" into our eyes and ears. Both my iPhone and my iMac, however, are physical objects of some consequence: designers and engineers at Apple have spent many thousands of hours crafting and testing every dimension of these products, from the buttons and keys to the materials; the metals and plastics in these objects are the product of human labor at a global scale, as is the manufacture and assembly of their various components. The explosion in digital technologies in the twenty-first century has collected and generated an astounding amount of information and entertainment: news, music, film, books, and television.

    A fundamental procedure of experimental and critical thinking is to compare two states: the familiar and the unfamiliar. In doing so with this experiment, we can understand how changes to our environment and the tools we use affect our thinking. This experiment will therefore ask you to choose an activity that you typically do digitally—listen to music, take a photograph, write, play a game—and find a way of doing the same thing with analog technology. The idea behind this is to use the process of comparison to understand whether and how our thinking differs based on the tools that we use.

Experiment Questions and Description

To explore and understand how I think with things, I wanted choose something that is fundamental to my thinking and working life: our present-day writing technologies. As a professor I write a lot: scholarly essays, textbooks like this one, emails to students and colleagues, comments on student papers. I would estimate that at least a third (and probably more than half) of my time working is spent on doing writing of one kind or another. The digital world has increased the amount of writing that we all do. It has, for instance, transformed personal communication, much of which once happened orally (in phone or in-person conversation), but now takes place over various messaging programs on our phones. We also have many more outlets for our writing than we once did: social media platforms, online discussion threads, digital publication sites, and interactive gaming all facilitate writing through a keyboard interface. "Writer" has a particular connotation in our society; it suggests a person who makes a living writing and selling articles, books, poems, and essays. Using that term more loosely, however, many of us could call ourselves writers.

I do a fair amount of writing by hand (I would guess 10-20% of my total writing output), but for the past 25 years, the main technology I have used for my writing is a computer with programs for word processing and emailing. For this experiment, I wanted to understand how my thinking and my writing both are influenced by the environment in which I do it and the tools that I use. What differences would I notice if I returned to technologies that preceded the word processor? What would be different about the writing experience if I used a typewriter or dictation? To structure the experiment, I gave myself a series of assignments replicate the work that I normally do when I write:

I wrote letters to friends and colleagues (instead of email)
I wrote a small section of a piece of scholarly writing that I was working on
I dictated a response to a piece of student writing
I dictated a draft of a course proposal document
I wrote an essay in response to a writing prompt for a website that publishes typewritten pages

I entered this experiment with a series of hypotheses that I wanted to test:

1) That non-digital composition would be less distracting. Without the distractions of email, web surfing, and other multitasking options available to me on a computer, I would find it easier to focus on my writing.
2) Writing on a typewriter or verbally composing would be more time consuming and laborious. Without the ability to copy and paste, easily delete, correct, and rewrite sentences, the process of writing would take longer and be more frustrating.
3) Writing on a typewriter or dictating would make me more creative. Related to hypothesis number one, I hypothesized that losing distractions, and possibly the novelty of using a technology that was new to me, would generate more creativity in my writing.

To measure these three hypotheses, I kept a log of my experiences with these tasks to record my detailed experiences and general reflections over the course of several days. I also kept track of how long each task took me and calculated basic words per minute rates to help me evaluate the differences in these various experiences.

Observations

My early experiences with these activities showed me that I needed to make adjustments to the way that I work, even in very simple ways. The typewriter I have does not fit on the same desk as my computer, so I needed to create a separate workspace where I could write with it. I moved to the dining room table, centrally located in our house. This created an immediate problem in my household—unlike my computer, whose keyboard produces only soft clicks and taps, the typewriter's manual arms smack into the page with a series of snaps that resonate throughout my home. A bell rings at the end of each line, and the carriage makes a raspy buzzing noise as I move it back to the start of the next line. "What is that?" my wife called out to me from her workspace, alarmed, as soon as I started using the typewriter. I needed to find a way to buffer the noise so that I wouldn't disturb family members doing their work. "The analog world has a different soundscape to it," I reflected in my notes from this first session. "We have replaced the percussive sound of the typewriter with the cool machine hum of the computer."

There was also a learning curve in using the technology itself. The equipment I used for this experiment was a 1956 Royal portable manual typewriter. I bought it from a local self-storage company that was selling off items that had been abandoned by their owners. It was in good condition and only needed to be cleaned up from a bad encounter with a bottle of Wite-Out. I spent an hour or so familiarizing myself with the various levers and controls on the machine so I would understand how to make it work properly. In doing so, I was reminded of how many of the terms used in our word processors harken back to this ancestral technology: "Shift" (which on the typewriter physically shifts the type hammers about 1/16" up to expose capital letters and other characters), "Tab," short for "Tabulators," a series of stops that can be assigned on the machine to help you space out columns of figures or text, and "Return," short for "carriage return," an arm-like mechanism on my typewriter that moves the roller and paper (which move across like a carriage) to the start of a line after the punchy "ding" indicating the line has ended. All of this makes the process of writing on a typewriter a much more conscious act: it is different from writing on a word processor in the way that driving a car with a manual transmission is different from operating one that is automatic.

One of the results of this difference is that it is physically more demanding to type on a typewriter. I have the experience when I type on the wireless keyboard of my Apple computer that my fingers quickly glide across the smooth, low-profile keys. It feels almost effortless. In contrast, striking the manual key on a typewriter requires a level of physical strength and dexterity to which my fingers and wrists were unaccustomed. "I need stronger hands/fingers," I commented during one of my sessions. The keyboard is tiered, rather than flat, and so my fingers had to move slightly up and down from the home row to get to the keys on upper or lower levels. And since the manual arms need to move through space to strike the paper when they make a mark, the arms regularly get jammed against each other. This effect was heightened for me, I am guessing, because I am used to typing very rapidly on my computer keyboard. I had to consciously slow myself down in order to avoid these jams. In fact, the original design of the QWERTY keyboard (for typists using English) was to minimize these keystroke jams by placing letters frequently used together in English physically far apart in the type carriage.

Thus, my experiences in thinking and writing with a typewriter was that everything slowed down noticeably. By my calculations I wrote at an average of about 18 words per minute over the sessions I worked with the typewriter. The way that I adjusted to the problem of key jams was to lift my hands just slightly from the keys and consciously hit each letter one at a time, creating for myself a kind of steady rhythm as I typed. This was interrupted whenever I fell back into my computer keyboard habit of fast typing, but as I got used to it, I found that I could adapt to the slower pace of my writing. The end line bell and carriage return gesture that happens roughly every 12 words also enforced that sense of rhythm, as it was impossible to get lost in a train of written thought in the way I do when writing on a digital word processor. Remarkably, I wasn't frustrated by this reduction in speed. My notes from one session speak to this: "The slower motor functions allow my thoughts to become more organized. Less flow, but more planning and integration of ideas." The contrast I was marking here is between the kind of stream-of-consciousness writing encouraged by the digital word processor, and the more meditative pacing of the typewriter. That, at least, was my experience: my first draft of the section later in this chapter on Nietzsche originated with a session in which I wrote in response to a reading I had just done on the famous philosopher's use of an early typewriter. I was writing without an outline or other notes, yet the page came together in a fairly logical order (I did revise it and rearrange a few sentences when I transferred the text into this book). The slower pace of the writing allowed me to organize my thoughts more cogently as I was writing, requiring less editing after the fact.

Writing through dictation also presented a notably different experience from either using a word processor or a typewriter. I did not have an amanuensis available to me (a secretary or scribe) so I used my computer's dictate function to compose a few different documents. I was impressed with how accurate the software was; one of my initial concerns was that the speech recognition would be inadequate to my work. But it recorded my sentences with accuracy—I only needed to clean up some punctuation and the spelling of one proper noun (the machine spelled Thomas More's name with the common spelling "Moore"). Dictation was fast: I averaged nearly 50 words a minute, slightly faster than the speed at which I type when I compose on a computer word processor. But removing the physical interaction between my hands and machine was an "odd feeling" that left me with the impression of being "disembodied," as I wrote in one of my observational notes. I also commented on another unanticipated effect of dictation that separated me from the machine: I found myself unable to look at the screen as the words were appearing, it was "too distracting" to see my words materialize before me as I was speaking. This also led to a feeling of separation from my writing that I am unaccustomed to. In one session I produced about 600 words for an administrative document I was working on, but reading over it afterwards I felt, strangely, as though I hadn't written those words.

Reflections

One of the most significant differences between a typewriter and computer word processor is your ability with the latter to edit mistakes and rewrite sentences as you compose them. (Just for example, I did a quick experiment with the previous sentence and found that I made six changes as I was writing it.) This happens, for me, without much thought after a while, and the process of composition really becomes a series of writings and rewritings of the same text. I wasn't even aware of how regularly I did this until I started paying attention to it through the observations of this experiment. Indeed, this pattern is so deeply ingrained in me that I at first found it almost painful to write without being able to edit. I had to overcome a strong physical urge to correct and rewrite in order to make the experience of composing on a typewriter work. The effect was stultifying at first, and I actually found myself unable to write very much in my first session with the typewriter. What surprised me, though, was how quickly I adapted to the restriction. I wrote down in my notes for one writing session that I just "go with it" when I make a mistake or when I begin a sentence or turn a phrase that I'm not completely satisfied with. In fact, I would speculate that this effect might actually make the process of using a typewriter less time-consuming, in the end, than writing on the computer. How many times have I had an experience of composing a paragraph, only to go back and hack away at it, responding to the immediate sense of dissatisfaction at having written it? Too many! This effect of the typewriter I found mimicked some of the experiences I had in using dictation. When we speak, we rarely feel the need to backtrack and correct something that we say. It is only in writing (especially formal writing) that we seek for a kind of perfection. Using a typewriter for drafting lessened that urge in ways that eventually became helpful, even freeing for me.

Other dimensions of composing on a typewriter were more challenging. It made me realize just how much I rely upon a fairly standard set of supports to help my writing: spellcheck, a digital thesaurus, Zotero (a research organization and scholarly citation program), Google, Google Books, my university library's website, and my computer's program for viewing PDF files. These technologies all replicate physical objects and materials that were once standard equipment for a writer's or scholar's workspace: print dictionaries and thesauri, paper copies of books and articles, note cards with citations, and reference resources such as a desk encyclopedia or the *New York Times Desk Reference*. I'm not arguing that these sources are necessarily better or worse than their electronic counterparts, but working with a typewriter made me realize that my workspace has become almost completely digitized. As a result, I was ill-equipped to do anything but the most basic (and brief) scholarly writing on my typewriter. I still work with some print books and paper, but my writing environment is very much of the twenty-first century. In order to fully carry out this experiment, I realized, I would need to adapt more than just the technology of the typewriter—I would require an entirely new workspace, one that would be difficult if not impossible to construct today.

My experiences with dictation made me realize that I may be overlooking a useful tool for certain kinds of writing. Not all writing requires the same level of thought or detail—I need to spend less time on writing a transactional email to a colleague or a student than I do crafting a paragraph in a scholarly essay. "An efficient method for composing," I noted after dictating an email. The close connection between oral speech and composition made the experience more like having a conversation with someone than writing to them. That's not necessarily a bad thing in that context, and I could also see employing dictation for "comments" that I make to students on their essays an effective way of sharing my ideas with them.

Conclusions

"Our writing tools are also working on our thoughts," Friedrich Nietzsche wrote at the end of the nineteenth century (Kittler 204). Nietzsche was probably among the first philosophers to use a machine for writing—not the familiar technology we know, but a "writing ball," as it was known, a Danish instrument named for its half-dome keyboard design (Kittler 203-06). He adopted the new technology after his sight began to deteriorate due to various eye ailments and the onset of debilitating migraines. The paper in this machine sat below the keys and so was invisible to its writer. For a brief time, he used the typewriter to compose mainly short pieces: poems, aphorisms, letters. He described these as written in a "telegram" style similar to messages created for that early form of electronic communication. Eventually the humid air of Genoa, Italy, where Nietzsche lived at the time, took a toll on the delicate ribbon of the machine and ended his use of the technology. "This machine," Nietzsche would write to a friend, "is as delicate as a little dog and causes a lot of trouble—and provides some entertainment" (Kittler 204). He eventually turned to human scribes (all women) who took dictation from him for what would be some of his most famous work (including *The Genealogy of Morals*).

We don't often think about how authors carry out the physical act of writing. I read a lot of Nietzsche in college (I was a philosophy major) and it never occurred to me even to ask the question. Particularly in philosophical study, the ideas of the text, it seemed, took absolute precedence to their production. That may still be the case for most readers, yet when I now think of Nietzsche giving dictation to a young graduate student (with whom he was also having an affair) the nature of his work shifts in my mind. The social interaction, the creation of the text as a performance, provides new context to the bold style that characterizes his work. The exchange between Nietzsche and his young female scribe is also based on power and privilege, and it bears pointing out that for much of the twentieth century typewriting was understood, in gendered terms, to be "women's work." There is a long history of this imbalanced power relationship—the etymology of the word "amanuensis," scribe or secretary, derives from the Latin phrase *servus a manu,* "servant/slave of the hand." It seems that it was not just the writing tools that were working on

Nietzsche's thoughts, but also the ecology of Mediterranean Italy that stifled the production of a temperamental machine, the social interactions of composition, the physical limitations that kept him from writing himself, and the social and gender dynamics of his relationships with his typists.

Nietzsche's story illustrates some of the key ideas of the extended mind. I find it notable, for instance, that the shift in writing technology away from longhand script and to the use of the mechanical "writing ball" led him to a different kind of composition. We might see parallels in the effects social media platforms like Twitter have had on contemporary writing practices: restricting the conditions of writing changes how you think. Whether it is through digital character limits or with a machine that doesn't allow you to see what you write, the effect is to condense thought into smaller, more potent expression. In Nietzsche's case, the effect was so immediate and notable that he began writing to friends about the new machine and its output. He was conducting his own experiment in thinking with things.

I remember a colleague at a conference joking that we should go around and affix gold stars to any book written before the internet. I thought about this quip while conducting my experiments: writing without the range of digital tools I now have available to me on the "Desktop" of my computer (there is one of those digital object metaphors again) was a significant challenge. But it may also be the case that the grass is always greener on the other side of the digital divide. Google makes it easier for me to quick-check citations or look up and document a fact that is just on the edge of memory, but it also presents us with any number of deep rabbit holes that can take us off track of our work and ideas. That kind of distraction is well documented in the press and in alarmist narratives likes Nicholas Carr's, who popularized the idea that the internet makes us dumber in his bestselling book *The Shallows: What the Internet is Doing to our Brains*. "Over the last few years I've had an uncomfortable sense that someone, or something, has been tinkering with my brain, remapping the neural circuitry, reprogramming the memory," Carr writes. "My mind isn't going—so far as I can tell—but it's changing. I'm not thinking the way I used to think" (6).

I began my experiment with a Carr-esque hypothesis that I would find typewriting or giving dictation less distracting than working on a computer as I usually do. Not being able to turn to internet resources as easily as I normal would was a different experience, to be sure. But I would point to two other significant interactions between my thinking and writing in a digital environment that I learned from this experiment:

1. As I explored in my observations, word processing makes it *too easy* for us to line edit as we write; it encourages a form of composition that is hesitant and self-judgmental (sometimes debilitatingly so).
2. Writing on a computer removes us from many of the material supports and collaborative structures that have supported the act of writing for centuries. The digital replacements for these tools do not exactly replicate the physical interactions with sources, people, and materials that guided writers for centuries before

the internet age. These physical connections may make writing both more cumbersome but, ultimately, easier on the individual writer.

As an illustration for this second point, I found myself returning to images of one of the great scholars in history: the translator of the Bible into Latin (and patron saint of librarians), St. Jerome. Paintings and drawings of Jerome often show him in the midst of writing, as depicted in this magnificent fresco from the Church of Ognissanti in Florence. Although Jerome is solitary, he is far from alone with his thoughts. His desk includes an elaborate set of tools that allow him to do his writing: a raised surface, ink pots installed for easy access at the sides of the writing desk (you can actually see the ink droplets splattered on the side of the desk), eye glasses, a candle, a pair of scissors for preparing his quill, and a tall ruler for drawing lines on his sheets of parchment. He has several books at hand, two of which are arranged at eye-level, including on a rotating shelf attached to his writing desk. Other notes and supplies surround him, including some carefully placed pieces of fruit for, I imagine, a quick snack break in the midst of his translations. Jerome's writing space is a marvelous fifteenth-century example of the extended mind—a material rich environment that creates the necessary conditions for his work to flourish (see. Fig. 8.1).

When we accept that material, social, technological, and environmental conditions are an essential part of thought and creation, it shows us how "writing" itself can have a wider meaning. It should also make us aware that the means and tools of creation are not always equitably distributed. There are often issues of power, gender, class, and even race at play that are also a part of the conditions at work supporting (or limiting) a writer in her work. In a previous chapter I quoted from Sojourner Truth, the African American woman who was born into slavery but became an early voice and actor in the abolitionist movement. Truth, so far as we know, was illiterate—she did not read and write—but she was able to publish her autobiography through collaboration with a Boston publisher who took dictation from her and put her words in print. The material conditions available to her and other African Americans in the nineteenth century made mainstream forms of communication largely inaccessible. Few could write, and even fewer had access to the privileges of time, space, and other physical materials needed for writing—the "room of one's own" that Virginia Woolf would later argue a writer needs. Yet, as the scholar of nineteenth-century literacy Elizabeth McHenry has shown, when we change our understanding of "literacy" to include oral performance, communal composition, and even important social institutions such as literary societies, book clubs, and Bible groups, we can see how African American "writing" came to be in this crucial time in history.

All tools have their benefits and costs. The ideology of the digital tends to smooth over the drawbacks of our new technologies, emphasizing instead the liquid flow of information our devices promise to create. If anything, this experiment made me appreciate the opportunities of the new technology and think more seriously about how to avoid the problems they create. I may, for instance, now try writing sessions where I write without looking at the screen, or disable my delete key to try to replicate the experience of the typewriter (in response to number one, above). I will also

Fig. 8.1 St. Jerome, Florence, the Church of Ognissanti. Image courtesy of Alamy.com

be more aware of how my desktop (physical or virtual) helps or hinders my ability to do my work. Applications like Freedom allow writers to take more control of their computers by turning off distractions (including, especially, an internet connection). Even within a digital experience it is still possible to borrow from the lessons of the analog world.

That said, I am far from giving up my computer or word processor, nor do I believe we should turn away from these technologies, even given their flaws. These are tools that have become a seamless part of my writing experience—the fundamental way in which I extend my mind into the world through language. On a broader level, it is also a technology that has given access to many writers and thinkers for whom writing on a typewriter or by hand is impossible. As I was carrying out this experiment, my thoughts at one point came to Stephen Hawking, the late cosmologist and remarkable public intellectual. Even though Dr. Hawking suffered from paralysis caused by a condition similar to ALS, he was able to use technologies that allowed him to write books, give lectures, surf the web, compose emails, and, generally, communicate with the outside world. Digital tools made his work possible, as they do for millions of people who work with varying degrees of visual, motor, or cognitive abilities. He wrote his now classic book *A Brief History of Time* using an early computer interface that could produce only 15 words per minute, a pace that makes my Royal typewriter seem blazingly fast. Yet his discussion of some of the most complex ideas known to humanity (black holes, the theory of relativity, quantum mechanics) found a wide readership. Based on my own experiments, I wonder if that slow pace of writing actually allowed for the conditions that could create such an important book. Did the restrictions of composition, ironically, allow Dr. Hawking to present these deep ideas more cogently?

Dr. Hawking also demonstrates the ethical dimension of extended mind theory that Clark and other philosophers raise in their arguments. Imagine, for a moment, that in an unimaginable act someone stole Dr. Hawking's computer from him. Would we say this is merely a crime of property destruction, or has something more fundamental been taken away from him? Would his personhood be compromised by losing these tools that gave him his voice and ability to communicate? If you find yourself thinking of such an act as a personal assault on Dr. Hawking, then what about Otto's notebook from a previous example? Would the loss or theft of that material object undermine his ability to think and operate in the world? Or, more personally, perhaps you have had the experience of losing or misplacing your smartphone. Did that leave you feeling that your sense of self was somehow unsettled?

When I think about my own uses of technology, I have to admit that my dependence on many of them runs deeper than simple utility. The companies that produce these products know this, too—most computer or smartphone companies use ads that tap into the feelings of identification we have with these objects. "Think different," the classic Apple ad campaign said, a slogan that resonates with my own experimentation in this chapter, but also with the idea that our choices in tools and technology make us into new thinking beings. My experimentation in this chapter has convinced me that our "thought" is more complicated than we accept, and that my material world is richly implicated in how I think.

Procedures and Methods

The procedures in this chapter were inspired, in part, by the psychologist Seth Roberts, who pioneered work in the psychological sciences through structured self-experimentation. His emphasis in this work was not so much on the outcomes of the experiments (although he was interested in that, too) but in the possibilities for "idea generation" provided by experimenting on yourself (227). His ideas and methods relate to a wider community of people interested in these methods of experimentation as a path to self-exploration and research. "The Quantified Self" is both a general description of this movement and a non-profit organization that helps facilitate this kind of research. Although there are many possibilities for larger studies involving objects and thought, on a practical level it may be easier to begin with self-experimentation. I followed this general outline, adapted from the Quantified Self community, to structure the research for my model essay:

1. **Overview/Introduction** Description and questions about the experiment: what are you hoping to find out?
2. **Observations** during experiment phase
3. **Reflection**—what do your observations show you? Do you have a baseline that you were working from? Do you see a pattern or patterns in your language of observation?
4. **Conclusion**—answer "What did you do? How did you do it? What did you learn?" Emphasize the failures as well as the successes. Were there any surprises for you? Did this experience lead you to any new ideas for other research projects or investigations? Emphasize the *idea generation* dimension of self-experimentation.

This structure can be adapted to various projects, but give some thought at the outset to the kind of data that you want to collect—will it be quantified (numerical, measurements, etc.) or qualitative (verbal descriptions). In my experiments I focused mainly on qualitative descriptions taken from my research notes. But I could also have quantified these experiments, for instance, by setting up simple experience scales to measure my experience of Distraction or Difficulty, or to count the number of new ideas I had in my writing (for Creativity).

This methodology is also based on a regular assignment that I do with my students based on David Sax's engaging book *The Revenge of Analog: Real Things and Why they Matter.* Sax writes compellingly about the recent cultural interest in record players, notebooks, tabletop games, and other retro-seeming technologies that have nonetheless persisted in the digital world. "Surrounded by digital, we now crave experiences that are more tactile and human-centric," Sax writes. "We want to interact with goods and services with all our senses, and many of us are willing to pay a premium to do so, even if it is more cumbersome and costly than its digital equivalent" (xvi-xvii). Sax makes an important *economic* claim here—that our feelings about objects make us more willing to spend money on a less technologically advanced option: we spend $20 on a new Moleskine notebook when we can at any time download, for free, Evernote onto our smartphones. In this chapter I wanted to frame that insight from a different perspective and view how the different experience of thought and creativity might also help explain why a 60-year-old typewriter could still be a useful tool for me as a writer.

Here is more comprehensive list of options that you could use to carry out your own analog experience:

Listen to music on an LP or cassette tape
Take photographs using film
Write a letter to someone
Have a conversation on the phone
Write a paper on a typewriter (there are typewriters available in many campus "Maker Labs" or spaces)
Keep a daily journal in a notebook
Play a table-top board game with some friends
Read a newspaper or magazine in print
Read a novel in print

This assignment will work best if you choose an experience that you rarely (or never) have in analog form. Thus, if you are already a record enthusiast with a large collection of LPs, or a photographer who works regularly with film, I would encourage you to choose a different experiment.

Resources and Research

To carry out the experiment described in this chapter, I had to take careful notes on the experience of using a typewriter. Thus, the research portion of this work involved significant work in recording and preserving details from the exercises I undertook. Ethnographers, art historians, archeologists, and other scholars who engage in extensive work in the field employ various methods for recording such "fieldnotes." In Object Studies, whether carrying out a self-experiment like the one described here or in making observations about an object, collection, or artifact, it can be useful to give some thought to the methods and structures of your note-taking practice.

In *FieldWorking*, their definitive textbook on field writing, Bonnie Sunstein and Elizabeth Chiseri-Strater recommend a two-columned "double-entry" note structure, with detailed information about the experience being recorded placed on the left (date and time, activity, specific observations) and reflections and personal commentary on the observations on the right side (77-79). The content of these notes, they recommend, should be detailed (including date and time for future reference) and, particularly important for this experiment, focus on "sensory impressions": "Sights, sounds, textures, smells, tastes" (83). Also important for this experiment is the experience you have, in the process, of working with the tool or technology that you chose. It can be helpful, for instance, to pair two of your experiments within close proximity in time: in my case, I switched from the typewriter to my computer immediately during one session so I could experience the clear comparison that came from the shock of this alteration in material practice.

Further Applications

In her excellent book on the practical applications of extended mind research, Annie Murphy Paul suggests a number of ways we can enhance our lives through the lessons of this scholarship. *The Extended Mind: The Power of Thinking Outside the Brain* is an accessible introduction to the topic that also includes a range of ideas for experiments that one could carry out:

- The use of a smartphone app called "ReTUNE" that suggests driving or walking routes that take the user past surroundings that increase experiences with nature. What effects do the environment and external world have on our thinking? (98)
- Imitating the famous biographer Robert Caro's use of wall-sized "maps" to organize his research and writing (144-46).
- Creating visual diagrams or three-dimensional models to explain complex systems or content (as James Watson did when describing the structure of DNA)—how much more do we learn when we transform abstract ideas into objects? (156-69)

Works Cited

Beach, King. "Becoming a Bartender: The Role of External Memory Cues in a Work-Directed Educational Activity." *Applied Cognitive Psychology*, vol. 7, 1993, pp. 191–204.

Carr, Nicholas. *The Shallows: What the Internet Is Doing to Our Brains*. Norton, 2010.

Clark, Andy. *Natural-Born Cyborgs: Minds, Technologies, and the Future of Human Intelligence*. Oxford UP, 2004.

Clark, Andy, and David Chalmers. "The Extended Mind." *Analysis*, vol. 58, 1998, pp. 7–19.

Kirsh, David. "The Intelligent Use of Space." *Artificial Intelligence*, vol. 73, 1995, pp. 31–68.

Kittler, Friedrich. *Gramophone, Film, Typewriter*. Stanford UP, 1999.

Maglio, Paul P., et al. "Interactive Skill in Scrabble." *Proceedings of Twenty-First Annual Conference of the Cognitive Science Society*, 1999. https://www.researchgate.net/publication/2518995_Interactive_Skill_in_Scrabble.

McHenry, Elizabeth. *Forgotten Readers: Recovering the Lost History of African American Literary Societies*. Duke UP, 2002.

Paul, Annie Murphy. *The Extended Mind: The Power of Thinking Outside the Brain*. Houghton Mifflin Harcourt, 2021.

Quantified Self, https://quantifiedself.com/.

Roberts, Seth. "Self-Experimentation as a Source of New Ideas: Ten Examples about Sleep, Mood, Health, and Weight." *Behavioral and Brain Sciences*, vol. 27, no. 2, 2004, pp. 227–88.

Sax, David. *The Revenge of Analog: Real Things and Why They Matter*. PublicAffairs, 2016.

Sunstein, Bonnie Stone, and Elizabeth Chiseri-Strater. *FieldWorking: Reading and Writing Research*. Macmillan, 2011.

Chapter 9
Epilogue: A Department of Object Studies?

What are the possibilities in the modern university for a widespread integration of Object Studies into our curricula? Could objects be an essential part of how we reimagine the "humanities"? This epilogue considers these questions and provides some further thoughts on the advantages of incorporating the study of material culture in today's academy.

A student, let's call her Maria, comes into my office at the end of the semester and declares: "I want to major in Objects." She has been taking my class in Object Studies and is excited by the prospect of deepening her exploration of the methods and topics we have been covering throughout the semester. I can easily envision what such a course of study might entail: a class in Creative Nonfiction Writing, a series of Art History and Anthropology courses, as well as classes in History and Philosophy. Maybe I would suggest a class taught by a colleague in Evolutionary Psychology. It would be an engaging progression of interdisciplinary study that would build from the lessons of our Introduction to Object Studies course and could result in a significant research project based on Maria's interests. Such a project might lead her to graduate school for a Ph.D., or perhaps through her research she would become connected with a museum or arts organization that offered her a job or internship.

At my university, Maria's real opportunities for pursuing a bachelor's degree with a focus in Object Studies would unfortunately be limited. At some larger university centers such a program may be available (though rare). But at most small or midsized colleges and universities like mine, there is not a department that offers such a major. Devising the plan of study outlined above through what we call a "contract major," while possible, would require a lot of creative maneuvering on Maria's part to get all the courses she would need. Moreover, there are undeniable social and cultural forces at work that discourage such curricular wayfinding. Students (and their parents) increasingly like to choose areas of study that they perceive employers will value: psychology, business, science. Even English is having a harder time attracting practically minded students to our major these days.

There are also institutional barriers that prevent the growth of Object Studies as an area of study. Our training as professors is highly specialized and tends to value that form of knowledge over more generalist or interdisciplinary approaches. Professors in my department are experts in Shakespeare, Virginia Woolf, or periods of literary history that typically cover only decades. Across campus departments are unified by this shared sense of expertise and discipline, and in the humanities, particularly, we view the perceived integrity and longevity of our fields as an asset. To study philosophy (or English, or sociology) is to embrace a long tradition of thinkers, writers, and methodologies within that field.

Dedicating a department to objects, then, would be a radical departure on a campus centered on humanistic study or the liberal arts. Our "brainbound" ways of thinking, to recall the philosopher Andy Clark's neologism, extends beyond ourselves and into the values we hold in our education. In the "humanities" as well as in the social sciences we remain beholden to the centuries-old project that began sometime in the Middle Ages with a reclamation of ancient Roman and Greek writings that celebrated human achievement. The honors college where I teach my Object Studies course requires all students to take a class called "The Individual and Society." This educational bias toward the human helps explain why the study of objects has been mostly a niche area for experts.

But what if this weren't the case? What if our current departments (many of which are not as old as we might think) were aligned around different topics or ways of knowing? The anthropologist Daniel Miller makes a remarkable observation in *Stuff*, one of his many books on material culture. "Yet no one thought to have an academic discipline whose specific area of study would be artefacts, the object world created by humanity. It could so easily have been otherwise...If material culture had existed for a century of established study in thousands of colleges, it would have been taken for granted as linguistics is today" (2). If we understand the rise of university departments (or governments, or economic systems) to be the product of historical forces, then we can be free to imagine future alternatives. What if we were to have departments of Object Studies?

The possibility might not be so far-fetched now. As we saw in Chap. 4, in the early decades of the twenty-first century there has been a growing interest in "object-oriented ontologies" and ways of thinking that are "posthuman." Scholars interested in Animal Studies, for instance, have called into question the Western tradition of anthropocentrism (human-centeredness) that dominates our narratives. In an era of climate change and ecological crisis, humanity's dominion over the planet looks more tenuous. The increasing role of technology in our lives has also led scholars to reimagine what it means to be "human": Donna Haraway's "Cyborg Manifesto" gave rise at the close of the twentieth century to various ways of reimagining what it means to be an "individual," including Clark's work on the "extended mind." And in the work of theorists ranging from Jane Bennett to Timothy Morton we see how looking at governments, ecosystems, or even novels as material systems displaces the role of the human to the periphery.

While this theoretical work is both fascinating and important, I hope that *Object Studies* has demonstrated the compelling educational reasons for giving material culture a more prominent place in our curriculum. To me this is no less of an urgent project as we seek to engage our students in new ways of seeing, learning, and writing. In his 2007 essay "Against Thinking," Peter Stallybrass makes the provocative claim that we should inculcate our students with forms of scholarship that encourage "working" over "thinking": unlike thinking, which is "hard" and ironically "indolent," working is "Easy, Exciting, a process of discovery" (1583). Object Studies is one way that we can relocate the energies of our pedagogy from brain-bound thinking into active scholarly working. This shift aligns with my vision for a new humanities: a study that is more inclusive and expansive than the name would suggest, but that still has a place for the "human" as a term in need of new definition through an increased network of relationships—including those between subjects and objects.

The point of *Object Studies* is not necessarily to argue for the creation of programs of study—that is beyond the scope and ambition of an introductory textbook. As Miller argues, too, it can be beneficial to be freed from the institutional apparatus that makes university departments surprisingly conservative. But I do hope that faculty and students who use this book will be inspired to seek out opportunities for new kinds of research questions, off-campus partnerships, conversations across disciplines, cross-departmental teaching, and other collaborations that expand our definition of the humanities. Doing so will help us to appreciate our indebtedness to a rich material world that our study of objects makes visible.

Works Cited

Miller, Daniel. *Stuff.* Polity, 2010.
Stallybrass, Peter. "Against Thinking." *PMLA*, vol. 122, no. 5, Oct. 2007, pp. 1580–87. https://doi.org/10.1632/pmla.2007.122.5.1580.

Index

A
Actor Network Theory (ANT), 73
Affordances, 46, 58, 71–73, 78, 100
Apple Computers, 84, 148
Archaeology, 20, 36
Asian Art Museum, San Francisco, 86–90

B
Belk, Russell, 85, 86
Benjamin, Walter, 81, 82
Bennett, Jane, 76, 110, 160
Bloom, Paul, 66
British empire, 60
British Museum, 43–47, 49–51, 57, 59, 60, 83, 90
Brundage, Avery, 86–91, 95, 100

C
Capitalism, 56, 65, 68, 69, 77, 93, 123–125, 130
Carr, Nicholas, 152
Chalmers, David, 144, 145
China porcelain and coffee cups, 44, 49–51, 57
Clark, Andy, 142, 144–146, 155, 160
Collections and collecting
  curation, x, 81, 86, 92
  and hoarding, 92–95
  and the holy grail, 84, 86
Colombia Coffee Federation, Juan Valdez as trademark, 56
Colonialism, 90
  empire and imperialism, 56, 90
Commodity(ies), 29, 32, 44, 50, 52–55, 59, 69, 70, 104, 124, 125, 127
Consumerism/consumer society, 44, 85, 123, 138

D
Dialectic, 67, 68, 73, 77
Descartes, Rene, 63, 65, 66, 68, 73, 74, 76–78, 145
De Waal, Edmund, 1, 2, 4, 14
Dualism, 65–66, 73, 77
Dutch East India Company (VOC), 50

E
Environmental/ecological impacts of objects
  mining and metals, 132
  recycling, 135, 136
Ethics
  collecting and ethics/ethics of collecting, 87, 100
  of consuming/ethical consumption, 133–136
  and extended mind theory, 155
Extended mind theory, 155

F
Fetish/commodity fetishism, 63, 69–71, 77, 124
Frankenstein
  manuscripts, 104–106
  publication history, 105, 120
  republicanism and politics in, 112–117
  tombs and monuments in, 104, 106, 116

Frankenstein (novel), 104–106, 110, 112, 116, 117, 120, 121
Freud, Sigmund, 63, 70
Fukushima nuclear disaster, 76

G
Genealogy, 4, 15
Gibson, James, 71–73
Godwin, William, 105–106, 110, 111, 116

H
Haitian Revolution, 56
Hampden, John, 103, 104, 106–117
Harman, Graham, 75, 76
Hartman, Saidiya, 22, 23
Hasbrouck family of New Paltz, 21, 25, 26, 29, 33, 34, 40
Hattox, Ralph, 48, 60
Hegel, Georg Wilhelm, 63, 67–71, 75–77
Heidegger, Martin, 75, 78
Herbert, Thomas, 47–49
Historical materialism, 66–68, 73
Hoarding and hoarders, 81–100
Huguenots, 20, 29, 33, 34, 36, 37
Hunt, Leigh, 110
Hyperobjects, 74–77

I
Immigrants/immigration, 4, 8, 9, 12, 91, 92
Imperial War Museum, London, 91
Inheritance, 4, 13, 114
Irving, Washington, 33, 34
Islam (and coffee), 48

J
Jim Crow Museum, Detroit, 92
Jones, Ann Rosalind, 53

K
Kastan, David Scott, 118
Katz-Hyman, Martha, 22–24, 40
Kimmerer, Robin Wall, 17
Kirsh, David, 145
Kondo, Marie, 133–136

L
Labor and manufacture of objects, 15
Lamott, Anne, 15

Latour, Bruno, 73, 74
LeFevre, Ralph, 23, 29–35
Literary studies, viii, 104, 119, 120

M
Maiklem, Lara, 16
Marx, Karl, 63, 66–71, 73, 75–77, 123–125, 130
Marxism, 71, 81, 123, 124
Material culture/material cultural studies, viii, ix, 21, 22, 25, 34–36, 39–40, 44, 45, 53, 56, 64–66, 77, 90, 91, 98, 104, 118, 119, 123, 141, 160, 161
Matory, L. Lorand, 71
McGann, Jerome, 118
Memoir, 1, 4, 14–17
Memory, 1, 4, 13, 15, 17, 23, 35, 56, 84, 91, 95–98, 109, 111, 113, 117, 125, 137, 145, 152
Merchants, 31, 32, 43, 44, 48, 50, 54, 55, 70
Metaphysics, 66, 75
Metropolitan Museum of Art, New York, 90, 95
Miles, Tiya, 17
Millburn, Joshua Fields, 133, 134
Miller, Daniel, 160, 161
Minimalism, 133–136
Monuments and memorials, 34, 35, 108, 111, 116
  naming of, 110
Morton, Timothy, 63, 73–76, 160
Munsee Indians, 23
Museum of German History, Berlin, 91
Museums
  activism in collections, 91
  decolonizing collections in museums, 86–90
  and hoarding, 95

N
Neuroscience, 141
Nicodemus, Ryan, 133, 134
Nietzsche, Friedrich, 149, 151, 152
9/11 Museum and Memorial, 97

O
Object-oriented ontology (OOO), 74–76, 78, 160
Objects
  and architecture and buildings, 13, 25, 34, 35, 39, 53, 83, 84, 99, 142

Index

books/novels as, viii, x, 1, 9, 11, 16, 60, 77, 78, 81, 104, 117–120, 141, 142, 160
clothing, vii, 1, 11, 53, 94, 119, 125, 127, 136
computers, 72, 84–86, 127, 130, 136, 139, 146–150, 152, 154, 155, 157
and distributed cognition, 143, 144
heirlooms, vii, 1, 15, 64
and human consciousness, 67, 74
and language, 46, 63, 69, 73, 77, 78, 81
mass production of, 123
as numinous or magical, 69, 85, 86, 100
paintings and representations of, viii, 52, 53, 61, 72, 90
sacred/sacralized objects, 85
as signifiers of social class, 94
and storytelling, 2, 13, 14, 117
and subjects in philosophy, 73, 78
as tools, vii, 75, 83, 145
Object Studies
archival research in, 19, 37–38, 40
and collaborative projects, ix
and descriptive writing, ix, x
digital exhibitions, 41, 90, 91
experiential learning, viii, ix
experiments in, ix, 15, 136, 157
observations and field notes, viii, x, 14, 75, 149, 157
research, ix, 15, 21, 35, 119
Orientalism/orientalists, 51
Ottoman Empire, 44, 54, 60

P
Pandemic, 9, 12, 13, 133
Paul, Annie Murphy, 158
Pilot Pen Corporation, 125, 136, 137
Posthuman, 73, 160
Provenance (in research), 7, 40, 51, 88
Psychology, viii, 72, 73, 81–100, 141, 159

R
Relic(s), 63, 64, 78, 117
Religion and objects, 69, 70
Richard, Jules (Mirza Riza), 51, 52

S
Safavid Empire, 46, 49, 54, 57, 83
Said, Edward, 51
Shakespeare, William Friedrich, 64, 65, 120, 134, 160
Shelley, Mary, 104–108, 110–117
Shelley, Percy Bysshe, 105, 110
Slavery and enslavement, 17, 20–23, 26, 32–39, 54, 55, 65, 67, 113, 119, 153
St. Jerome, 153, 154
Stallybrass, Peter, 53, 161
Starbucks Coffee, 44, 59

T
Technology
analogue and digital, 84, 141, 146–155
and marketing, 56, 118, 130
Thelwall, John, 110
Trentmann, Frank, 134–136, 138, 139
Truth, Sojourner, 23, 24, 29, 35, 118, 119, 153

V
Van Loo, Charles-André, 52, 53, 56, 57
Victoria and Albert Museum, London, 92

W
Williams, Raymond, 78
Wollstonecraft, Mary, 110, 112, 116
Writing and materiality
computers, 72, 84–86, 127, 130, 136, 139, 146–150, 152, 154, 155, 157
pens, vii, 5, 125–132, 136, 137, 142–144
typewriters, 130, 144, 147–151, 153–157

Z
Zauner, Michelle, 17

The manufacturer's authorised representative in the EU is Springer Nature Customer Service Centre GmbH, Europaplatz 3, 69115 Heidelberg, Germany. If you have any concerns regarding our products, please contact ProductSafety@springernature.com

Printed and bound by CPI Group (UK) Ltd, Croydon, CR0 4YY

15/12/2025

02019781-0001